First Workshop on Natural Language Processing for Political Sciences (PoliticalNLP)

Held at LREC 2022

Marseille, France
20 – 25 June 2022

Editors:

Haithem Afli
Mehwish Alam
Houda Bouamor
Cristina Blasi Casagran
Colleen Boland
Sahar Ghannay

ISBN: 978-1-7138-6133-1

Printed from e-media with permission by:

Curran Associates, Inc.
57 Morehouse Lane
Red Hook, NY 12571

Some format issues inherent in the e-media version may also appear in this print version.

Printed with permission by Curran Associates, Inc. (2023)

For permission requests, please contact the Association for Computational Linguistics at the address below.

Association for Computational Linguistics
209 N. Eighth Street
Stroudsburg, Pennsylvania 18360

Phone: 1-570-476-8006
Fax: 1-570-476-0860

acl@aclweb.org

Additional copies of this publication are available from:

Curran Associates, Inc.
57 Morehouse Lane
Red Hook, NY 12571 USA
Phone: 845-758-0400
Fax: 845-758-2633
Email: curran@proceedings.com
Web: www.proceedings.com

LREC 2022 Workshop
Language Resources and Evaluation Conference
20-25 June 2022

First Workshop on Natural Language Processing for Political Sciences (PoliticalNLP)

PROCEEDINGS

Editors:

Haithem Afli (General Chair), Mehwish Alam, Houda Bouamor Cristina Blasi Casagran, Colleen Boland and Sahar Ghannay.

Proceedings of the LREC 2022 workshop on Natural Language Processing for Political Sciences (PoliticalNLP)

Edited by:
Haithem Afli (General Chair), Mehwish Alam, Houda Bouamor, Cristina Blasi Casagran, Colleen Boland and Sahar Ghannay.

For more information:
European Language Resources Association (ELRA)
9 rue des Cordelières
75013, Paris
France
http://www.elra.info
Email: lrec@elda.org

Message from the General Chair

The First Workshop on Natural Language Processing for Political Sciences (PoliticalNLP) took place on Friday, June 24, 2022, in Marseille, France, immediately after the 13th Edition of the Language Resources and Evaluation Conference (LREC 2022). The focus of our workshop was to explore the multifarious aspects of effective Natural Language Processing (NLP) techniques for socio-political data. The workshop provided a research platform dedicated to new methods and techniques for text processing of socio-political content and exploring the use of such methods in information extraction and analysis.

It was a venue for discussing the implementation of language technologies in the social and political sciences domain. Computational Social and Political scientists reported and discussed their NLP tools in comparison to their traditional coding approaches. Computational linguistics and machine learning practitioners and researchers investigated the challenges of real-world use cases in these domains.

Cristina Blasi Casagran from Universidad Autónoma de Barcelona gave the invited talk on "The Role of Emerging Predictive IT Tools in Effective Migration Governance".

We would like to thank the members of the Program Committee for their timely reviews. We also would like to thank the participants of the workshop for the interesting discussions around our PoliticalNLP topics, and our sponsors: the Horizon 2020 project ITFLOWS (Grant Agreement No. 882986) and the Science Foundation Ireland Research Centre ADAPT (Grant Agreement No.13/RC/2106).

Haithem Afli

Organizers

Haithem Afli – ADAPT Centre, Munster Technological University (Ireland)
Mehwish Alam – FIZ Karlsruhe - Leibniz Institute for Information Infrastructure (Germany)
Colleen Boland – Universidad Autónoma de Barcelona (Spain)
Houda Bouamor – Carnegie Mellon University (Qatar)
Sahar Ghannay – Université Paris-Saclay, CNRS, LISN (France)
Cristina Blasi Casagran – Universidad Autónoma de Barcelona (Spain)

Program Committee:

Yiyi Chen, FIZ Karlsruhe - Leibniz Institute for Information Infrastructure, Germany
Adam Zebrowski, Microsoft, Saudi Arabia
Bruno Andrade, Munster Technological University, Ireland
Lenka Dražanová, European University Institute, Italy
Georgios Stavropoulos, The Centre for Research and Technology, Greece
Mohammed Hasanuzzaman, Munster Technological University, Ireland
Amira Barhoumi, LIUM, Le Mans Université, France
Colleen Boland, Universidad Autónoma de Barcelona, Spain
Andrea Iana, University of Mannheim, Germany
Nikolaos Gkevrekis, CERTH, Greece
Praveen Joshi, Munster Technological University, Ireland
Patrick Paroubek, Université Paris-Saclay, CNRS, LISN, France
Ilias Iliopoulos, CERTH, Greece
Zsolt Kardkovacs, Munster Technological University, Ireland
Pintu Lohar, Dublin City University, Ireland
Suman Adhya, Indian Association for the Cultivation of Science, India
Valentin Barriere, Joint Research Center, Italy

Table of Contents

Workshop Program

Friday, June 24, 2022

09:00–09:10	**Opening and Welcome by Haithem Afli**
09:10–09:45	**Keynote Speech by Cristina Blasi Casagran: The Role of Emerging Predictive IT Tools in Effective Migration Governance**
09:45–10:45	**Oral session 1: chaired by Houda Bouamor**
09:45–10:05	Debating Europe: A Multilingual Multi-Target Stance Classification Dataset of Online Debates Valentin Barriere, Alexandra Balahur, and Brian Ravenet
10:05–10:25	Cause and Effect in Governmental Reports: Two Data Sets for Causality Detection in Swedish Luise Dürlich, Sebastian Reimann, gustav finnveden, Joakim Nivre, and Sara Stymne
10:25–10:45	An Unsupervised Approach to Discover Media Frames Sha Lai, Yanru Jiang, Lei Guo, Margrit Betke, Prakash Ishwar, and Derry Tanti Wijaya
10:45–11:45	**Poster session: chaired by Mehwish Alam**
11:45–12:45	**Oral session 2: chaired by Sahar Ghannay**
11:45–12:05	Electoral Agitation Dataset: The Use Case of the Polish Election Mateusz Baran, Mateusz Andrzej Wójcik, Piotr Kolebski, Michał Bernaczyk, Krzysztof Rajda, Lukasz Augustyniak and Tomasz Kajdanowicz
12:05–12:25	Does Twitter know your political views? POLiTweets dataset and semi-automatic method for political leaning discovery Joanna Baran, Michał Kajstura, Maciej Ziolkowski and Krzysztof Rajda
12:25–12:45	Political Communities on Twitter: Case Study of the 2022 French Presidential Election Hadi Abdine, Yanzhu Guo, Virgile E. Rennard and Michalis Vazirgiannis
12:45–13:00	**Closing remarks by Haithem Afli**

Proceedings of the First Workshop on Natural Language Processing for Political Sciences (PoliticalNLP), pages 1–7
Marseille, 24 June 2022

NewYeS: A Corpus of New Year's Speeches with a Comparative Analysis

Anna Tramarin, Carlo Strapparava
University of Trento, FBK-IRST
anna.tramarin@studenti.unitn.it, strappa@fbk.eu

Abstract

This paper introduces the NewYeS corpus, a multilingual corpus that contains the Christmas messages and New Year's speeches held at the end of the year by the heads of state of different European countries (namely Denmark, France, Italy, Norway, Spain and the United Kingdom). The corpus was collected via web scraping of the speech transcripts available online. A comparative analysis was conducted to examine some of the cultural differences showing through the texts, namely a frequency distribution analysis of the term *"God"* and the identification of the three most frequent content words per year, with a focus on years in which significant historical events happened. An analysis of positive and negative emotion scores, examined along with the frequency of religious references, was carried out for those countries whose languages are supported by LIWC, a tool for sentiment analysis. The corpus is available for further analyses, both comparative (across countries) and diachronic (over the years).

Keywords: Political Speeches, Multilingual Corpus, Text Analysis, Computational Social Science

1. Introduction

In many European countries, it is traditional for the head of state to hold a speech towards the end of the year, which may take place on Christmas Day or on New Year's Eve. The tradition generally started in the second post-war period - with exceptions such as the United Kingdom, where it started in 1932 (Catsiapis, 2001). The speeches were first broadcast on radio and later on television, and the tradition still continues today.

It is mainly a moment of reflection on the events of the year that is about to end, which is concluded with the head of state usually expressing a positive message for the upcoming year. It is a ritual event in a country's political life, not made to convince or persuade the audience, but to create a sense of community and national identity in a moment of passage. At the same time, it serves as an implicit legitimacy of the institutions and political system that the head of state represents (Tuzzi, 2008).

Within the framework of a ritual ceremony, the personality and subjectiveness of the speaker still emerges in the choice of tone, topics and vocabulary, which is particularly noticeable in the case of elected representatives - e.g., the Italian and French presidents, who are elected every seven and five years, respectively (formerly seven in France until the year 2000) - compared to monarchs' lifetime positions. Nevertheless, the institutional tone and cultural framework is maintained across representatives, while diachronic change is perceivable in the chronological evolution of style and vocabulary (Leblanc, 2016).

In this work, we introduce the NewYeS corpus, a collection of transcripts of Christmas messages and New Year's speeches from various European countries, that cover different periods of time starting between 1946 and 1960 (depending on transcript availability online) until 2020.

This paper is organised as follows: section 2 describes the formal structure of this particular kind of speech, drawing from relevant literature; section 3 illustrates how the dataset was built; section 4 explains the analysis conducted on the texts. In section 5 we present and discuss the results, whereas in section 6 we outline possible future directions.

Country	Speech held by
Denmark	King/Queen of Denmark
France	President of the French Republic
Italy	President of the Italian Republic
Norway	King of Norway
Spain	Francisco Franco (until 1974) King of Spain
United Kingdom	Queen of the United Kingdom

Table 1: List of countries and country representatives holding the speech at the end of the year.

2. Background

The final speech of the year is usually held by the king or queen of the country - in case the country's form of government is a constitutional monarchy - or by the elected president in case of a democracy (see Table 1 for more details about the countries considered in this paper), with the notable exception of dictator Francisco Franco who held the Christmas Message in Spain until 1974.

Analysis of political discourse has been drawing increasing attention in the field of Natural Language Processing (NLP). Some work has been carried out with regard to political stance detection (Diermeier et al., 2012; Zirn, 2014; Glavaš et al., 2017; Lehmann and Derczynski, 2019), analysis of persuasiveness in political speeches (Guerini et al., 2008), political affiliation (Navarretta and Hansen, 2020), sentiment analysis (Onyimadu et al., 2013; Abercrombie and Batista-Navarro, 2018) and topic classification in political manifestos (Zirn et al., 2016).

However, New Year's speeches represent a specific type of "institutional speech", as they are a ritual of seasonal passage between a "before" and an "after" (Tuzzi, 2008). The monarch or president also act as a symbol of the institutions, and therefore contribute to legitimise the political system they represent in front of the entire nation. Their speech emphasises a particular notion of national identity - i.e., the power's representation of national identity, addressed to an audience that is believed - and lead to - share that sense of belonging (Madsen, 2017). It aims at building the "We" in a moment of passage and potential change, hence carrier of inherent uncertainty (Van Gennep, 2013). At the same time, it tries to make sense of past events and to point out the priorities for the coming year (Leblanc, 2016). As a political ritual, the speeches present some text characteristics that may be similar across countries. For instance, a possibly fixed opening line that mainly depends on the person pronouncing the speech - e.g., the Norwegian *"Kjære landsmenn"* ("Dear countrymen"), Francisco Franco's *"Españoles!"* ("Spanish people!") or the greetings of some Italian presidents *"Italiani"* ("Italians"), *"Care Italiane, cari Italiani"* ("Dear Italian women, dear Italian men"). Sometimes even a simple "good evening" can open the speech (Spain and Italy). All the speeches usually end with the speaker wishing a merry Christmas or a happy New Year, and possibly invoking God's protection (Denmark).

The nation building effort also goes through an appeal to national values - or the values the nation is supposed to identify itself with - and an overview of the year's events as a common and shared experience.

A comparative analysis of these speeches may thus reveal both cultural differences and possible similarities, providing some insight into a tradition that for decades has been carried on in parallel in several European countries.

3. Dataset

The NewYeS corpus comprises transcripts of Christmas messages and New Year's speeches held by the heads of state - presidents or monarchs - of six different European countries (Italy, France, Spain, United Kingdom, Denmark and Norway), spanning from varying starting years to 2020. The Danish corpus is the largest, as it begins with the 1946 speech, whereas the French one is the smallest, since transcripts were available only starting from 1960.

The corpus was collected from various web sources, mainly constituted by - but not limited to - the official royal or presidential websites. In some cases the scraped texts needed a thorough cleaning before being used for NLP analysis. A primary condition for the dataset creation has therefore been the availability of the speech transcripts online.

4. Analysis

The analysis was carried out on 366 speeches (61 per country), spanning a time period of sixty years - from 1960 until 2020. This time span was chosen because speeches covering this period were available for each country, thus allowing a uniform analysis. However, some of the collected corpora contain speeches dating back to before 1960.

A first level of analysis consisted of examining the absolute frequency (i.e., the absolute number of occurrences for each year) of the word "God" throughout the texts, as shown in figure 1.

We further considered the three most frequent content words for each year - i.e., nouns, verbs (excluding auxiliary verbs), adjectives and adverbs. In particular, the word lemmas were considered for this analysis. Adverbs with a more grammatical role in the sentence, that could therefore be considered as function words (e.g., *so, too, yet, then*) were excluded. An essential step for this analysis was part-of-speech (POS) tagging, which was performed using Stanza[1], an NLP toolkit developed by Stanford University (Qi et al., 2020). An example of the three most frequent words for the year 1989 can be seen in table 2, whereas a more comprehensive comparison between years is illustrated in table 4.

Year	Country	Most frequent words (lemmas)
1989	Denmark	år (year) **frihed (freedom)** ny (new)
	France	**liberté (freedom)** pays (country) est (East)
	Italy	**libertà (freedom)** popolo (people) nuovo (new)
	Norway	mange (many) år (year) stor (big)
	Spain	desear (to wish) buen (good) hacer (to do/to make)
	UK	child world make

Table 2: Examples of the top three most frequent content words (nouns, adjectives, verbs or adverbs) as lemmas in the speeches of the year 1989.

[1]https://stanfordnlp.github.io/stanza/

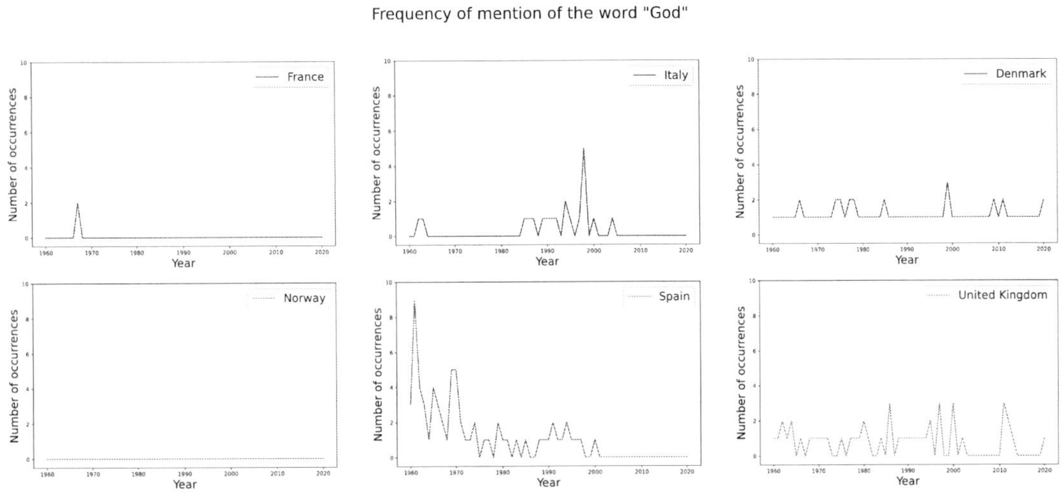

Figure 1: Absolute frequency of mention of the word "God" across countries over the years. It can be observed how the green line, representing Spain, spikes in the early '60s and slightly peaks again in the early '70s, when Franco was in power, then drops to a level that is comparable to other countries when the king of Spain started holding the speech. On the other hand, the word "God" was never mentioned in Norwegian speeches and barely in French ones (the only mention happened when some lines by the French poet Paul Verlaine were quoted, in 1967).

In addition, we applied Linguistic Inquiry and Word Count 2015 (LIWC2015)[2] for speech sentiment analysis. LIWC2015 is an application that relies on internal dictionaries in which words have been classified in different categories, according to psychological theories and emotion-measuring scales (Pennebaker et al., 2015). The tool processes the text sequentially, comparing each encountered word to the words in the dictionary and assigning scores depending on the category (or categories) a word is assigned to. The result is a speech psychometric analysis with percentage scores for each conceptual dimension. LIWC has been used in the past to identify texts written by people with mental disorders (Coppersmith et al., 2014), to analyse the correlation between narcissism and language (Holtzman et al., 2019), in social psychology (Klauke et al., 2020) and political science studies (Bond et al., 2017), among others.

The speech sentiment analysis was carried out for English, French, Italian and Spanish, as LIWC is available for these languages and has been deemed a valuable tool for multilingual analysis (Dudău and Sava, 2021). In particular, positive and negative emotion scores for specific years were extracted and compared (see Table 3), together with religion-related words. Figure 2 shows the change of positive emotion rate over time, whereas figure 3 presents the frequency of religion-related words.

[2]The LIWC2015 website: http://liwc.wpengine.com/

5. Discussion

The first analysis regarded the absolute frequency of mention of the word *"God"* in the texts. Figure 1 shows the absolute frequency of occurrence of the word *"God"* over the years. It stands out how in Spanish Christmas messages, God was mentioned significantly more often in Francisco Franco's speeches (until 1974, the year of his last speech), compared to the speeches pronounced later by the kings of Spain. A peak can also be observed in Italian speeches in 1998, when President Oscar Luigi Scalfaro held his last New Year's speech, whereas mentioning God dropped with the following Italian presidents. An interesting case is represented by Norway, as the kings never mentioned the word *"God"*. The Norwegian case is followed closely by France, since the only mention of God in 1967 was due to Charles De Gaulle quoting a line by the poet Paul Verlaine.

With regard to the most frequent content words per year, table 2 shows that *"freedom"* was one of the most repeated words in 1989, likely related to the events of that year.

A more comprehensive comparison, which takes into account different years that are representative of the whole period, can be seen in table 4. Perhaps unsurprisingly, *"year"* is one of the most repeated words overall. It is also interesting to see how *"all"* (which taken as a lemma, could stand for "every", "everything" or "everybody") seems to be a recurring word in Danish speeches, and also makes it to the top three in one French speech. It is most likely expression of an attempt to address and embrace the whole nation, in or-

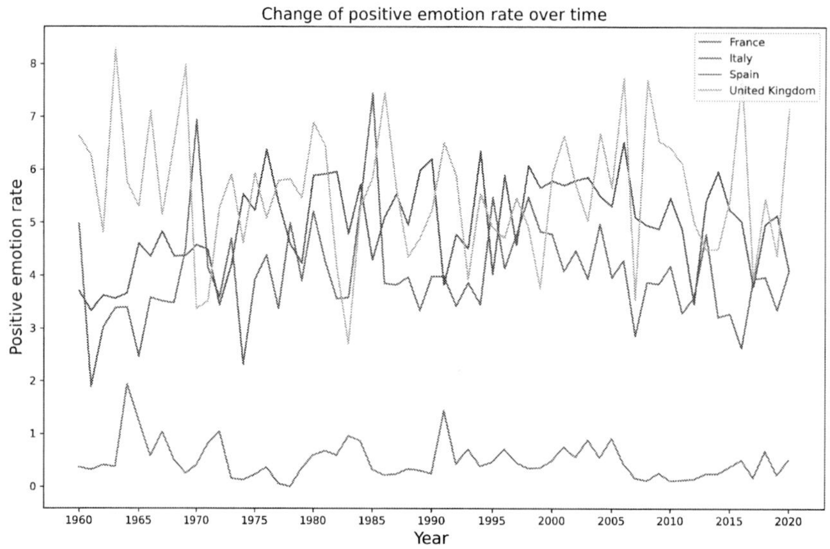

Figure 2: Change of positive emotion rate over the years

der to build a sense of community.
In addition, it can be observed how the adjective *"French"* is a recurring word in earlier French speeches, whereas the shift from *"Italian"* in 1980 to *"European"* in 2020 with respect to Italian speeches is certainly a sign of changing times.
On the other hand, some word occurrences are simply related to peculiarities of that year's speech, such as the repetition of the verb *"ring"* in the UK speech of 1980, which is due to the Queen quoting a poem by Alfred Tennyson[3].
Figure 2 gives an overview of how the positive emotion rate changed over the years, whereas table 3 shows positive and negative emotion scores assigned to New Year's speeches held in pivotal years of recent history, compared across countries. It is interesting to observe how Italy always scores very low with respect to positive emotion, regardless of the president, whereas other countries - in particular the United Kingdom - score fairly high on the positive emotion scale. This may be due to a tendency of Italian Presidents to talk about problems and challenges encountered throughout the year, whereas other speakers seem to lean more towards optimism and hope for the future.
The diachronic frequency of religion-related words is featured in figure 3. It can be seen that France presents the lowest score, followed by Italy. In line with the frequency of mention of the word *"God"*, Spain presents a higher rate of religious references when the Christmas speeches were held by Francisco Franco. Perhaps unsurprisingly, since the Queen of the United Kingdom is also head of the Church of England, her Christmas messages tend to mix political and religious elements. This distinctive trait may also contribute to the peaks in positive emotion scores, as a speech held on Christmas Day would likely be characterised by positive feelings

[3]Some verses from the poem "In Memoriam (Ring out, wild bells)"

Year	France		Italy		Spain		United Kingdom	
	Pos	Neg	Pos	Neg	Pos	Neg	Pos	Neg
1968	3.48	2.39	**0.51**	1.28	4.36	1.52	**6.52**	1.78
1973	4.70	1.46	**0.16**	2.56	4.20	2.18	**5.91**	1.43
1989	3.34	0.92	**0.31**	2.09	**5.98**	1.84	4.70	1.86
2000	4.78	1.66	**0.49**	1.03	5.79	1.42	**5.92**	1.15
2008	3.87	3.06	**0.12**	2.21	4.95	1.93	**7.69**	1.16
2020	4.09	1.64	**0.52**	1.22	4.10	1.80	**7.15**	1.16

Table 3: Positive and negative emotion scores per country in different years, in which significant historical events happened (i.e., protests of 1968, oil crisis of 1973, fall of the Berlin wall in 1989, turn of the millennium in the year 2000, financial crisis of 2008, COVID-19 pandemic in 2020).

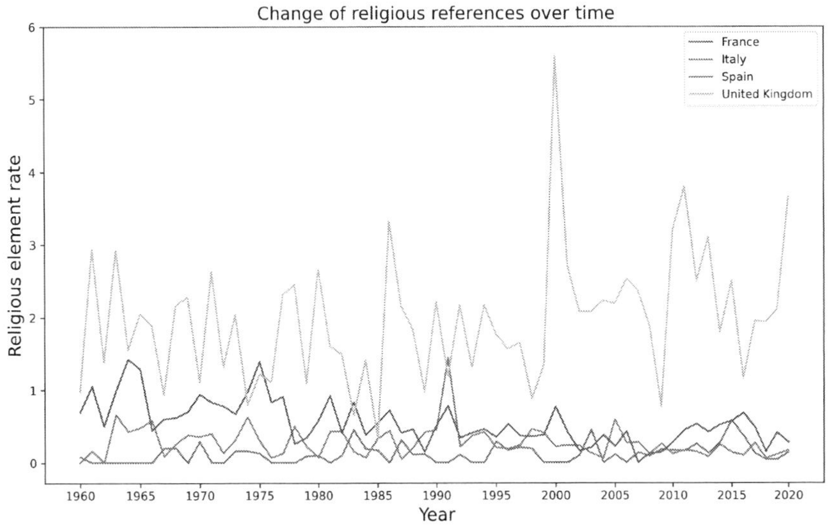

Figure 3: Frequency of religion-related words over the years

and good wishes. The highest peak of religious references can be observed in the message of the year 2000, which features the highest number of occurrences of words such as *"Christ"*, *"Christian"* and *"faith"*.

6. Conclusion

In this paper, we collected and analysed the texts of Christmas messages and New Year's speeches from six European countries. For the analysis we selected speeches that covered the same time span, namely 61 years from 1960 to 2020, for a total amount of 366 speeches. We examined the absolute frequency of mention of the word *"God"* and extracted the three most frequent content words in the speeches of specific years, which revealed some remarkable cultural differences among countries. We further implemented the LIWC2015 application for the analysis of positive and negative emotion scores for four countries (France, Italy, Spain and the United Kingdom).

This work has been an exploratory study of a subgenre of political speeches that differ considerably from the usual political talks, whose main goal is generally to convince and persuade the audience to share the speaker's opinion. New Year's speeches are a more "institutional" kind of speech held by the head of state, whose role is to represent a country's political institutions in front of the nation in a ritual way. The analysis that was implemented is an experimental example of how this corpus could be used in the framework of political analysis in NLP.

The NewYeS corpus can certainly be expanded to other countries that present a Christmas or New Year's speech tradition. For instance, at the moment transcripts of German speeches are available only from the late Eighties until today, but they would constitute a valuable addition.

With regard to future directions, focusing on one country would allow for a deeper diachronic analysis - e.g., how the vocabulary, syntax complexity and way of addressing the nation have changed over time. From a cross-cultural perspective, a detailed analysis of discourse and rhetorical strategies could highlight further differences or similarities among countries. The NewYeS corpus is publicly available for research purposes upon request to the authors.

7. Bibliographical References

Abercrombie, G. and Batista-Navarro, R. (2018). A sentiment-labelled corpus of hansard parliamentary debate speeches. *Proceedings of ParlaCLARIN. Common Language Resources and Technology Infrastructure (CLARIN).*

Bond, G. D., Holman, R. D., Eggert, J.-A. L., Speller, L. F., Garcia, O. N., Mejia, S. C., Mcinnes, K. W., Ceniceros, E. C., and Rustige, R. (2017). 'Lyin'Ted', 'Crooked Hillary', and 'Deceptive Donald': Language of lies in the 2016 US presidential debates. *Applied Cognitive Psychology*, 31(6):668–677.

Catsiapis, H. (2001). The Queen's Christmas messages. In *Seeing things: Literature and the visual. Papers from the Fifth International British Council Symposium*, pages 73–88.

Coppersmith, G., Dredze, M., and Harman, C. (2014). Quantifying mental health signals in Twitter. In *Proceedings of the workshop on computational linguistics and clinical psychology: From linguistic signal to clinical reality*, pages 51–60.

Diermeier, D., Godbout, J.-F., Yu, B., and Kaufmann,

Year	Country	Most frequent words (lemmas)	Year	Country	Most frequent words (lemmas)
1960	Denmark	**år (year)** **al (all)** stor (big)	1980	Denmark	**år (year)** tid (time) land (country)
	France	**français (French)** bien (good/well) **tout (all)**		France	**année (year)** pays (country) **français (French)**
	Italy	problema (problem) popolo (people) **anno (year)**		Italy	**italiano (Italian)** popolo (people) giovane (young)
	Norway	**år (year)** menneske (man/human being) god (good)		Norway	**år (year)** dag (day) bli (to become)
	Spain	político (political) **año (year)** social (social)		Spain	esfuerzo (effort) querer (to want) mejor (better)
	UK	time good **year**		UK	service ring (Verb) many
2000	Denmark	**al (all)** familie (family) god (good)	2020	Denmark	mange (many) **år (year)** **al (all)**
	France	**année (year)** nouveau (new) avoir (to have)		France	**année (year)** avoir (to have) vie (life)
	Italy	**anno (year)** avere (to have) fare (to do)		Italy	**anno (year)** paese (country) **europeo (European)**
	Norway	stor (big) **år (year)** tid (time)		Norway	**år (year)** bli (to become) god (good)
	Spain	**año (year)** hoy (today) noche (evening/night)		Spain	gran (big) sociedad (society) tener (to have/to have to)
	UK	**year** life man		UK	light hope **year**

Table 4: Examples of the top three most frequent content words (nouns, adjectives, verbs and adverbs) as lemmas from the speeches of four different years, with the corresponding translation for languages other than English.

S. (2012). Language and ideology in Congress. *British Journal of Political Science*, 42(1):31–55.

Dudău, D. P. and Sava, F. A. (2021). Performing multilingual analysis with Linguistic Inquiry and Word Count 2015 (liwc2015). an equivalence study of four languages. *Frontiers in Psychology*, 12:2860.

Glavaš, G., Nanni, F., and Ponzetto, S. P. (2017). Unsupervised cross-lingual scaling of political texts. In *Proceedings of the 15th Conference of the European Chapter of the Association for Computational Linguistics: Volume 2, Short Papers*, pages 688–693.

Guerini, M., Strapparava, C., and Stock, O. (2008). Trusting politicians' words (for persuasive NLP). In *International Conference on Intelligent Text Processing and Computational Linguistics*, pages 263–274. Springer.

Holtzman, N. S., Tackman, A. M., Carey, A. L., Brucks, M. S., Küfner, A. C., Deters, F. G., Back, M. D., Donnellan, M. B., Pennebaker, J. W., Sherman, R. A., et al. (2019). Linguistic markers of grandiose narcissism: A LIWC analysis of 15 samples. *Journal of Language and Social Psychology*, 38(5-6):773–786.

Klauke, F., Müller-Frommeyer, L. C., and Kauffeld, S. (2020). Writing about the silence: identifying the language of ostracism. *Journal of Language and Social Psychology*, 39(5-6):751–763.

Leblanc, J.-M. (2016). *Analyses lexicométriques des vœux présidentiels*. ISTE Group.

Lehmann, R. and Derczynski, L. (2019). Political Stance in Danish. In *Proceedings of the 22nd Nordic Conference on Computational Linguistics*, pages

197–207.

Madsen, C. (2017). Magtens repræsentation af danskhed. konstitueringen af nationalidentitet i Dronning Margrethes nytårstaler. *Passage-Tidsskrift for litteratur og kritik*, 31(76).

Navarretta, C. and Hansen, D. H. (2020). Identifying parties in manifestos and parliament speeches. In *Proceedings of the Second ParlaCLARIN Workshop*, pages 51–57.

Onyimadu, O., Nakata, K., Wilson, T., Macken, D., and Liu, K. (2013). Towards sentiment analysis on parliamentary debates in hansard. In *Joint international semantic technology conference*, pages 48–50. Springer.

Pennebaker, J. W., Boyd, R. L., Jordan, K., and Blackburn, K. (2015). The development and psychometric properties of LIWC2015. Technical report.

Qi, P., Zhang, Y., Zhang, Y., Bolton, J., and Manning, C. D. (2020). Stanza: A Python natural language processing toolkit for many human languages. *arXiv preprint arXiv:2003.07082*.

Tuzzi, A. (2008). Messaggi dal Colle: l'analisi statistica dei dati testuali e il discorso di fine anno del Presidente della Repubblica Italiana. *Messaggi dal Colle*, pages 1000–1021.

Van Gennep, A. (2013). *The rites of passage*. Routledge.

Zirn, C., Glavaš, G., Nanni, F., Eichorts, J., and Stuckenschmidt, H. (2016). *Classifying topics and detecting topic shifts in political manifestos*. University of Zagreb.

Zirn, C. (2014). Analyzing positions and topics in political discussions of the German Bundestag. In *Proceedings of the ACL 2014 Student Research Workshop*, pages 26–33.

Proceedings of the First Workshop on Natural Language Processing for Political Sciences (PoliticalNLP), pages 8–15
Marseille, 24 June 2022

Correlating Political Party Names in Tweets, Newspapers and Election Results

Eric Sanders, Antal van den Bosch
CLS/CLST Radboud University, KNAW Meertens Institute
e.sanders@let.ru.nl, antal.van.den.bosch@meertens.knaw.nl

Abstract

Twitter has been used as a textual resource to attempt to predict the outcome of elections for over a decade. A body of literature suggests that this is not consistently possible. In this paper we test the hypothesis that mentions of political parties in tweets are better correlated with the appearance of party names in newspapers than to the intention of the tweeter to vote for that party. Five Dutch national elections are used in this study. We find only a small positive, negligible difference in Pearson's correlation coefficient as well as in the absolute error of the relation between tweets and news, and between tweets and elections. However, we find a larger correlation and a smaller absolute error between party mentions in newspapers and the outcome of the elections in four of the five elections. This suggests that newspapers are a better starting point for predicting the election outcome than tweets.

Keywords: social media, Twitter, newspapers, elections

1. Introduction

For over a decade researchers have attempted to predict (political) election results on the basis of Twitter. Some results from the beginning of that period looked promising (Tumasjan et al., 2010; Sanders and Van den Bosch, 2013), but soon papers appeared that expressed doubts about the ability to correctly predict the election outcome based on tweets (Gayo-Avello, 2012). Although there are findings that support these doubts (e.g. (Sanders and van den Bosch, 2019)), still studies appear that report on attempts to forecast the elections with tweets, often including sentiment analysis (Nugroho, 2021; Batra et al., 2020; Rao et al., 2020) and others with mixing in additional information, such as economic indicators (Liu et al., 2020).

In his paper on the predictive power of tweets with regards to election results, Murthy concludes: "Twitter frequency and sentiment are hardly measures of 'victory'. They are better indicators of the social media 'buzz' around a candidate. Twitter also tends to act as a reactive rather than predictive media platform." (Murthy, 2015). Based on this finding we intended to investigate whether the mentioning of party names in tweets might be more influenced by what Twitter users hear in the media than their political preference. We did this by studying the correlation of the mentions of political party names in tweets and party mentions in the news, and compare these to the correlation of party mentions in tweets and election results. If Murthy's conclusion is right, we expect the former correlation to be larger than the latter.

For news we restricted ourselves to newspaper articles. The reason for this is that this is a relative limited textual resource that is relatively well accessible and searchable, in contrast with for example television or radio news broadcasts. We are supported in this choice by Druckman who writes in his paper "More important, I find that newspapers, and not television news, play a significant, although potentially limited, role in informing the electorate." (Druckman, 2005).

In earlier studies about the relation between tweets and newspapers, we find opposing findings. In 2015 Murthy concludes "Using the 2011–2012 U.S. Republican primary as a case study, this article evaluates whether the sentiment of traditional print media coverage of candidates is related to the frequency of their mentions on Twitter. We found that the two are generally not related." (Murthy and Petto, 2015), where Su finds in a study about climate change in the news in 2019 "The findings imply that Twitter is more likely to influence newspapers' agenda in terms of breaking news, whereas newspapers are more likely to lead Twitter's agenda in terms of ongoing discussions during non-breaking news periods." and "Overall, the agendas of Twitter and newspapers were significantly correlated." (Su and Borah, 2019).

To investigate our research question whether tweets are more influenced by news than by political preference we counted how often political party names occur in tweets, newspaper articles and how the parties score in the elections of five Dutch elections of national importance, and compare their percentages. The paper is organised as follows: in section 2 we present how we got our data, in section 3 we explain how we conducted our experiment, in section 4 we show our results and in sections 5 and 6 we discuss our findings and draw conclusions.

2. Data

2.1. TwiNL

The tweets we used in our study are taken from TwiNL (Tjong Kim Sang and Van den Bosch, 2013), a project in which Dutch tweets are collected since December 2010. The archive creators claim a coverage of about 60% to 80% of all Dutch tweets (based on the number of replies to a tweet that also appears in the collection). These are tweets that are either in the Dutch language or posted by a set of users known to post in Dutch. Language detection separates the Dutch from the non-Dutch tweets. In our experiments we only use the tweets that were detected as written in Dutch, which is not flawless, but sufficiently accurate for trustworthy numbers. Until February 2021, over 4.1 billion Dutch written tweets were collected.

2.2. LexisNexis

For newspaper articles we used a huge online collection of Dutch newspapers provided by LexisNexis. It has a special service for academia, called LexisUni (Knapp, 2018). It contains an archive of forty years of weekly and daily newspapers. All major Dutch national newspapers (*Telegraaf, Volkskrant, Algemeen Dagblad, NRC, Parool, Trouw, Financieel Dagblad*) and many regional newspapers are present[1]. In contrast to the tweets we do not have the texts of the newspaper articles. We use the search engine of LexisNexis that returns the number of newspapers in which a search term was found within an indicated date range. This number was used in our experiments.

2.3. Elections and Parties

We studied five Dutch elections of national importance. In 2012 and 2017 elections were held for the *Tweede Kamer* (comparable to the House of Representatives in the USA) and in 2011, 2015 and 2019 elections were held for the *Eerste Kamer* (comparable to the Senate in the USA). Eleven political parties participated in all five elections. These are the parties that were taken into account in our experiments. Table 1 shows the eleven parties. See (Sanders and van den Bosch, 2019) for a more detailed description of the Dutch electoral system and the various political parties.

3. Experiments

3.1. Counting Political Party Names

To find the ("political") correlation between tweets and newspapers, we count how often political party names appear in them. We use case insensitive pattern matching of different manners of writing of the party names. For tweets we use more elaborate regular expression to find the party names, for an extensive description, see (Sanders and van den Bosch, 2019). For the newspapers, we use a simpler set, because newspaper are much more unambiguous in their way of spelling party names and misspelling will be so infrequent that they can safely be ignored. Table 1 shows the political parties that gained at least one seat in all five elections under study. In 2017 and 2019, two other parties also gained seats in the elections: FvD and DENK. We decided to not include these in our experiments for two reasons: 1) By having the same set of parties over all elections makes it much easier to compare between the different elections. 2) 'Denk' is also a conjugation of the Dutch verb 'Denken' (to think), which is very common in the Dutch language. For tweets, we can disambiguate between the party name and the verb by means of automatic classification, but for newspaper articles this is not possible, because we do not have the texts of the articles.

We did some sample searches with all party names that might be used in the newspapers (also with their full names) and for most parties only their common abbreviation was sufficient to catch almost all news paper articles in which this party was mentioned. For a few parties we needed both the abbreviation as well as the full name. Note that the party *50Plus* is sometimes also written as *50+*, but this is not a possible search term in LexisNexis, because the plus-sign is ignored. Our estimation is that we did not miss many newspaper articles because of this.

Table 1: Search terms in LexisNexis of the political parties.

Party Name	Search Terms LexisNexis (case insensitive)
VVD	VVD
PvdA	PVDA
CDA	CDA
PVV	PVV
SP	SP
D66	D66
GroenLinks	GroenLinks "Groen Links" GL
ChristenUnie	ChristenUnie "Christen Unie" CU
50Plus	50Plus "50 Plus"
SGP	SGP
PvdD	PvdD "Partij voor de Dieren"

3.2. Correlation and Absolute Error

To determine the correlation between the number of party names mentioned in tweets on the one hand and in newspaper articles on the other hand, we counted mentions of the names in a period of ten days before election day. This period is long enough to smooth out fluctuations in reporting about specific parties, effects of one source influencing the other and the fact that in the Netherlands newspapers do not appear on Sundays. It is also short enough to make sure that the mentioning of parties is likely related to the elections.

We decided to take only singular copies of tweets and newspaper articles into account. Thus, we leave out

[1] https://www.lexisnexis.nl/over-lexisnexis/dutch-news-content

all retweets and replies to a tweet in which a party is mentioned out of our counts; also, we count identical articles, in which a party is mentioned, that appear in several newspapers as one. It is to be expected that including duplications will normalise over all parties and an earlier study showed that there is no substantial difference in including or excluding retweets with respect to the relation between party mentions in tweets and the outcome of elections (Sanders and van den Bosch, 2019).

Figure 1 shows the number of tweets per day in the ten days before election day. Retweets and replies to tweets are excluded from this set. For the elections in 2011 and 2012 there are considerably more tweets in the set than for the later elections, although we will see later that the number of tweets with party names in them are more comparable over the years. For every day and for every election there are at least 450,000 tweets in the collection.

Our research question as posed in the introduction is whether the correlation between political parties mentioned in tweets and in newspaper articles is bigger than the correlation between parties mentioned in tweets and the outcome of elections. To complete the triangular relation between these measurements, we also computed the correlation between parties mentioned in newspaper articles and the outcome of elections and compared these to the other two correlations.

We use two measurements to investigate the relationship between tweets and newspaper articles: Pearson correlation and Absolute error. Pearson correlation (Benesty et al., 2009) is a well known way to indicate the strength of the relation between two series of numbers. In our case we relate the percentages of the number of times the parties are mentioned in two different sources, tweets and newspaper articles.

The absolute error is a measurement used to express the difference between a measured value and a real value. In earlier studies, we used this measurement to compute the distance between a prediction and the real outcome of elections (Sanders and van den Bosch, 2019). In these experiments we use the absolute error to measure the relation between mentions of political parties in tweets and newspapers. See equation 1 for the computation of the absolute error.

$$AE = \sum_{i=1}^{N} |Perc_1(i) - Perc_2(i)| \quad (1)$$

Where AE is the Absolute Error, $Perc_1(i)$, the percentage of the mentions of party i in data stream 1, $Perc_2(i)$ the percentage of mentions of party i in data stream 2 and N is the total number of parties.

4. Results

The total number of tweets and newspaper articles in which one or more political parties were mentioned in the ten days before the elections are shown in Table 2. For newspaper articles, these numbers vary roughly between 7,000 and 16,000. For tweets these numbers are a factor 30 higher and vary roughly between 200,000 and 700,000. Figure 2 shows the number of tweets with party names per day in the ten days before the elections. From Table 2 and Figure 2 it can be observed that in 2012 and 2017 most tweets and newspaper articles with party names are found. This is to be expected, since these were the years that the elections for the *Tweede Kamer* took place, which are the most important elections in the Netherlands. In Figure 2 it can be seen that in the last one or two days before election day the number of tweets in which a party is mentioned increase substantially, which is also to be expected.

Table 2: Number of tweets and newspaper articles in which political parties were mentioned, for five elections.

year	#tweets	#newspaper articles
2011	304,933	11,175
2012	570,452	15,917
2015	413,967	10,928
2017	669,515	13,561
2019	206,159	7,261
total	2,165,026	58,842

For the five elections the percentages of party mentions in tweets and newspaper articles and the percentages of votes per party can be found in Figures 3, 4 and 5 respectively.

Comparing these figures it becomes apparent that they correlate to some extent. The largest parties (VVD, PvdA, PVV, CDA) have the largest percentages in all graphs, while the smaller parties (PvdD, SGP, 50Plus) are represented by small percentages in all graphs. Figure 6 confirms the visual correlation, showing Pearson's correlation coefficient for the three data pairs (news-tweets, tweets-elections, news-elections) for the five elections.

All Pearson's correlation coefficients lie between 0.67 and 0.95, which means that there is always at least a strong correlation. The correlation between newspaper articles and tweets is almost equal or higher than the correlation between tweets and election results in all cases. The hypothesis that tweets and news are more correlated than tweets and elections is not falsified by these results, but the differences are minimal.

At the same time we find that the correlation between newspaper articles and the election outcome is the highest in four of the five elections. This effect is clearer from Figure 7 in which the absolute errors for the three data pairs for the five elections are shown.

Figure 7 shows the same pattern as Figure 6: where the Pearson's correlation coefficient is higher, the absolute error is lower and vice versa. We observe that the absolute error of the news-elections relation is markedly lower in all elections except the one in 2012.

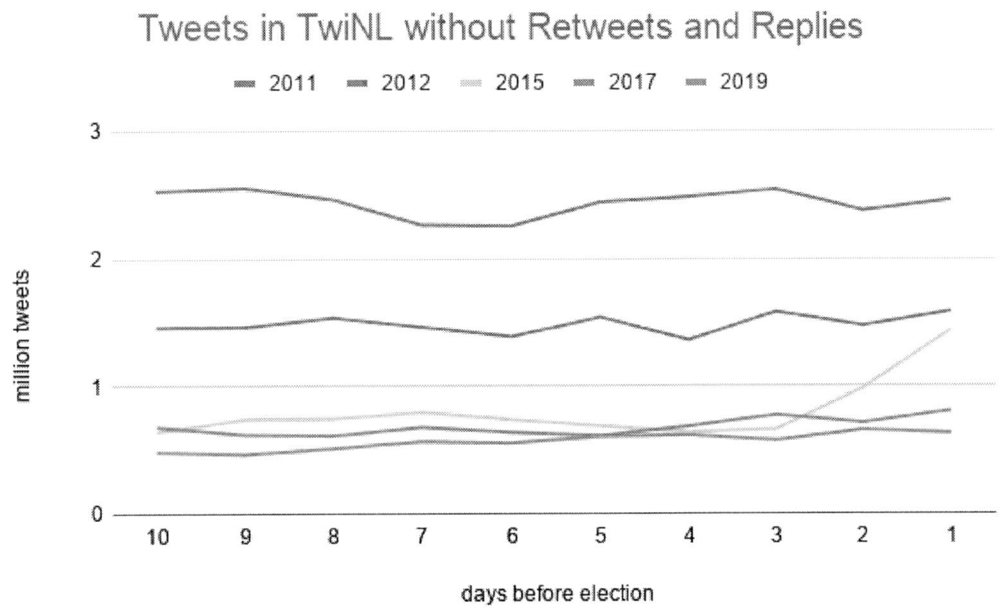

Figure 1: Number of million Dutch tweets per day in TwiNL in the 10 days before the election, excluding retweets and replies

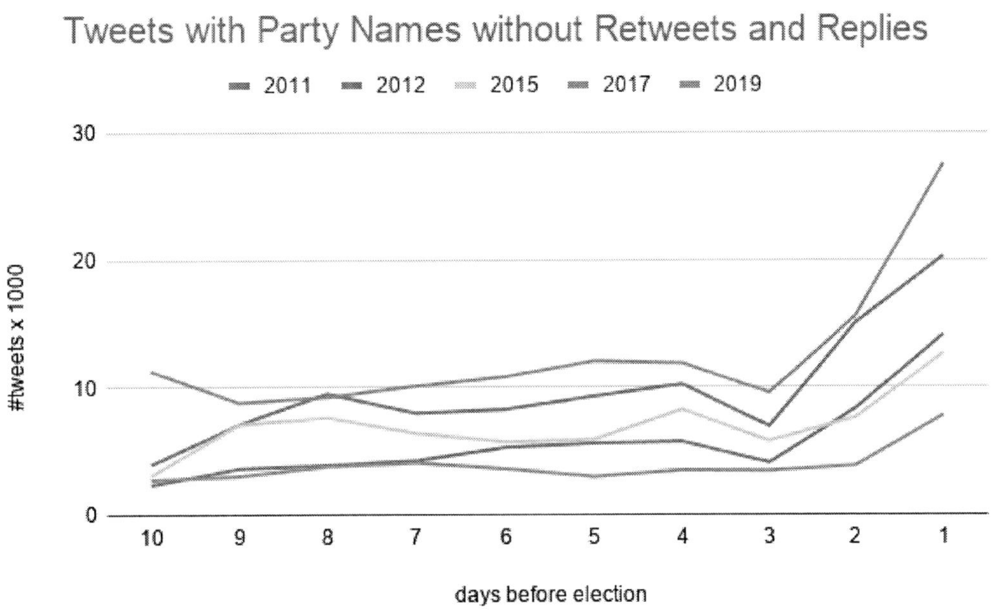

Figure 2: Number of tweets (excluding retweets and replies) with one or more party names in the ten days before the elections, for the five elections.

5. Discussion

Both a larger Pearson correlation (in four of the five elections) and a smaller absolute error (in all elections)

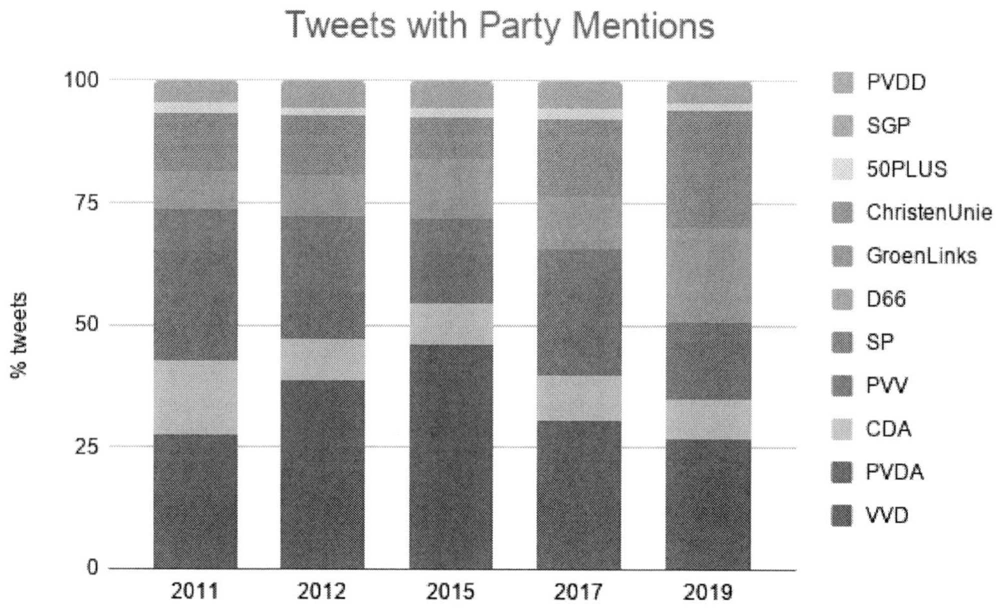

Figure 3: Percentages that indicate how often a political party was mentioned in tweets, for five elections.

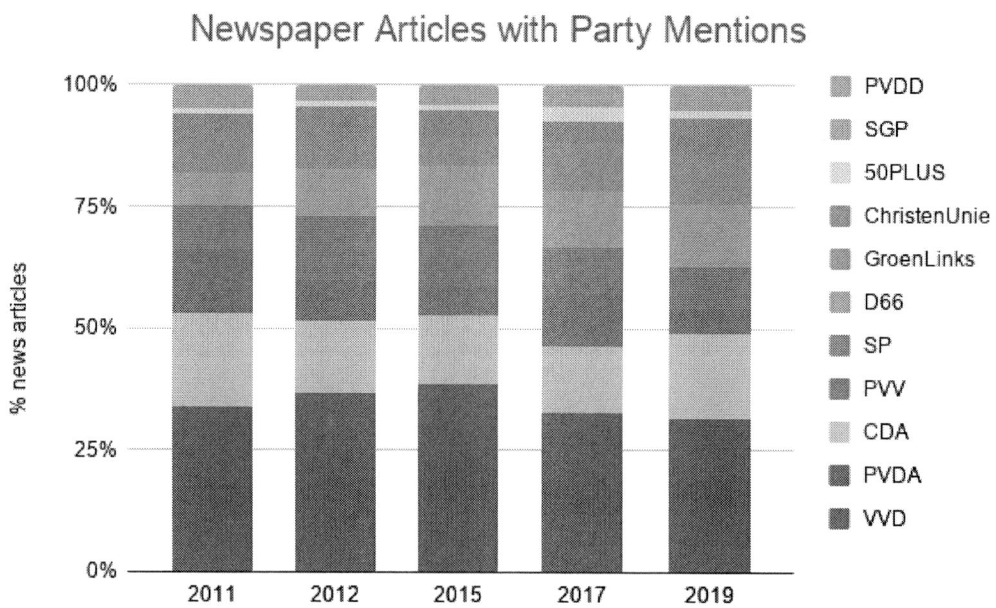

Figure 4: Percentages that indicate how often a political party was mentioned in newspaper articles, for five elections.

of the relation tweets—newspapers compared to the relation tweets—election results would confirm our assumption that party mentions in tweets are more influenced by the news than the political preferences of Twitter users, but the differences are overall very small.

Although it was not the focus of our research, we found that the correlation between party mentions in newspaper articles and the election results is the largest in four

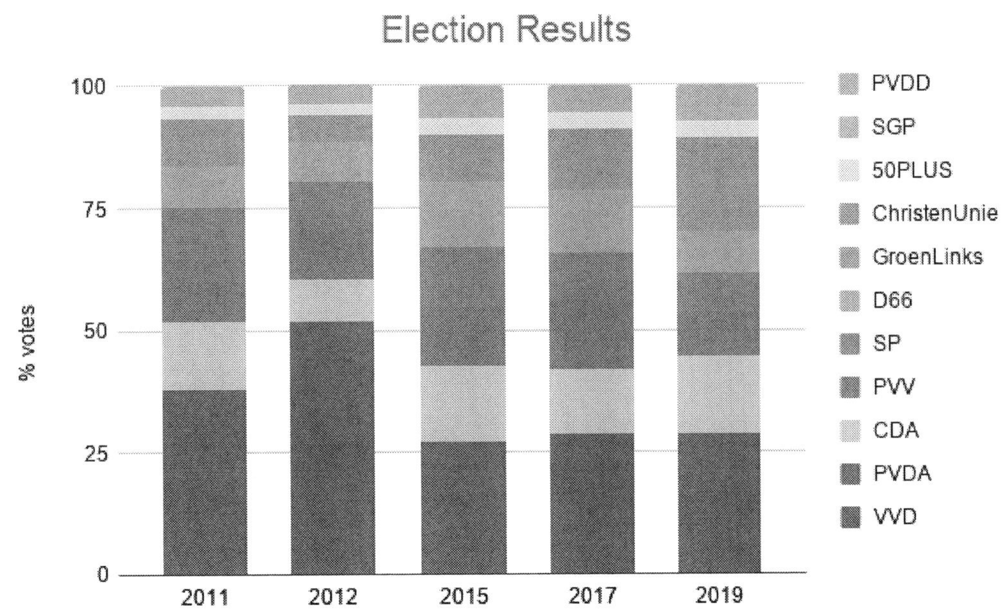

Figure 5: Percentages that indicate how many votes a political party got, for five elections.

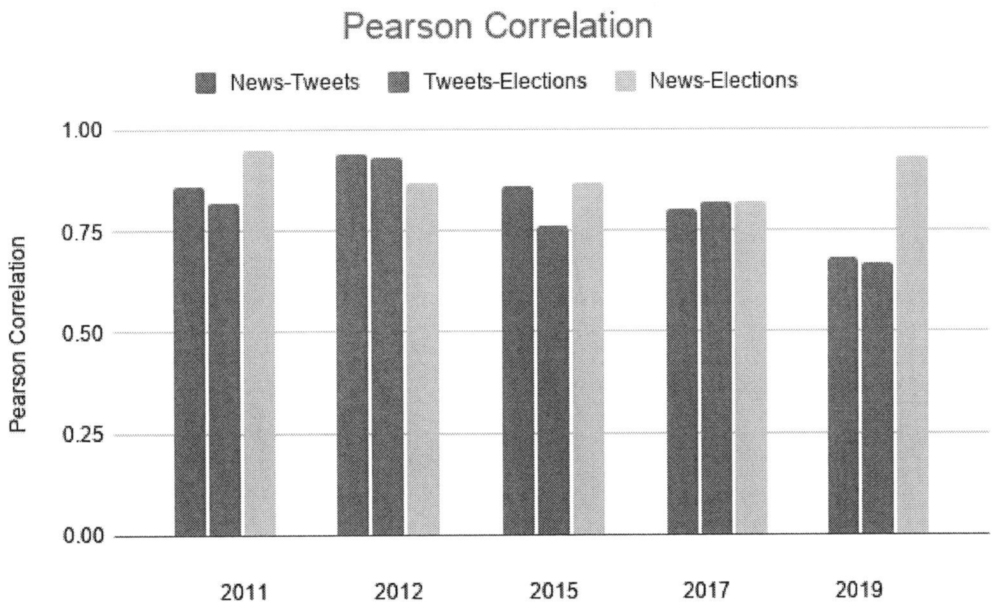

Figure 6: Pearson's correlation coefficients for the relation pairs between newspaper articles, tweets and election results for five elections.

of the five elections. Especially the absolute error is significantly lower in these four cases. The exception is in 2012 when two parties were in a duel to become the largest. It seems that newspapers reflect the political preferences in society better than tweets do. That would make them a better basic predictor of the election results. This is in accordance to what Barclay et al. conclude in their paper about the political bias of In-

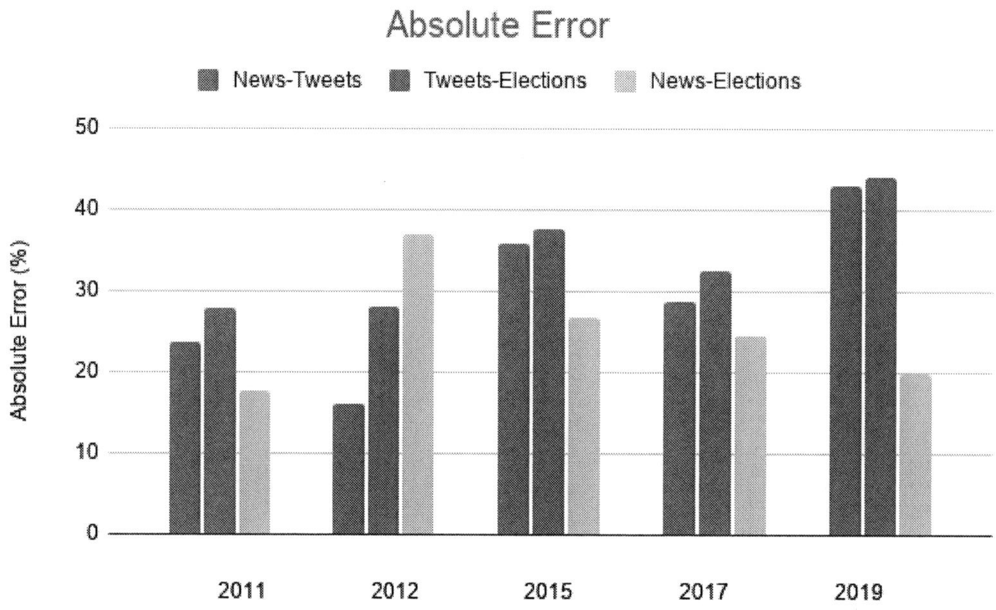

Figure 7: Absolute error for the relation pairs between newspaper articles, tweets and election results for five elections.

dian English newspapers in the 2014 elections in India: "This overall Press bias was observed to have a strong and positive correlation with the vote count, supporting the strong effects paradigm." (Barclay et al., 2015).

We were investigating whether news has a bigger impact on which political party people tweet about than their intention to vote for that party. The first step to find out was to look at the correlations and absolute errors. We realise that these measurements in itself do not tell anything about the influence of one data stream on the other. To be able to have more insight in the direction of influence we would need to take a closer look to the chronological order in which the parties are mentioned in different media and in what context they are mentioned.

When we take a closer look at the mentions of the individual parties in the newspapers and tweets in graphs 3, 4, 5, we see that PVV (an anti-islam party) is consistently underrepresented in the newspapers while CDA (Christian democrats) is over-represented. PVV has for a long time been a party that people typically will not say they will vote for. CDA on the other hand is a party in the middle of the political spectrum that has been the largest party for large periods in the previous century that is declining in support since a few decades, but still talked about in the newspapers. The same goes for PvdA (social democrats), but the over-representation in the newspapers is smaller than that of CDA.

We restricted ourselves to newspapers because of feasibility reasons. It would be interesting to study the difference with respect to party mentions in other media, such as radio, television and news websites. Unfortunately we do not have access to searchable resources that contain the transcriptions of radio and television broadcasts and news websites are often behind a paywall or very difficult if not impossible to search. We conjecture that they are likely to be correlated strongly to our newspaper measurements.

For our comparisons, we used raw counts of political party mentions in tweets and newspapers. This is very crude. Of course it would be best to normalise for all kinds of demographic variations of the tweeters, as that could help improving the results as the demographics of Twitter users are different (and changing over time) from the general voting populace; being able to correct for that would strengthen the assumption that when Twitter users mention a party, they often express their political preference for that party. However, as far as such a correction is technically possible, we have indications it does not offer an improvement (Sanders et al., 2016). Also taking context and sentiment into account does not appear to improve the preciseness of the counts, as we concluded in (Sanders and van den Bosch, 2020).

6. Conclusion

The goal of our research was to investigate the hypothesis that mentions of political party names in tweets are more influenced by what people read from the me-

dia (i.e. the news) than by what they (intend to) vote for. A first step in this investigation is to look at the correlation of party mentions in tweets and newspaper articles and the election results. Pearson correlation between party mentions in tweets and newspaper articles is larger than that of party mentions in tweets and the election results in four of the five elections and the absolute errors is smaller in all elections, which indicates that our hypothesis is confirmed. However, the differences are overall too small to be able to draw definitive conclusions.
It appeared that the correlation between the party mentions in the news and the election results are significantly higher and the absolute error significantly lower in four of the five cases. This leads us to conclude that newspaper articles might be a better predictor of the election outcome than tweets.

7. Bibliographical References

Barclay, F. P., Venkat, A., and Pichandy, C. (2015). Media effect: correlation between press trends and election results. *Media Asia*, 42(3-4):192–208.

Batra, P. K., Saxena, A., Goel, C., et al. (2020). Election Result Prediction Using Twitter Sentiments Analysis. In *2020 Sixth International Conference on Parallel, Distributed and Grid Computing (PDGC)*, pages 182–185. IEEE.

Benesty, J., Chen, J., Huang, Y., and Cohen, I. (2009). Pearson correlation coefficient. In *Noise reduction in speech processing*, pages 37–40. Springer.

Druckman, J. N. (2005). Media matter: How newspapers and television news cover campaigns and influence voters. *Political communication*, 22(4):463–481.

Gayo-Avello, D. (2012). No, you cannot predict elections with Twitter. *IEEE Internet Computing*, 16(6):91–94.

Knapp, J. A. (2018). Nexis Uni. *The Charleston Advisor*, 19(3):31–34.

Liu, R., Yao, X., Guo, C., and Wei, X. (2020). Can We Forecast Presidential Election Using Twitter Data? An Integrative Modelling Approach. *Annals of GIS*, pages 1–14.

Murthy, D. and Petto, L. R. (2015). Comparing print coverage and tweets in elections: A case study of the 2011–2012 US Republican primaries. *Social science computer review*, 33(3):298–314.

Murthy, D. (2015). Twitter and elections: are tweets, predictive, reactive, or a form of buzz? *Information, Communication & Society*, 18(7):816–831.

Nugroho, D. K. (2021). US presidential election 2020 prediction based on Twitter data using lexicon-based sentiment analysis. In *2021 11th International Conference on Cloud Computing, Data Science & Engineering (Confluence)*, pages 136–141. IEEE.

Rao, D. D. R., Usha, S., Krishna, S., Ramya, M. S., Charan, G., and Jeevan, U. (2020). Result Prediction for Political Parties Using Twitter Sentiment Analysis. *International Journal of Computer Engineering and Technology*, 11(4).

Sanders, E. and Van den Bosch, A. (2013). Relating Political Party Mentions on Twitter with Polls and Election Results. In *Proceedings of DIR-2013*, pages 68–71.

Sanders, E. and van den Bosch, A. (2019). A Longitudinal Study on Twitter-Based Forecasting of Five Dutch National Elections. In *International Conference on Social Informatics*, pages 128–142. Springer.

Sanders, E. and van den Bosch, A. (2020). Optimising Twitter-based Political Election Prediction with Relevance and Sentiment Filters. In *Proceedings of The 12th Language Resources and Evaluation Conference*, pages 6158–6165.

Sanders, E., de Gier, M., and van den Bosch, A. (2016). Using Demographics in Predicting Election Results with Twitter. In *International Conference on Social Informatics*, pages 259–268. Springer.

Su, Y. and Borah, P. (2019). Who is the agenda setter? Examining the intermedia agenda-setting effect between Twitter and newspapers. *Journal of Information Technology & Politics*, 16(3):236–249.

Tjong Kim Sang, E. and Van den Bosch, A. (2013). Dealing with big data: The case of Twitter. *Computational Linguistics in the Netherlands Journal*, 3:121–134, 12/2013.

Tumasjan, A., Sprenger, T. O., Sandner, P. G., and Welpe, I. M. (2010). Predicting Elections with Twitter: What 140 Characters Reveal about Political Sentiment. *ICWSM*, 10:178–185.

Proceedings of the First Workshop on Natural Language Processing for Political Sciences (PoliticalNLP), pages 16–21
Marseille, 24 June 2022

Debating Europe: A Multilingual Multi-Target Stance Classification Dataset of Online Debates

Valentin Barriere*, Alexandra Balahur*, Brian Ravenet†
*European Commission – DG-JRC, via Enrico Fermi 2749, 21027 Ispra (VA), Italy
†University Paris-Saclay, CNRS, LISN, CPU Team, 91400, Orsay, France
name.surname@ec.europa.eu, brian.ravenet@upsaclay.fr

Abstract

We present a new dataset of online debates in English, annotated with stance. The dataset was scraped from the "*Debating Europe*" platform, where users exchange opinions over different subjects related to the European Union. The dataset is composed of 2600 comments pertaining to 18 debates related to the "*European Green Deal*", in a conversational setting. After presenting the dataset and the annotated sub-part, we pre-train a model for a multilingual stance classification over the X-stance dataset before fine-tuning it over our dataset, and vice-versa. The fine-tuned models are shown to improve stance classification performance on each of the datasets, even though they have different languages, topics and targets. Subsequently, we propose to enhance the performances over "*Debating Europe*" with an interaction-aware model, taking advantage of the online debate structure of the platform. We also propose a semi-supervised self-training method to take advantage of the imbalanced and unlabeled data from the whole website, leading to a final improvement of accuracy by 3.4% over a Vanilla XLM-R model.

Keywords: Stance Classification, Online Debates, Multilingual

1. Introduction

Stance detection and classification in online debates have been tackled by various approaches. Some of the first ones employed linguistics-based methods inside debates using pre-defined opposed targets such as "*iPhone vs BlackBerry*" (Somasundaran and Wiebe, 2009), classifying ideological debates (Somasundaran and Wiebe, 2010) and on social justice subjects such as "*Abortion*" or "*Gay Rights*". They were followed by more complex probabilistic graphic systems (Sridhar et al., 2015), allowing to model the dynamics of the debate and the disagreements between speech turns, and finally deep neural methods (Augenstein et al., 2016; Allaway and McKeown, 2020), allowing efficient multi-target and zero-shot classification.

Recently, most of the work in this area focused on stance detection over tweets either in a non-interactional manner, like the SemEval-2016 task (Mohammad et al., 2016), or by including the interactions between the users (Barriere et al., 2018; Barriere, 2017) and applying stance detection over the whole thread (Gorrell et al., 2019). Building on seminal work in stance, the SemEval 2016 task was capable of targeting abstract concepts (e.g. "*Atheism*" or "*Abortion*"), as well as persons (e.g. "*Hillary Clinton*" or "*Donald Trump*"). On multilingual stance analysis over tweets, (Lai et al., 2020) present a model using mainly high-level linguistic features like stylistic, structural, affective or contextual knowledge, but no dense contextual vectors.

In (Vamvas and Sennrich, 2020), the authors propose the X-stance dataset, containing 67k comments over 150 political issues in 3 languages. Their approach was to reformulate the target in a natural question in order to easily train one multilingual multi-target model on the entire dataset. Similarly, in the *procon* dataset, containing 6,019 comments over 419 controversial issues, each target was also reformulated as a question (Hosseinia et al., 2020). However, none of these datasets contains interactional data.

The integration of the debate's dynamics in the model can be done in many ways. It can be achieved using dialogic features (Abbott et al., 2011) or intrinsically in the shape of a graphical model (Walker et al., 2012; Sridhar et al., 2015), allowing to represent the dialogic structure of the debates which is important in term of agreements. Eventually, this integration was accomplished with transformer models like BERT (Prakash and Madabushi, 2020; Yu et al., 2020; Devlin et al., 2018). To the best of our knowledge, no work with transformers so far investigates the use of a context window, like us, for multi-target stance detection in debates. Self-training (ST) (Yarowsky, 1995) is interesting when annotation is scarce, but however rarely used for stance detection and even less with imbalanced data. A recent work is the one of (Glandt et al., 2021) that use Knowledge Distillation on COVID tweets. (Wei et al., 2021) propose an interesting self-training method for imbalanced images on CIFAR, but they assume the distributions of the unlabeled and labeled datasets are the same, which is not true in our case.

Motivations and Positioning The first motivation of this work relates to the lack of an appropriate multilingual multi-target stance-annotated debate dataset. We created such a corpus, together with the appropriate annotation schema and guidelines. It is composed of contemporary questions that can be debated in the Conference on the Future of Europe.[1] The contributions of this paper are four-fold. Firstly, we propose a new dataset of annotated stance in online debates. Secondly,

[1] https://futureu.europa.eu/?locale=en

Figure 1: Examples of comments from 3 debates of the Debating Europe Dataset

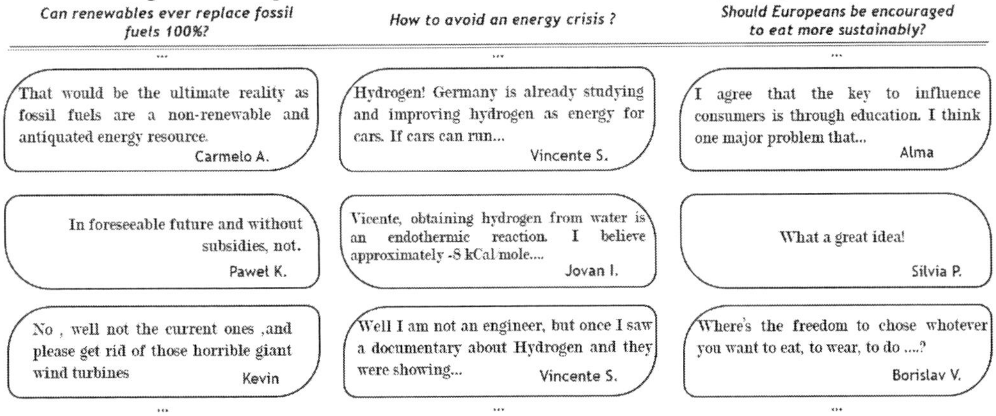

Label	% DE	Unit	μ_{com}	μ_{deb}	Σ
✗	100%	Comments	∅	89.5	125,798
		Words	51.7	4,623	6,499,625
✓	2.0%	Comments	∅	140	2,523
		Words	33.4	4,683	84,289

Table 1: Low-level statistics on the DE dataset, regarding there is label annotation or not. μ_{com}/μ_{deb} is the average mean of the respective units (comments or words) at the comment/debate-level.

we assess the quality of the data and annotation by showing that our dataset can be used to improve stance classification in non-English languages. Indeed, pre-training on English text stemming from Debating Europe (DE) allows us to reach better results on the multilingual X-stance dataset (Vamvas and Sennrich, 2020). Thirdly, we take advantage of the debate structure inside the learning model and analyze its impact on the performances. Finally, we show that self-training can be used on the unlabeled part of the dataset to enhance the model performances.

We differ from the existing works for three reasons. Firstly the dataset we are proposing allows to study stance in online debates in a multi-target and multi-lingual way. Secondly, we propose to use a context window in order to integrate the dynamics of the debate in a context-aware transformer model Finally, we not only release an annotated dataset for one domain, but also a larger dataset of unlabeled data on other topics, and show how to enhance a multilingual stance classifier with a simple, yet efficient semi-supervised learning method for imbalanced and unlabeled datasets.

2. Datasets Overview

2.1. The Debating Europe dataset

We release the Debating Europe (DE) dataset which is composed of online debates annotated with stance annotations at the comment level.

2.1.1. Debating Europe and Extraction

The DE dataset is composed of debates scraped in September 2020 from the *"Debating Europe"* platform[2]. Most of the debates are related to questions such as *"Should we have a European healthcare system?"*, which can generally be reformulated as a yes/no question. Each debate is composed of a topic tag, a text paragraph with the context of the debate, as well as comments, either about the main context or about previous comments.

The dataset contains 125,798 comments for 1,406 debates. More statistics are shown in Table 1

2.1.2. Annotation

Subset selection We annotated 18 debates from the whole dataset scraped from Debating Europe. The criteria chosen to select those debates are the number of comments associated to each debate and the relevance to one or more of the policy areas of the new *"European Green Deal"*.[3]

When needed, the debate question was reformulated into a closed question in order to make it compatible with our framework. We discarded the debates with less than 25 comments. More information about the debates and policy areas are available in the Appendix.

Annotation scheme The annotation scheme and corresponding guidelines aimed to capture citizens' stance towards the debate question, at the comment-level. To achieve this, four labels were defined: *Yes*, *No*, *Neutral* and *Not answering*. For each comment, the annotation regarded whether the user replied to the answer and if so, whether if he/she was in favour or not, or neutral with respect to the original question. The questions of the annotated debates are shown in Appendix. The annotation has been done by one unique expert using the INCEpTION software (Klie et al., 2018).

Final annotations We obtained 2,523 labels over the 18 debates, with 4 classes: *Yes* (40.1%), *No* (19.4%), *Neutral* (11.2%) and *Not answering* (29.3%). We chose to add the last category in order to check if the commenter was interested in answering the debate question. In the following experiments we merged the *Neu-*

[2]https://www.debatingeurope.eu/

[3]https://tinyurl.com/GreenDealEC

	Intra-target			X-question			X-Topic			X-lingual
	DE	FR	Mean	DE	FR	Mean	DE	FR	Mean	IT
M-BERT (Vamvas2020)	76.8	76.6	76.6	68.5	68.4	68.4	68.9	70.9	69.9	70.2
XLM-R	76.3	78.0	77.1	71.5	72.9	72.2	71.2	73.7	72.4	73.0
XLM-R_{ft}	77.3	79.0	**78.1**	71.5	74.8	**73.1**	72.2	74.7	**73.4**	**73.9**

Table 2: Results over X-Stance dataset for a binary classification

tral and *Not answering* classes into a unique class in order to simplify the work (Mohammad et al., 2016; Küçük and Fazli, 2020). The validation using classical inter-annotator-agreement metrics was impossible with one unique expert annotations, hence we validated the dataset by showing its usefulness for cross-dataset, cross-topic and cross-lingual transfer learning in Subsection 3.1.
More information about the general distribution of the words is available Table 1 and in the Appendix, Table 5.

2.2. X-stance: A Multilingual multi-target stance detection dataset

The X-stance (XS) dataset (Vamvas and Sennrich, 2020) contains 67,271 comments in French, German and Italian on more than 150 political issues (*targets*) retrieved from the Swiss application *Smartvote*. To tackle stance classification in this setting, the authors propose to integrate the target inside a natural question which can be seen as a debate's title. This approach allows the model to learn across targets, to remain efficient in a zero-shot learning setting and to use the semantics information contained inside the pre-trained model (Yin et al., 2019). The 4 labels have been merged into 2 classes: *favor* and *against* the proposition, which can be seen as *yes* or *no* when the proposition is formulated as a question.

3. Experiments and Results

The 3 experiments below are complementary. The first experiment focuses on transfer learning across topics, targets and languages. The second one focuses on the interactive aspect of online debates. The last one highlights the value of the unlabeled DE dataset, with a self-training method handling unlabeled and imbalanced data.

3.1. Multilingual stance detection using transfer learning

It is known that when the source and target domains are dissimilar, standard transfer learning may fail and hurt the performance by conducting to a negative transfer (Rosenstein et al., 2005). Hence, showing the small DE dataset can improve the results on a bigger dataset via transfer learning across topics and language is a way to validate the annotations. The XS dataset, which is composed of multilingual comments answering to political debate questions from several topics, is the perfect candidate. We used a XLM-R (Conneau et al., 2020) as multilingual learning model, and call it XLM-R_{ft} when it has been already trained over one dataset.

3.2. Context-aware model

In order to model the dynamics aspect of a debate, we decided to use a context window to integrate an interactional context of variable size. We separated the different sentences using [SEP] tokens, rendering for a context window of size 2: `[CLS] Debate Question [SEP] Sent n [SEP] Sent n-1 [SEP] Sent n-2 [SEP]`.

3.3. Data-augmentation with semi-supervised learning

As seen in Subsection 2.1, we annotated only a small part of the available DE dataset, leaving unlabeled a large amount of data that could potentially be useful to increase model performance. To maximise the potential of this unlabeled dataset, we propose to use a self-training method (Yarowsky, 1995). The general principle we follow is to leverage some of the model's own prediction on unlabeled data by adding pseudo-examples in the training set. We compare two classical methods, using a threshold on the model's class probability and taking the k predictions with the highest probability (resp. *thresh* and *k-best* in Table 3). When doing so, we keep aware of the downside of self-training such as the fact that the model is not able to correct its own mistakes and that errors are amplified (Ruder, 2019). Thus, if the unlabeled dataset is imbalanced, the classifier bias will be amplified by the pseudo-labels and the class-imbalance issue will be aggravated (Wei et al., 2021).
To mitigate this risk, we propose to combine both techniques, by adding a definite and balanced number of k_{max} examples chosen randomly amongst those which have a probability above the threshold, at each iteration of the SSL algorithm. Our technique makes no assumption on the label distribution of the unlabeled dataset and can thus help to prevent an overflowing of the training set with pseudo-examples from outer domains.

3.4. Methodological protocol

We followed the protocol of (Barriere and Balahur, 2020; Barriere and Jacquet, 2021) for the transformers' learning phase, already used in the past for multilingual sentiment analysis and text classification. The pre-trained models that we used were made available online using the `transformers` library (Wolf et al., 2019).We used the Adam algorithm (Kingma and Ba, 2014) with early stopping for the optimization of the training loss, using a learning rate of $2e^{-6}$ for the first training of the model on a stance task, and $5e^{-7}$ when fine-tuning on another dataset for the transfer learning.

Unsupervised Method	Threshold	k_{max}	Balanced	Model	Prec.	Rec.	F1	Acc
✗	✗	✗	✗	XLM-R	68.6	69.3	68.9	70.1
				XLM-R_{ft}	70.7	69.9	**70.2**	**72.1**
thresh-0.99	0.99	✗	✗	XLM-R	68.6	69.8	69.1	70.7
				XLM-R_{ft}	68.9	69.6	69.0	70.9
k-best-2000	✗	2000	✗	XLM-R	67.5	68.3	67.8	69.3
				XLM-R_{ft}	70.4	69.9	69.8	71.9
k-best-600	✗	600	✗	XLM-R	69.4	68.5	68.0	69.5
				XLM-R_{ft}	72.5	70.3	71.1	73.3
our-2000	0.99	2000	✓	XLM-R	69.5	69.4	69.4	71.3
				XLM-R_{ft}	70.5	69.9	69.3	71.7
our-600	0.99	600	✓	XLM-R	70.9	71.6	71.1	72.7
				XLM-R_{ft}	71.5	71.5	**71.4**	**73.5**

Table 3: Results over the Debating Europe dataset for a 3-class classification using SSL

Ctxt	Prec	Rec.	F1	Acc
0	70.7	69.9	70.2	72.1
1	72.1	70.5	**71.2**	**72.7**
2	70.7	69.8	70.2	**72.7**

Table 4: Results over DE for different context windows. All the models were pre-trained over XS (XLM-R_{ft})

Figure 2: Distribution of the pseudo-labels

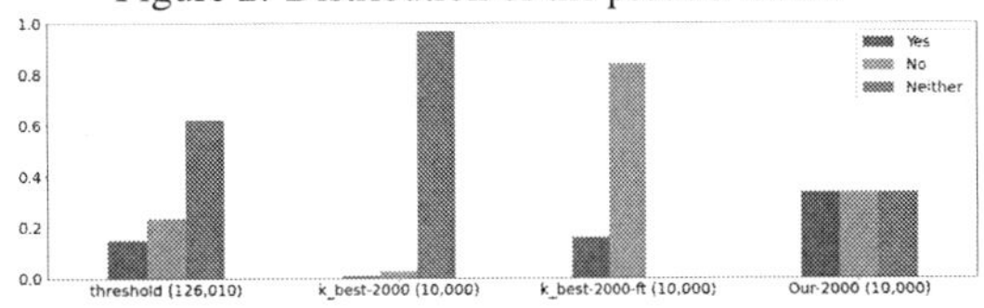

In contrast to (Vamvas and Sennrich, 2020), we do not perform any hyperparameter optimization on dev and use a shorter maximum sequence length (128 vs 512) to speed up training and evaluation.

We divided the DE dataset into 3 train/validation/test sets in a stratified way with a ratio of 75/5/20. To compare results, we proceeded the same partition as (Vamvas and Sennrich, 2020) for the XS dataset. For the SSL, we stopped at 5 iterations, used 0.99 for probability threshold, and 600 and 2000 as maximum number of examples added at each iteration when applicable.

3.5. Results

The 3 experiments are complementary. The first one gives an insight of the effect of a pre-training over a non-English multi-lingual dataset from another domain. The second one investigated the impact of the integration of the dialogic context inside the model, using context windows of variable sizes. The third experiment uses a self-training method applicable on a dataset of unlabeled and imbalanced data.

Cross-datasets This experiment gives an insight of the effect of a pre-training over a non-English multilingual dataset from another domain. As can be seen in Table 3 and 2, the transfer learning approach is efficient for both the datasets, even though they have different languages, topics and targets.

Impact of a context window This experiment investigated the impact of integrating dialogic context of variable size inside the model, using a context window. The results (Table 4) show that a context window can enhance the model and a context window of size 1 is optimal.

ST setting The results in Table 2 show that the ST setups were not all successful. To understand the causes of this failure, Figure 2 shows the distribution (and amounts) of the pseudo-labels. Analysing the distribution, we can clearly observe the weaknesses of each method and draw a conclusion on why our method is working: it does not flood the gold labels with weak labels as pair with a balanced distribution.

The threshold method does not improve the performances of the model because of the small size of our dataset and the lack of model calibration. Too many pseudo-examples added at each iteration significantly degrade the performances of the model. The k-best method allows diminishing the number of examples added at every iteration and it performs well for the XLM-R_{ft}, as it has seen way more training examples and seems more robust.

4. Conclusion and Future work

In this work, we presented "*Debating Europe*" - a new dataset for stance detection and classification, composed of online debates and partly annotated for stance at the comment-level. This is as far as we know the first multi-target stance dataset in the literature. Although it has been annotated by one unique expert, we validated the quality of the annotation by showing the DE dataset is useful for transfer learning across languages and domains, and reaching a new state-of-the-art on the multilingual multi-target X-stance dataset. Additionally, we proposed and validated two methods to improve over the baseline results by integrating the interactional context inside a transformer models, and by utilising the imbalanced and unlabeled dataset with a home-made self-training algorithm that makes no assumption on the label distribution. The dataset and labels will be available online after publication. Future work includes extending DE dataset to further languages and domains, as well as testing the impact of annotation granularity.

5. Bibliographical References

Abbott, R., Walker, M., Anand, P., Fox Tree, J. E., Bowmani, R., and King, J. (2011). How can you say such things?!?: recognizing disagreement in informal political argument. *Proceedings of the Workshop on Languages in Social Media*, pages 2–11.

Allaway, E. and McKeown, K. (2020). Zero-Shot Stance Detection: A Dataset and Model using Generalized Topic Representations.

Augenstein, I., Rocktäschel, T., Vlachos, A., and Bontcheva, K. (2016). Stance detection with bidirectional conditional encoding. *EMNLP 2016 - Conference on Empirical Methods in Natural Language Processing, Proceedings*, pages 876–885.

Barriere, V. and Balahur, A. (2020). Improving Sentiment Analysis over non-English Tweets using Multilingual Transformers and Automatic Translation for Data-Augmentation. In *COLING*.

Barriere, V. and Jacquet, G. (2021). How does a pretrained transformer integrate contextual keywords? Application to humanitarian computing. *Proceedings of the International ISCRAM Conference*, 2021-May(May):766–771.

Barriere, V., Clavel, C., and Essid, S. (2018). Attitude Classification in Adjacency Pairs of a Human-Agent Interaction with Hidden Conditional Random Fields. In *ICASSP*.

Barriere, V. (2017). Hybrid Models for Opinion Analysis in Speech Interactions. In *ICMI*, pages 647–651.

Conneau, A., Khandelwal, K., Goyal, N., Chaudhary, V., Wenzek, G., Guzmán, F., Grave, E., Ott, M., Zettlemoyer, L., and Stoyanov, V. (2020). Unsupervised Cross-Lingual Representation Learning at Scale. pages 31–38.

Devlin, J., Chang, M.-w., Lee, K., and Toutanova, K. (2018). BERT: Pre-training of Deep Bidirectional Transformers for Language Understanding.

Glandt, K., Khanal, S., Li, Y., Caragea, D., and Caragea, C. (2021). Stance Detection in COVID-19 Tweets. In *ACL-IJCNLP*, pages 1596–1611.

Gorrell, G., Bontcheva, K., Derczynski, L., Kochkina, E., Liakata, M., and Zubiaga, A. (2019). RumourEval 2019: Determining rumour veracity and support for rumours. In *SemEval 2019*, pages 845–854.

Hosseinia, M., Dragut, E., and Mukherjee, A. (2020). Stance Prediction for Contemporary Issues: Data and Experiments.

Kingma, D. and Ba, J. (2014). Adam: A Method for Stochastic Optimization. *International Conference on Learning Representations*, pages 1–13.

Klie, J.-C., Bugert, M., Boullosa, B., de Castilho, R. E., and Gurevych, I. (2018). The INCEpTION Platform: Machine-Assisted and Knowledge-Oriented Interactive Annotation. *Proceedings of the International Conference on Computational Linguistics*, pages 5–9.

Küçük, D. and Fazli, C. A. (2020). Stance detection: A survey. *ACM Computing Surveys*, 53(1).

Lai, M., Cignarella, A. T., Hernández Farías, D. I., Bosco, C., Patti, V., and Rosso, P. (2020). Multilingual stance detection in social media political debates. *Computer Speech and Language*, 63.

Mohammad, S. M., Kiritchenko, S., Sobhani, P., Zhu, X., and Cherry, C. (2016). A Dataset for Detecting Stance in Tweets.

Prakash, A. and Madabushi, H. T. (2020). Incorporating Count-Based Features into Pre-Trained Models for Improved Stance Detection. *COLING*, pages 22–32.

Rosenstein, M. T., Marx, Z., Kaelbling, L. P., and Dietterich, T. G. (2005). To transfer or not to transfer. *NIPS 2005 workshop on transfer learning*, 898:3.

Ruder, S. (2019). Neural Transfer Learning for Natural Language Processing.

Somasundaran, S. and Wiebe, J. (2009). Recognizing stances in online debates. *ACL-IJCNLP 2009*, pages 226–234.

Somasundaran, S. and Wiebe, J. (2010). Recognizing Stances in Ideological On-Line Debates. In *NAACL Workshop*.

Sridhar, D., Foulds, J., Huang, B., Getoor, L., and Walker, M. (2015). Joint Models of Disagreement and Stance in Online Debate. *Proceedings of the 53rd Annual Meeting of the Association for Computational Linguistics and the 7th International Joint Conference on Natural Language Processing*, pages 116–125.

Vamvas, J. and Sennrich, R. (2020). X-stance: A Multilingual Multi-Target Dataset for Stance Detection. In *SwissText*.

Walker, M. A., Anand, P., Abbott, R., and Grant, R. (2012). Stance classification using dialogic properties of persuasion. *NAACL HLT 2012 - 2012 Conference of the North American Chapter of the Association for Computational Linguistics*, pages 592–596.

Wei, C., Sohn, K., Mellina, C., Yuille, A., and Yang, F. (2021). CReST : A Class-Rebalancing Self-Training Framework for Imbalanced Semi-Supervised Learning. In *CVPR*.

Wolf, T., Debut, L., Sanh, V., Chaumond, J., Delangue, C., Moi, A., Cistac, P., Rault, T., Louf, R., Funtowicz, M., and Brew, J. (2019). HuggingFace's Transformers: State-of-the-art Natural Language Processing.

Yarowsky, D. (1995). Unsupervised word sense disambiguation rivaling supervised methods. In *ACL*, pages 189–196.

Yin, W., Hay, J., and Roth, D. (2019). Benchmarking zero-shot text classification: Datasets, evaluation and entailment approach. *EMNLP-IJCNLP 2019*, pages 3914–3923.

Yu, J., Jiang, J., Khoo, L. M. S., Chieu, H. L., and Xia, R. (2020). Coupled Hierarchical Transformer for Stance-Aware Rumor Verification in Social Media Conversations. In *EMNLP*, pages 1392–1401.

Aggregation-level		Debate			Comment			All
Units	Label	μ	σ	med	μ	σ	med	Σ
Comments	All	140	99	101	1	0	1	2,523
	Yes	56	37	39	1	0	1	1,012
	No	29	39	14	1	0	1	489
	Neutral	18	18	11	1	0	1	282
	Not answering	41	23	35	1	0	1	740
Words	All	4,683	2,721	3,794	33	60	16	84,289
	Yes	1,933	1,221	1,772	34	74	13	34,790
	No	942	1,157	554	33	43	19	16,012
	Neutral	814	808	478	46	73	23	13,023
	Not answering	1,137	627	972	28	39	16	20,464

Table 5: Low-level statistics on the Debating Europe dataset. Here, μ represents the average mean, σ the standard deviation, med the median and Σ the sum.

Appendix

A. European Green Deal

We chose to select the debates that were falling under the scope of the European Green Deal European Commission's priority.

The policy areas comprised in the European Green Deal are 9 and are the following: Biodiversity, From Farm to Fork, Sustainable agriculture, Clean Energy, Sustainable industry, Building and renovating, Sustainable mobility, Eliminating pollution and Climate action. More details are available online.[4]

B. Questions of the annotated debates

The debates chosen for the annotation are the ones below: *Should we consume less energy?*, *Should we make the cities greener?*, *Can renewables ever replace fossil fuels 100?*, *Should we invest more in clean energies to avoid an energy crisis?*, *Should we cut CO2 emission and invest into clean energies?*, *Should we think about the real cost of the food we eat?*, *Should all cars be electric by 2025?*, *Does organic food really make a difference?*, *Should Europeans be encouraged to eat more sustainably?*, *Sustainable agriculture: With or without pesticides?*, *Should all EU countries abandon nuclear power?*, *Should we stop flying to help the environment?*, *Should plastic packaging be banned?*, *Should we all eat less meat?*, *Should we invest in cheap and clean energies?*, *Should we move towards a low-carbon economy or invest into clean energies?*, *Should the European Union ban plastic bags?* and *Should plastic water bottles be banned?*.

C. Debating Europe Dataset Statistics

More low-level statistics on the Debating Europe dataset are available in Table 5.

[4]https://ec.europa.eu/info/strategy/priorities-2019-2024/european-green-deal_en

Proceedings of the First Workshop on Natural Language Processing for Political Sciences (PoliticalNLP), pages 22–31
Marseille, 24 June 2022

An Unsupervised Approach to Discover Media Frames

Sha Lai[1], Yanru Jiang[4], Lei Guo[3], Margrit Betke[1], Prakash Ishwar[2], Derry T. Wijaya[1]
[1] Department of Computer Science, [2] Department of Electrical and Computer Engineering, and
[3] College of Communication, Boston University
[4] Department of Communication, University of California Los Angeles
lais823@bu.edu, yanrujiang@g.ucla.edu, guolei@bu.edu, betke@bu.edu, pi@bu.edu, wijaya@bu.edu

Abstract

Media framing refers to highlighting certain aspect of an issue in the news to promote a particular interpretation to the audience. Supervised learning has often been used to recognize frames in news articles, requiring a known pool of frames for a particular issue, which must be identified by communication researchers through thorough manual content analysis. In this work, we devise an unsupervised learning approach to discover the frames in news articles automatically. Given a set of news articles for a given issue, e.g., gun violence, our method first extracts frame elements from these articles using related Wikipedia articles and the Wikipedia category system. It then uses a community detection approach to identify frames from these frame elements. We discuss the effectiveness of our approach by comparing the frames it generates in an unsupervised manner to the domain-expert-derived frames for the issue of gun violence, for which a supervised learning model for frame recognition exists.

Keywords: unsupervised learning, natural language processing, frame

1. Introduction

Framing, in the communication context, means selecting certain aspect of a perceived reality to improve its salience among the audience (Entman, 1993). By carefully selecting frames, some authors can encourage certain interpretations of an issue; others may even promote a political agenda. Communication researchers have been studying ways to recognize frames in news articles. Currently, their approach is mostly based on manual content analysis. Given an issue, researchers need to create a list of possible frames based on the existing literature and/or by examining a sample of news items. Then human coders are recruited and trained to annotate frames. Such approach has a few limitations. First, since the frames are created about a certain issue, they are limited within some scope. Second, the resulting frames may be subjective, as there is no standard of creating or naming frames. Third, the processes of manually determining and annotating frames can be very time consuming. Though some automatic methods exist have been applied in communication research such as supervised machine learning, they still require substantial expert intervention and human labor. In this article, we propose a framing analysis method that can be widely adapted to different issues, with little human intervention, and largely unsupervised.

Our proposed method, which is our main contribution of this paper, is based on two concepts: general news frames and frame elements. We define general news frames as frames applied to news articles of any issue. To be clear, our proposed "general news frames" are different from "generic news frames" defined in the communication literature such as conflict, economic consequences, and morality (Semetko and Valkenburg, 2000), which are pre-determined by communication scholars. General news frames, as will be discussed later, are identified in an unsupervised way. We define frame elements as ingredients of the general news frames. In communication research, common framing elements include "themes, subthemes, types of actors, actions and setting, qualification, statistics, charts, graphs, appeals, etc" (Van Gorp and others, 2010). Using Wikipedia categories, framing elements in our approach are also identified automatically rather than predetermined. In addition, general news frames are mutually exclusive subsets of all frame elements.

With these two concepts defined, we can describe our proposed approach as a pipeline:

1. Pass a news article to a frame element generator, which makes use of the Wikipedia category system, to obtain a list of frame elements.
2. Pass the list of frame elements to a frame generator, in which we apply graph community detection algorithms, to obtain a list of frames.

A diagram of this pipeline is shown in Figure 1.

2. Related Work

While we study framing in communication research, there exist similar concepts in other domains. In linguistics, for example, semantic frames are defined as a coherent structure of concepts that are related such that without knowledge of all of them, one does not have complete knowledge of any one. Tools like FrameNet (Ruppenhofer et al., 2016) have been developed to recognize these semantic frames from text, but we cannot use them since our task is different due to the difference in definition of frames.

Since our proposed method involves formulation of media frames and the usage of Wikipedia category system, in this section, we will review works related to computational methods used in media framing research and the application of Wikipedia categories in computational linguistic research.

2.1. Media Framing Analysis

We can categorize the computational methods as the following: lexicon-based methods and machine learning (ML) methods. Furthermore, the ML methods can be split into supervised methods and unsupervised ones. In frame extraction research problems, the frames can either be defined by researchers manually or be modeled and constructed automatically. In the tasks where frames are predefined, a common goal is to recognize the frames from media sources using some lexicon-based or supervised ML methods, while in the event where frames are not explicitly defined, unsupervised ML methods are applied to model them.

2.1.1. Lexicon-based Methods

The lexicon-based methods center around term frequency as well as mapping from keywords to categories. Such methods is widely used in sentiment analysis. For example, Turney (2002) computes similarity between phrases and two lists of predefined words corresponding to positive and negative semantics orientations using Pointwise Mutual Information and Information Retrieval. An example of lexicon-based methods is the development of keywords for frames regarding immigrants by Lind et al. (2019). One major disadvantage of such methods is the requirement of expert knowledge in creating the keywords, which are largely tied to issues, limits the application scope.

2.1.2. Supervised ML Methods

The supervised methods do not gain much popularity in framing analysis, despite of the fact that models like Support Vector Machine (SVM) and Random Forest have been proved successful in other communication research problems (Opperhuizen et al., 2019; Adamu et al., 2021). Burscher et al. (2014) discover that an ensemble algorithm combining two linear SVM models, a polynomial SVM model and a perceptron model can lead to higher accuracy in predicting the four generic frames than using these individual classifiers alone.
Another supervised ML example is the recent work by Tourni et al. (2021), which shows that combining a transformer model to process news headlines and a residual network model to process news images in tandem leads to accurate headline frame prediction.

2.1.3. Unsupervised ML Methods

Despite of the popularity of framing theory in communication research, what constitutes framing remains an open question. Nonetheless, that it being open-ended allows a diverse range of formulation of frames under unsupervised ML approaches.
One popular unsupervised ML method is the Latent Dirichlet Allocation (LDA) based topic modeling. Blei et al. (2003) develop LDA as a probabilistic model that discovers keywords to represent topics in an article. Walter and Ophir (2019) construct frames based on the topics returned by LDA. We would like to emphasize that topics are not equivalent to frames, though they appear to be similar in some cases. One key difference is that frames should be "persistent over time" (Reese et al., 2001) while topics naturally do not have to be so. While we focus on frames in news articles and model them as a collection of frame elements obtained from Wikipedia categories, others may formulate frames in a diverse range of applications. For instance, Ajjour et al. (2019) model frames as mutually exclusive clusters of arguments. They develop a two-level clustering method which takes a set of arguments as input and yields a partition of the arguments as output. Of the two levels of clustering, one aims to remove topics in the arguments and the other aims to produce a partition. Though like us, they model frames as sets, their formulation applies to arguments, which typically contain only one or two sentences and strongly focus on one aspect of the corresponding topic.

2.2. Framing via Community Detection

We construct frames by applying community detection algorithms on a graph formed by frame elements. The community detection has been used extensively in graph analysis and applications. In social science, this technique is frequently applied on social media networks, as a number of reviews and surveys on this type of application have been published (Wang et al., 2015a; Wang et al., 2015b; Bedi and Sharma, 2016; Kumar et al., 2018; Souravlas et al., 2021).
In framing analysis, Walter and Ophir (2019) treat the topics returned by LDA as frame elements. They create a graph using the frame elements and applied community detection on the graph. Such approach is very similar to ours, while the key difference lies in the source of frame elements.

2.3. Usage of Wikipedia Category System

Our approach involves the Wikipedia category system. Many works have adopted this system, but few aim at solving a similar problem as ours. Nastase and Strube (2008) use the system to study the relation between concepts stored on Wikipedia. Pasca (2018) developes a method to recognize classes of Wikipedia articles, where the categories are used as part of the approach. Allahyari and Kochut (2016) integrate the Wikipedia categories as topics into the LDA probabilistic model to perform semantic tagging on online articles.
A number of works use this system to perform topic modeling. Schönhofen (2009) uses Wikipedia categories and Wikipedia article titles to identify document topics. Mirylenka and Passerini (2013) propose a method to create topic summaries for documents by mapping them to Wikipedia articles and the related categories. Kumar et al. (2017) build an automated topic identification model, which is trained on the Wikipedia category graph, to generate topic trees from text data.

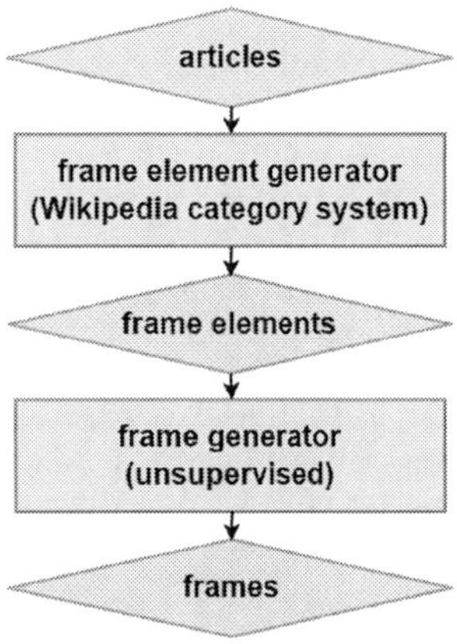

Figure 1: The pipeline of our approach.

Nevertheless, we again stress that topics and frames are different in terms of scope.

3. Methodology

Out proposed pipeline, as described in section 1 and shown in Figure 1, contains two major parts: frame element generator and frame generator. This section presents the two generators in detail.

3.1. Frame Element Generator

The goal of this part is to extract frame elements from the articles. To do so, we first associate each news article to some Wikipedia articles, and then use the Wikipedia category system to create frame elements.

3.1.1. From News Articles to Wikipedia Articles

The bridge between the news articles and the Wikipedia ones is built with computational linguistics techniques. We use a Doc2Vec model (Le and Mikolov, 2014) to create a document embedding for each news article and each Wikipedia one. Then, for each news article embedding, we find the top K_p most similar Wikipedia article embeddings based on cosine similarity. Thus, each news article is linked to K_p Wikipedia ones.

3.1.2. From Wikipedia Articles to Categories

This step involves the category system on Wikipedia. Due to the system's complex nature, we will briefly introduce it with an example before describing how we make use of it.

Wikipedia's Category System Wikipedia is a gigantic online database with free access. For every recorded item, there is a page containing an article describing it. To help the readers better navigate through the database to find relevant items, a hierarchical category system is used to group the articles. Each article has a list of categories, which can be found at the bottom of the article webpage. Furthermore, each category may have its own list of categories.

Example An example that starts from the article "computer science" is illustrated in Figure 2. In this example, the Wikipedia article "computer science" has

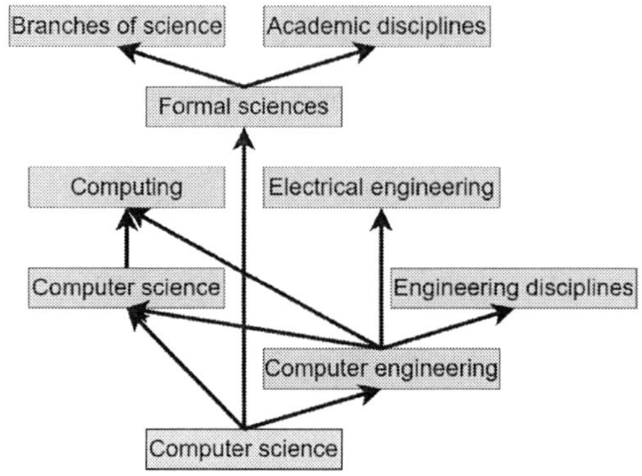

Figure 2: Example Wikipedia categories obtained from two levels of recursion from the Wikipedia article titled "Computer science" (green box).

the following categories: "computer science", "formal sciences", and "computer engineering". The category with the same name, "computer science", has the following categories: "formal sciences", "computing", "categories requiring diffusion", and "commons category link is on Wikidata". The last two of these categories are called "hidden categories" which are mainly used by the Wikipedia's internal system for maintenance purposes. Furthermore, that "formal sciences" is the category of both the article page as well as the category page of "computer science" shows the non-trivial nature of the hierarchical system.

Obtaining Categories The example suggests that one can follow the category links to retrieve the categories recursively starting from any page. Our method performs a recursive retrieval of categories for each page with a maximum recursion depth D.

Processing Categories The retrieved categories need to be cleaned up to reduce noise for further analysis. We first remove the categories for Wikipedia administration or maintenance, including the hidden categories mentioned in the example, since they are not helpful in our study. Then, we merge the categories sharing the same key words via an NLP technique called dependency parsing (DP). DP analyzes the relation between words in a sentence and assigns a grammar role for each word. The main subject is selected uniquely and is called ***root***. All categories are mapped to some ***roots*** and merging occurs among the categories sharing the same ***root***, as these categories document the same subject from different aspects. For example, there are categories such as "suicides by city," "suicides by country," and "suicides by method." In each of them, DP recognizes the word "suicide" as the main subject and labels it ***root***. Then, all three categories can be merged into "suicide."

Forming Frame Elements After processing, we sort the roots by the number of Wikipedia articles they are associated with and choose a list of most popular ones to become frame elements.

3.2. Frame Generator

The frame generator takes the frame elements obtained from the previous steps as inputs and yields frames as outputs. In particular, we build a graph using frame elements and apply graph community detection to partition the frame elements. As a result, each partition will be a frame. In this section, we first define our frame element graph, and then introduce the algorithms used to group the frame elements.

3.2.1. Frame Element Graph

We define a weighted undirected complete graph $G = (V, E, W)$ where the nodes are the frame elements and the edges represent the similarity between the frame elements. The similarity is a combination of two measurement score and is encoded in the edge weight

$$w(u, v) = \mathit{ExSim}(u, v) + \mathit{SemSim}(u, v).$$

The functions *ExSim* and *SemSim* will be explained next.

ExSim By construction, a frame element is a ***root*** of some Wikipedia categories and the categories are associated with Wikipedia articles. Hence, with an arbitrary ordering of the Wikipedia articles fixed, for each frame element we can define an indicator vector e where $e_i = 1$ if the frame element is associated with the ith article. We call such vector the *existence vector*. The function *ExSim*, where "*Ex*" stands for "existence" and "*Sim*" stands for "similarity", measures the coexistence between two frame elements u and v by computing the cosine similarity of their *existence vectors*.

SemSim Since the frame elements are in the form of text, a natural way to measure their connection is by their semantics meanings. Hence, the function *SemSim*, where "*Sem*" stands for "semantics" and "*Sim*" again stands for "similarity", is added to the weight function. This function computes the cosine similarity between two frame elements' semantics embeddings. To create embeddings, we input the text of each frame element into a pretrained BERT (Devlin et al., 2018) model and extract the outputs of the last layer of the network.

3.2.2. Community Detection

Several algorithms have been developed for different types of graphs, as one algorithm simply cannot perform in all graphs (Javed et al., 2018). We apply two community detection methods : Spectral Clustering (SC), a traditional algorithm that utilizes the eigenvalues and eigenvectors of the graph Laplacian, and Community Discovery via Node Embedding (VEC), a novel method proposed by Ding et al. (2017).

3.3. Summary

We here briefly summarize the relations between the main concepts mentioned so far. Wikipedia categories are reduced and merged into ***roots***, some of which are our frame elements. We build a graph using these frame elements and group them via community detection, and the resulting communities are defined as frames.

Index	Frame
1	2nd Amendment (Gun Rights)
2	Gun Control
3	Politics
4	Mental Health
5	School/Public Space Safety (Public Safety)
6	Race/Ethnicity
7	Public Opinion
8	Society/Culture
9	Economic Consequence

Table 1: The nine headline frames in the Gun Violence Frame Corpus dataset that we used.

4. Experiments

In this section, we will describe the data, our pipeline implementation, the experiments and some intermediate outputs. Since each part of our pipeline involves a number of variables to explore and yields individual outputs, after the data subsection below, we will follow the workflow of the pipeline as in Figure 1 by dividing the subsections similar to the method section. In addition, the code and results are publicly available [1].

4.1. Data

The dataset we used is a subset of the extended Gun Violence Frame Corpus (Liu et al., 2019). The dataset contains 1,300 samples of news articles about gun violence in United States. Each sample has a headline and the main body content. Furthermore, each headline is labeled with one of the nine frames shown in Table 1.

4.2. Frame Element Generator

There are two main steps in the frame element generator we will detail them one at a time below.

4.2.1. From News Articles to Wikipedia Articles

When creating embeddings for our news articles and the Wikipedia ones, we ran a Gensim (Řehůřek and Sojka, 2010) Doc2Vec model and each embedding vector is of length 200, an arbitrary number. There are two common variants of Doc2Vec model: one uses the Distributed Bag of Words version of Paragraph Vector (PV-DBOW) and the other uses the Distributed Memory version of Paragraph Vector (PV-DM) (Le and Mikolov, 2014). PV-DM usually yields more accurate performance in classification tasks while PV-DBOW is faster if the corpus is large. Since the corpus we used to train our Doc2Vec model was a snapshot of all Wikipedia articles taken in June 2021, we chose PV-DBOW for the sake of speed.

For every news article embedding, we found $K_p = 10$ most similar Wikipedia article ones by cosine similarity. A natural way to decide the value to K_p is to examine the overall sorted similarity scores and choose a point where a significant drop locates. However, we observed that the curve went down smoothly from the

[1] https://github.com/slai7880/unsupervised-media-frame-discovery

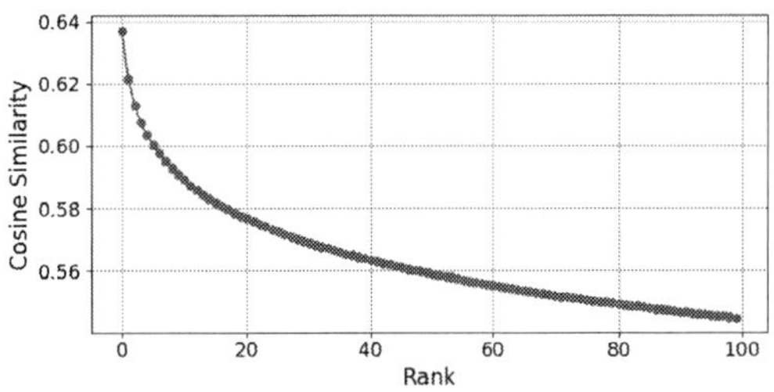

Figure 3: The average top 100 scores of cosine similarity between all news articles and Wikipedia articles. To generate this plot, for each news article, we selected the Wikipedia articles with the 100 highest cosine similarity scores, and, for rank 1 to 100, we averaged the scores across articles. The average scores do not have a sudden decrease in this range.

highest to the 100th, as depicted in Figure 3. Thus, an arbitrary number 10 was chosen for this part.

4.2.2. From Wikipedia Articles to Categories

This part involves retrieving and cleaning categories.

Obtaining Categories As described in section 3.1.2, we retrieved categories recursively with a maximum depth D. In our implementation, we set $D = 4$. Our observation of the Wikepedia category system suggested that if D is too small, the retrieved categories might be too specific, while our communication experts recommended more general categories for better framing quality. Furthermore, as shown in Figure 2, since each category can also have a list of its own categories, the farther the exploration goes, the more categories to examine. This means the time it takes to retrieve the categories can increase drastically. Therefore, in this study, we fixed this upper bound D to be 4, with which the retrieval process could finish in a reasonable amount of time and the outcomes were deemed satisfactory by our communication experts.

Processing Categories The category retrieval process returned 74,281 categories. After the administrative and maintenance categories were removed, 71,303 remained. We then applied a dependency parser developed by Qi et al. (2020) to obtain 4,797 root words. Next, we sorted the root words by the size of the union of the directly associated Wikipedia articles and chose the top 100 root words to become our frame elements. We consider a root word and a Wikipedia article is directly associated if the root word is a category of the article or one of the categories of the article is merged into the root word by dependency parsing.

4.3. Community Detection

With the selected root words being our frame elements, we began building the graph as described in 3.2.1 for community detection. In this phase, we explored different numbers of communities, as there is no common method to predetermine the right value for this parameter. More specifically, for each integer N_c between 2 and 20, we ran the two community detection algorithms with the community number set to N_c.

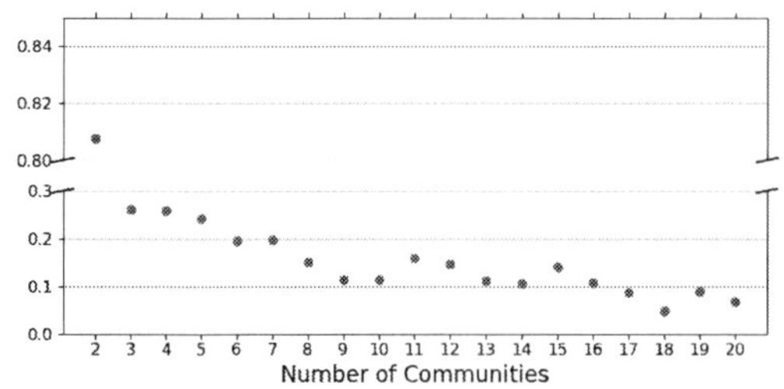

Figure 4: Adjusted Rand index score between the community labels produced by SC and VEC.

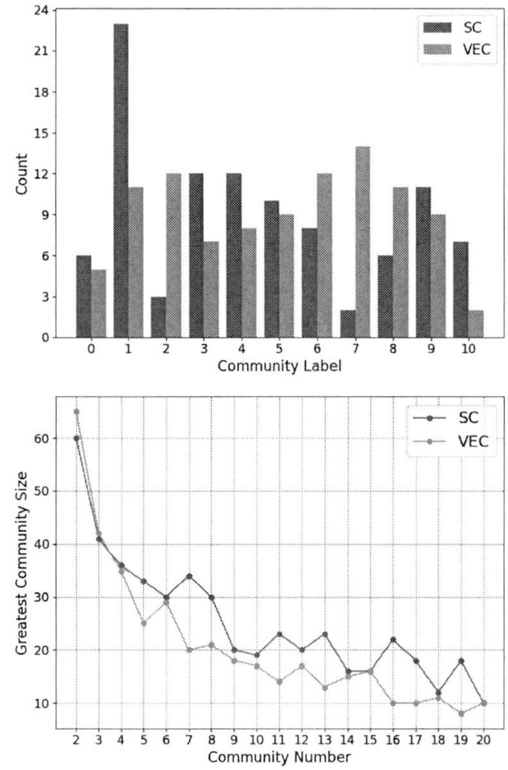

Figure 5: Top: The number of frame elements in each community with total community number N_c fixed to be 11. For this example, SC produces a dominant communit. Bottom: The greatest community sizes for each community number from 2 to 20. SC tends to produce a dominant community while VEC is less likely to do so, as the VEC curve is mostly below the SC one.

We examined the community detection results both from data science and communication perspectives.

4.3.1. Analysis from Data Science Perspective

Our first impression is that the clustering results are very different between the two algorithms for any community number. This can be verified by adjusted Rand index (Hubert and Arabie, 1985) shown in Figure 4, where the majority of the values appear to be very low. Furthermore, we observe that SC tends to produce a community with size dominating the results. For example, as seen in the top plot in Figure 5, among the communities produced by SC, community 1 dwarfs the rest by size. Such situation, however, is not seen in the results produced by VEC. The bottom plot in Figure 5, where we show the maximum community size in each community number setting, suggests that such dominating community is common in SC results.

4.3.2. Analysis from Communication Perspective

Our communication experts examined the results by determining how coherent and how interpretable each community is. In particular, a group of frame elements are coherent if they are distinct from each other and semantically meaningful, and elements within a cluster represent a core frame (Guo et al., 2016; Van Gorp and others, 2010).

Overall, a good range for the community number appears to be between 7 and 16 for both SC and VEC. The results with community number $N_c < 7$ are too broad to identify meaningful frame clusters, while the ones with $N_c > 16$ are too sporadic.

SC tends to outperform VEC for all community numbers, particularly in terms of coherency, despite of the presence of the dominating community. In fact, most communities from SC are coherent and interpretable except for the dominating ones. Interestingly, since usually smaller communities are more coherent than larger ones, the existence of dominating communities, which results in the smaller ones in the same set of outputs, is likely the reason why SC is overall better than VEC. Furthermore, the best community numbers, judging from SC results, are 12, 14, 15, and 16, with 12 and 14 being slightly better.

5. Evaluation

The final part is to evaluate the community frames. However, the evaluation is not simple, because the communities do not have labels and neither do the news contents. Nevertheless, we devised an evaluation approach that made use of the nine headline frames.

Our evaluation strategy aims to create "soft labels" based on the nine headline frames for both the articles and the communities. Thus, this requires us to first obtain frames from the main body of each article and then associate the communities to the nine frames. The first part was achieved by predicting the frame for each sentence in the articles while the second part was achieved by associating the communities to the nine headline frames. We applied a BERT model in both parts, but in each part the model and usage were different. We will detail them one at a time below.

5.1. Acquiring Article Frames

Since it has been shown by Tourni et al. (2021) that BERT can accurately predict the frames of the headlines in the same dataset we used, we adopted the model and a training process similar as in that work.

Training BERT We created a training set for BERT using 2,911 news headlines from the Gun Violence Frame Corpus dataset. Among these headlines, 1,300 were the samples we used in our current framing analysis and each of them has one of the nine frames as listed in Table 1, while the rest were labeled by our communication experts as "no frame". We assumed that the set of frames present in the articles are the same as those in the headlines, and that there exist a substantial number of sentences not having one of the nine frames. In fact, many sentences do not even have a frame. An example is a quote from a conversation. We finetuned the epoch number and the learning rate using stratified 5-fold cross validation. The optimal values for these two parameters are 12 and 2×10^{-5} respectively, and the corresponding optimal validation F1 score is 0.817.

Preprocessing Articles Before predicting the sentence frames, we first tokenized each article into sentences using the NLTK (Loper and Bird, 2002) package, and then we removed sentences of length less than 20 characters, since we observed that most sentences shorter than 20 characters did not contain any frame. After removal, we found that every news article had at least one sentence left while the majority (77%) still had more than 10 sentences left.

Prediction Outputs The prediction results are shown in Figure 6. An interesting observation from these histograms is that the distribution shape of the frames in the prediction roughly resembles that in the training set.

Creating Soft Labels Finally, we created a soft label L_s for each article where the ith entry $L_s(i)$ is the proportion of sentences in the article that were classified as headline frame i. These soft labels would serve as ground truth.

5.2. Community-Frame Association

In this part, we need to associate the communities to the nine headline frames. We again use BERT.

Creating Community Embeddings For each frame element, we built a BERT embedding by extracting the outputs of the last layer of the model. Note that the BERT used for this task was pretrained but not finetuned on any problem. Then, we computed the embedding centroid by averaging all frame element embeddings in each community. Next, for each centroid i, we computed a vector S_i where each entry s_{ij} is the cosine similarity between centroid i and headline frame embedding j. This gave us a measurement of how close each community is to the nine known frames.

Creating Soft Labels Because every news article is linked to a list of communities, for each news article, we computed the average of the similarity vectors corresponding to the communities linked to the article and then normalized the resulting vector. The final output vector, denoted as L_c, would be the soft label of the article from community detection.

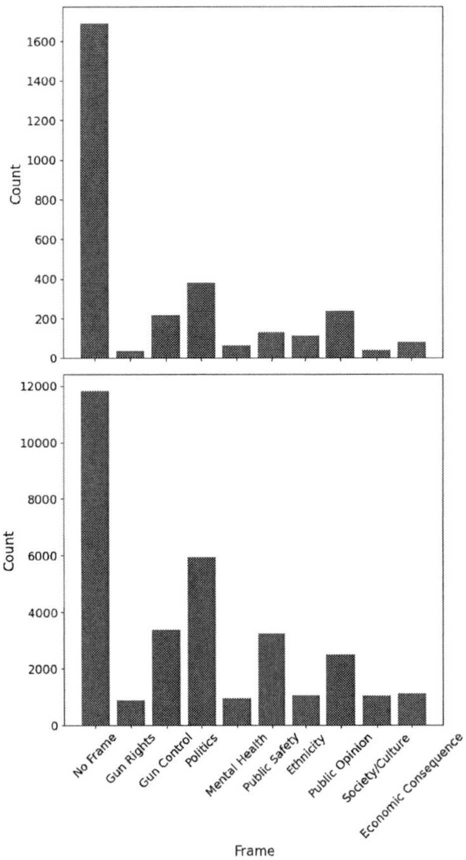

Figure 6: Top: Frame population among the headlines used to train BERT. Bottom: The sentence frame distribution predicted by BERT.

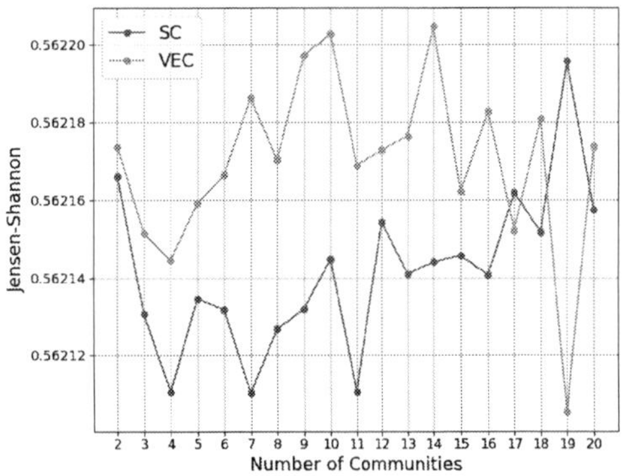

Figure 7: The average Jensen-Shannon distance.

5.3. Comparing Soft Labels

The evaluation is to compare the soft labels from the two sources described above. We present in Figure 7 the results in Jensen-Shannon distance. In the case of SC, there are three values for the number of communities N_c where the distance is minimized: 4, 7 and 11. Whereas there is only one obvious minimum for VEC: $N_c = 19$. It's interesting that the minimum of the VEC curve is exactly the maximum of the SC one.

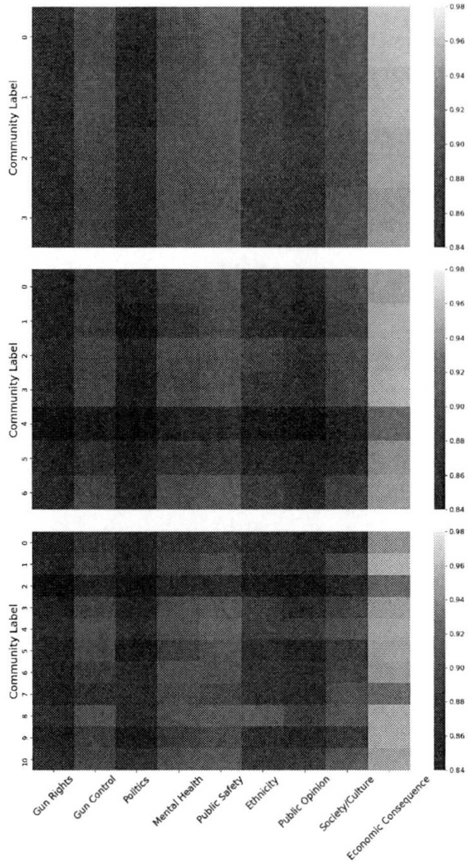

Figure 8: From top to bottom: soft labels corresponding to $N_c = 4$, $N_c = 7$ and $N_c = 11$. Note that the community labels are zero-based.

5.4. Examining Soft Labels

Because each soft label of a community is a vector of similarity towards the headline frames, we can visualize the soft labels using heatmap as shown in Figure 8 and in Figure 9. In particular, Figure 8 shows the soft label heatmaps corresponding to $N_c = 4, 7$ and 11 on the SC curve, and Figure 9 shows the soft label heatmap at $N_c = 19$ on the VEC one.

A common feature among these figures is that the frame ***Economic Consequence*** always has the highest similarity score towards any community, regardless of the community detection method used. In fact, we observe such dominance in the rest of the results as well. However, as shown in Figure 6, according to BERT, the frame ***Economic Consequence*** is among the low-popularity frames. A similar and more surprising phenomenon can be observed in frames ***Politics*** and ***Public Opinion***, which are both popular in the predicted sentence frames but almost always have low similarity scores towards the communities.

After examining the frame elements and their original Wikipedia categories, we found a possible cause of such difference for frame ***Politics***: many words that are apparently related to this frame were dropped by

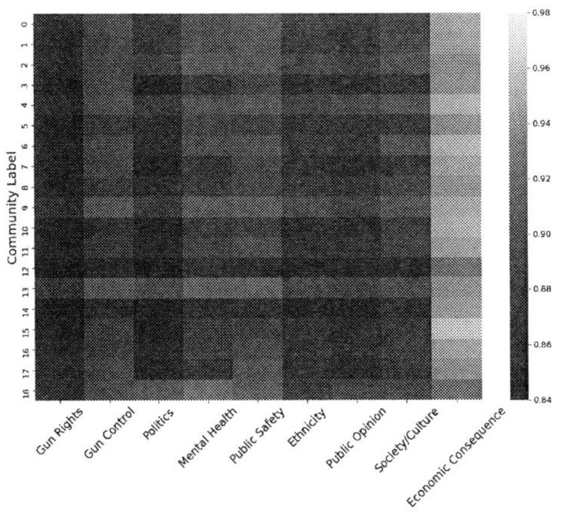

Figure 9: The soft label heatmap of the VEC results where $N_c = 19$.

DP. For example, the category "Political positions of United States senators", which is obviously related to ***Politics***, was reduced by the parser to "position", which has little similarity to that frame. Such loss of information appears to be a limitation of applying DP.

6. Discussion

The pipeline we propose can be beneficial in both the communication and computational linguistic fields.

In communication research, lexicon-based methods and supervised ML are most commonly used in automatic framing analysis. As mentioned in 2.1.1, the nature of lexicon-based methods requires researchers to create keywords and dictionaries to map the keywords to frames. Supervised ML also requires human annotations. Our pipeline, however, requires much less labor, as the process is unsupervised. Furthermore, since the frame elements we choose are essentially Wikipedia categories, they are not tied to any specific issues. Hence, the frames constructed using these frame elements are more general and can be applied to articles of any issue. We, however, recommend that researchers should consider using our method as an exploratory approach examine the text rather than use it for hypothesis testing. More future research should be conducted to test the validity of the proposed approach.

In computational linguistic research, our idea of forming frame elements based on Wikipedia categories adds another novel usage of this gigantic knowledge database. Other researchers can use a similar approach to formulate abstract concepts from text like we do with Wikipedia categories. Our proposed evaluation method can be an example of using a pretrained model to create ground truth information for comparison when such information does not exist in some scenario. In addition, the performance presented in Figure 7 can serve as a baseline for future unsupervised automatic framing research. Furthermore, since Wikipedia is a multilingual knowledge database, we can adopt our pipeline in analyzing text in non-English languages.

Our work can also be applied on text other than news articles. For instance, as pointed out by Odebiyi and Sunal (2020), some textbooks used in U.S. schools seem to be portraying Africa nations falsely. The authors approach this framing problem in textbooks by analyzing themes. More specifically, they identify three main categories of themes: 1) the framing of Nigeria(ns), which includes a) "resources and poverty" and b) underdevelopment and conflicts as sub-frames; 2) demographic features and framing of Nigeria(ns); and 3) cultural practices (mis)understanding and ecological framing of Nigeria(ns). The process is done through three rounds of manual coding. First round, the coders locate the text relevant to Nigeria. Second, the coders examine the relevant portions sentence by sentence. Third, the coders "conduct focused coding to create meta-codes for different patterns and themes based on how each textbook framed Nigerian people, places and practices" found in the previous rounds. Such process is time consuming and heavily human-labor involving. If we adopt our proposed pipeline into this problem, we can simplify the work by inputting the textbook articles into our model, as we do with news articles, and obtaining the frames as clusters of frame elements. Some post-processing work may be required, as the clusters by themselves do not have names. Moreover, the thematic approach used by the authors is bound to the specific nation, while ours can produce more robust frames that can extend the analysis to more Africa countries.

7. Conclusion and Future Work

In this work, we have presented a novel unsupervised pipeline method to produce frames for news articles. We have proposed using Wikipedia categories to create frame elements. We have formulated the frame construction as a graph community detection problem where the frame elements serve as graph nodes. We have demonstrated an example of our pipeline using the news from Gun Violence Frame Corpus. Lastly, we have proposed an evaluation strategy to compare our community frames and the news article ones.

Automatic framing, especially when pairing with an unsupervised method, remains a challenging task. Our future work involves improvement and exploration in many steps of our pipeline. In particular, we seek better handling of the Wikipedia categories, as simply merging them by dependency parsing can result in loss of helpful information. Furthermore, since the two community detection methods we used only assign one community label for each graph node, we plan to explore methods that allow multiple labels.

Acknowledgements Funding from the National Science Foundation, grant 1838193, is gratefully acknowledged.

8. Bibliographical References

Adamu, H., Lutfi, S. L., Malim, N. H. A. H., Hassan, R., Di Vaio, A., and Mohamed, A. S. A. (2021). Framing twitter public sentiment on nigerian government covid-19 palliatives distribution using machine learning. Sustainability, 13(6):3497.

Ajjour, Y., Alshomary, M., Wachsmuth, H., and Stein, B. (2019). Modeling frames in argumentation. In Proceedings of the 2019 Conference on Empirical Methods in Natural Language Processing and 9th International Joint Conference on Natural Language Processing (EMNLP/IJCNLP), pages 2922–2932. pdf.

Allahyari, M. and Kochut, K. (2016). Semantic tagging using topic models exploiting wikipedia category network. In 2016 IEEE Tenth International Conference on Semantic Computing (ICSC), pages 63–70.

Bedi, P. and Sharma, C. (2016). Community detection in social networks. Wiley Interdisciplinary Reviews: Data Mining and Knowledge Discovery, 6(3):115–135.

Blei, D. M., Ng, A. Y., and Jordan, M. I. (2003). Latent dirichlet allocation. Journal of machine Learning research, 3(Jan):993–1022.

Burscher, B., Odijk, D., Vliegenthart, R., De Rijke, M., and De Vreese, C. H. (2014). Teaching the computer to code frames in news: Comparing two supervised machine learning approaches to frame analysis. Communication Methods and Measures, 8(3):190–206.

Devlin, J., Chang, M., Lee, K., and Toutanova, K. (2018). BERT: pre-training of deep bidirectional transformers for language understanding. CoRR, abs/1810.04805.

Ding, W., Lin, C., and Ishwar, P. (2017). Node embedding via word embedding for network community discovery. IEEE Transactions on Signal and Information Processing over Networks, 3(3):539–552.

Entman, R. M. (1993). Framing: Toward clarification of a fractured paradigm. Journal of communication, 43(4):51–58.

Guo, L., Vargo, C. J., Pan, Z., Ding, W., and Ishwar, P. (2016). Big social data analytics in journalism and mass communication: Comparing dictionary-based text analysis and unsupervised topic modeling. Journalism & Mass Communication Quarterly, 93(2):332–359.

Hubert, L. and Arabie, P. (1985). Comparing partitions. Journal of classification, 2(1):193–218.

Javed, M. A., Younis, M. S., Latif, S., Qadir, J., and Baig, A. (2018). Community detection in networks: A multidisciplinary review. Journal of Network and Computer Applications, 108:87–111.

Kumar, S., Rengarajan, P., and Annie, A. X. (2017). Wikitop: Using wikipedia category network to generate topic trees. In Thirty-First AAAI Conference on Artificial Intelligence.

Kumar, P., Chawla, P., and Rana, A. (2018). A review on community detection algorithms in social networks. In 2018 4th International Conference on Applied and Theoretical Computing and Communication Technology (iCATccT), pages 304–309. IEEE.

Le, Q. and Mikolov, T. (2014). Distributed representations of sentences and documents. In International conference on machine learning, pages 1188–1196. PMLR.

Lind, F., Eberl, J.-M., Heidenreich, T., and Boomgaarden, H. G. (2019). Computational communication science— when the journey is as important as the goal: A roadmap to multilingual dictionary construction. International Journal of Communication, 13:21.

Liu, S., Guo, L., Mays, K., Betke, M., and Wijaya, D. T. (2019). Detecting frames in news headlines and its application to analyzing news framing trends surrounding U.S. gun violence. In Proceedings of the 23rd Conference on Computational Natural Language Learning (CoNLL), pages 504–514, Hong Kong, China, November. Association for Computational Linguistics.

Loper, E. and Bird, S. (2002). Nltk: The natural language toolkit. CoRR, cs.CL/0205028.

Mirylenka, D. and Passerini, A. (2013). Navigating the topical structure of academic search results via the wikipedia category network. In Proceedings of the 22nd ACM international conference on Information & Knowledge Management, pages 891–896.

Nastase, V. and Strube, M. (2008). Decoding wikipedia categories for knowledge acquisition. In AAAI, volume 8, pages 1219–1224.

Odebiyi, O. M. and Sunal, C. S. (2020). A global perspective? framing analysis of us textbooks' discussion of nigeria. The Journal of Social Studies Research, 44(2):239–248.

Opperhuizen, A. E., Schouten, K., and Klijn, E. H. (2019). Framing a conflict! how media report on earthquake risks caused by gas drilling: a longitudinal analysis using machine learning techniques of media reporting on gas drilling from 1990 to 2015. Journalism Studies, 20(5):714–734.

Pasca, M. (2018). Finding needles in an encyclopedic haystack: Detecting classes among wikipedia articles. In Proceedings of the 2018 World Wide Web Conference, pages 1267–1276.

Qi, P., Zhang, Y., Zhang, Y., Bolton, J., and Manning, C. D. (2020). Stanza: A Python natural language processing toolkit for many human languages. In Proceedings of the 58th Annual Meeting of the Association for Computational Linguistics: System Demonstrations.

Reese, S. D., Gandy Jr, O. H., and Grant, A. E. (2001).

Framing public life: Perspectives on media and our understanding of the social world. Routledge.

Řehůřek, R. and Sojka, P. (2010). Software Framework for Topic Modelling with Large Corpora. In Proceedings of the LREC 2010 Workshop on New Challenges for NLP Frameworks, pages 45–50, Valletta, Malta, May. ELRA. http://is.muni.cz/publication/884893/en.

Ruppenhofer, J., Ellsworth, M., Schwarzer-Petruck, M., Johnson, C. R., and Scheffczyk, J. (2016). Framenet ii: Extended theory and practice. Technical report, International Computer Science Institute.

Schönhofen, P. (2009). Identifying document topics using the wikipedia category network. Web Intelligence and Agent Systems: An International Journal, 7(2):195–207.

Semetko, H. A. and Valkenburg, P. M. (2000). Framing european politics: A content analysis of press and television news. Journal of communication, 50(2):93–109.

Souravlas, S., Sifaleras, A., Tsintogianni, M., and Katsavounis, S. (2021). A classification of community detection methods in social networks: a survey. International Journal of General Systems, 50(1):63–91.

Tourni, I., Guo, L., Daryanto, T. H., Zhafransyah, F., Halim, E. E., Jalal, M., Chen, B., Lai, S., Hu, H., Betke, M., Ishwar, P., and Wijaya, D. T. (2021). Detecting frames in news headlines and lead images in U.S. gun violence coverage. In Findings of the Association for Computational Linguistics: EMNLP 2021, pages 4037–4050, Punta Cana, Dominican Republic, November. Association for Computational Linguistics.

Turney, P. D. (2002). Thumbs up or thumbs down? semantic orientation applied to unsupervised classification of reviews. arXiv preprint cs/0212032.

Van Gorp, B. et al. (2010). Strategies to take subjectivity out of framing analysis. Doing news framing analysis: Empirical and theoretical perspectives, pages 84–109.

Walter, D. and Ophir, Y. (2019). News frame analysis: An inductive mixed-method computational approach. Communication Methods and Measures, 13(4):248–266.

Wang, C., Tang, W., Sun, B., Fang, J., and Wang, Y. (2015a). Review on community detection algorithms in social networks. In 2015 IEEE international conference on progress in informatics and computing (PIC), pages 551–555. IEEE.

Wang, M., Wang, C., Yu, J. X., and Zhang, J. (2015b). Community detection in social networks: an in-depth benchmarking study with a procedure-oriented framework. Proceedings of the VLDB Endowment, 8(10):998–1009.

Proceedings of the First Workshop on Natural Language Processing for Political Sciences (PoliticalNLP), pages 32–36
Marseille, 24 June 2022

Electoral Agitation Data Set: The Use Case of the Polish Election

Mateusz Baran, Mateusz Wójcik, Piotr Kolebski,
Michał Bernaczyk, Krzysztof Rajda, Łukasz Augustyniak, Tomasz Kajdanowicz
Wrocław University of Science and Technology
Department of Computational Intelligence, Wrocław, Poland
{mateusz.baran, mateusz.wojcik, piotr.kolebski}@pwr.edu.pl
{krzysztof.rajda, lukasz.augustyniak, tomasz.kajdanowicz}@pwr.edu.pl
Wrocław University
Faculty of Law, Administration and Economics, Wrocław, Poland
michal.bernaczyk@uwr.edu.pl

Abstract

The popularity of social media makes politicians use it for political advertisement. Therefore, social media is full of electoral agitation (electioneering), especially during the election campaigns. The election administration cannot track the spread and quantity of messages that count as agitation under the election code. It addresses a crucial problem, while also uncovering a niche that has not been effectively targeted so far. Hence, we present the first publicly open data set for detecting electoral agitation in the Polish language. It contains 6,112 human-annotated tweets tagged with four legally conditioned categories. We achieved a 0.66 inter-annotator agreement (Cohen's kappa score). An additional annotator resolved the mismatches between the first two improving the consistency and complexity of the annotation process. The newly created data set was used to fine-tune a Polish Language Model called HerBERT (achieving a 68% F1 score). We also present a number of potential use cases for such data sets and models, enriching the paper with an analysis of the Polish 2020 Presidential Election on Twitter.

Keywords: Electoral Agitation, Data Set, HerBERT, Natural Language Processing

1. Introduction

The use of social media in politics varies between two extremes: from creating an ethically debatable illusion of mass support to the brutal fight against political opponents in coordinated hate campaigns (Kearney, 2013). The scope of identified actions ranges from mass trolling, hate-speech, harassment, and intimidation to the spread of manipulative, defamatory, or false content (fake news) (Skogerbø and Krumsvik, 2015; Rashkin et al., 2017). From a legal perspective they do not necessarily constitute a novelty, since most European States, including Poland, criminalize the abuse of freedom of expression (which includes political speech) or impose other forms of liability (Rosenfeld, 2003). The Polish Election Code of 2011 (PEC, 2011) requires the oversight of the National Elections Committee (*Państwowa Komisja Wyborcza*, hereinafter "NEC"), a supreme and permanent body charged with overseeing the implementation of electoral law. Unfortunately, the Polish election administration lacks the ability to track the spread and quantity of messages that count as electoral agitation (electioneering) under the Polish Election Code. In this paper, we present a data set and model that allows us to identify not just any political speech on Polish Twitter but precisely content categorized as regulated political speech in Polish law. It may provide valuable information, e.g., on the number of posts campaigning in favor of a specific candidate, the number of breaches of pre-election silence, as well as the vast number of data used for political science, journalists, international observers, and other parties following national politics. In the long term, it may help courts and the NEC to verify whether election campaigns comply with free and fair election standards (required by the Polish Constitution and article 3 of the 1st Protocol to the European Convention on Human Rights ("right to free and fair elections").

Some natural language resources addressing political content analysis in social media already exist. These include collections related to elections in countries such as Spain (Taulé et al., 2018), France (Lai, 2019), and Italy (Lai et al., 2018). While the data sets on political campaigning are fundamental for studies on social media manipulation (Aral and Eckles, 2019), there are very limited resources (Augustyniak et al., 2020) that allow us to understand the agitation phenomena in Polish. Thus, there is a strong need to acquire data annotated in accordance with legal conditions. We want to fill this gap and present a textual data set of agitation during the 2020 Polish Presidential Election that was annotated in terms of precise, legally conditioned categories. Our contributions are as follows: (1) a novel, publicly open data set for detecting electoral agitation in the Polish language, (2) a publicly available neural-based model for classifying social media content with electioneering that achieves a 68% F1 score, and (3) an analysis of the agitation during the Polish 2020 Presidential Election campaign.

2. Motivation and Legal Framework

In the 21 July 2009 (case no. K 7/09) ruling, the Polish Constitutional Tribunal explained that free elections constitute the core element of the rule of law creating a positive obligation for parliament "to establish rules which provide citizens with access to truthful information on public matters and about candidates. The election campaign shall lead to a free formation of electorate will and conclusive decision expressed by an act of voting". What rivets the attention of the doctrine is the Tribunal's emphasis on a certain quality of information ("truthful") and its unconstrained exchange "by all citizens". This demand for an inclusive, democratic debate creates a difficult situation when it comes to balancing the freedom of expression and the demand for truthful, regulated political campaigns on social media platforms - a medium that was practically unknown at the time of issuing those judgments. In Poland, electioneering may commonly be called "political advertising", a form of corporate jargon originating from areas such as Twitter's or Facebook's terms of service. Primarily, however, it has a normative definition in Article 105 of the Election Code. The Election Code defines electioneering as "public encouraging to vote a certain way or for a candidate of the election committee" (Article 105 sec. 1 EC). Public posts or tweets fall under this category, but it is still unclear whether "public" would apply to political micro- or nanotargeting as long as they remain personalized messages targeting individual recipients (the existing case law suggests that the adjective "public" in electoral agitation may not refer exclusively to "open, unrestricted" access to political ads but also to a message distributed to a "considerable" number of recipients, regardless of possible personalization by means of microtargeting). During the 2019 parliamentary campaign, the OSCE Office for Democratic Institutions and Human Rights pointed out the lack of an official monitoring mechanism (OSCE, 2019). Addressing this research gap, we believe our data set helps to identify tweets that contain public encouraging, as well as those trying to target election participation in general.

3. Data Set Creation Process

3.1. Data collection

The data set was obtained from the social network Twitter and contains 9,819,490 tweets. They come from the 2020 presidential election campaign, which was defined by the official time frame from 05.02.2020 to 12.07.2020. The texts were collected based on the following hashtags: *biedron2020, bosak2020, druzynakosiniaka, czasdecyzji, duda2020, ekipaszymona, głosuj, hołownia2020, idziemynawybory, kosiniak2020, kosiniakkamysz, mimowszystkoduda, NieKłamRafał, pis, po, polska2050, PrezydentRP, rafał, rafałniekłam, trzaskowski2020, wybory, wybory2020, wyboryprezydenckie2020, wyboryprezydenckie, wypad.* Duplicated texts (retweets) and tweets in languages other than Polish were filtered out, which resulted in 4,952,804 tweets. We also excluded all tweets shorter than 100 characters (without counting mentions, links and hashtags, to make each text likely to be more informative). After consulting with domain experts, tweets containing a hashtag related to a candidate (e.g. *#Duda2020*, *#Trzaskowski2020*) were also filtered out, as such hashtags that directly point to candidates and most likely indicate a direct link to electoral agitation activity. Finally, after careful data cleaning, the number of samples in the data set was 15,790 tweets, which included hashtags with a neutral tinge (without a direct candidate or party mention). This set was prepared as the main corpus for annotation.

3.2. Annotation method

In order to solve the problem of detecting electoral agitation, texts can be divided into two categories: agitated and not agitated. However, relying directly on the definition of electoral agitation in Article 105 of the Polish Election Code and analysis of data characteristics, we adopted four mutually exclusive categories for the annotation:

Inducement – explicitly convincing or advising voting for/against a particular candidate. It must be clear from the content which person the text is about and it may also include tweets regarding a political party. This is the most significant category, which focuses on agitation in the intuitive sense – e.g.: "Vote for Duda!".
Encouragement – assigning good or bad associations and characteristics to a person. This category includes tweets that refer to candidates or parties directly but are not agitation in a literal sense. These are usually positive or negative statements about politicians – e.g.: "Holownia makes a good impression, maybe he will be a new hope for Poland.".
Voting turnout – refers to encouraging or discouraging people from participating in the vote itself, e.g.: "Poles, go vote!".
Normal – non-agitated text or text that does not qualify as the other groups. A neutral statement or discussion piece that does not fall into any of the above groups. e.g.: "I'm curious about this election, the fight will go on until the very end.".

The *inducement* and the *encouragement* categories are both considered as electoral agitation. In contrast, encouraging people to participate in voting itself (without intending to influence the voter's decision) is not treated as agitation based on current legal regulations in the Electoral Code. The correctness of the selection and interpretation of the above categories was confirmed by a constitutional and legal field expert. The categories chosen in the presented way cover the most relevant needs for interpreting texts in the problem of classifying electoral agitation. However, to extend the data set application, we made an effort to assign tweets with additional metadata that is independent of agitation categories. Each tweet can have multiple additional pieces of information assigned as follows:

Satire – a statement that is deemed as satire. Intentionally changing the name of a candidate/party to a satirical term (e.g. Duda – pen, etc.). Various types

Label	S	C	M	Total
Inducement	114	130	17	**735**
Encouragement	181	356	96	**1 517**
Voting turnout	5	50	9	**314**
Normal	156	571	743	**3 546**
Total	456	1 107	865	**6 112**

Table 1: The number of examples in the data set. Tweets' metadata: S – satirical, C – missing context, and M – media report.

of rhymes, statements overtly indicating so-called *bait*, which are usually specific to a particular language.

Missing context – the text requires additional knowledge to assign it to a given category. These are often hard-to-catch allusions or statements that refer to a URL or attachment that we don't know about - e.g. "Let him finish already, I can't stand this steak of nonsense..." with a URL attached.

Media report – a statement from a media entity, e.g. TV, radio, newspaper. The statement has an informative purpose. Most often it is a quotation, paraphrase or citation of the full statement – e.g. "#czasdecyzji – Minister Łukasz Szumowski will be our guest today.".

Before annotation, the data was pre-processed by removing emoticons and hyperlinks as they did not add any relevant information to the target classes. All hashtags and mentions were kept in the text, making them an integral part of the sentences due to the fact that they carry important contextual information.

Five native speakers took part in the annotation process. Two annotators labeled each example. We disambiguated and improved the annotation via an additional pass by a third annotator, who resolved the mismatches between the first two annotators and made the data set more consistent and comprehensive. Due to the pioneering nature of the data set being created and concern for its potential usefulness, approaches to interpreting difficult texts during annotation were consulted and coordinated under the supervision of the domain expert. After 4,529 examples had been annotated, when Cohen's kappa score stabilized at a satisfactory level, each sample was labeled by one annotator only. In total, we annotated 6,112 tweets that were randomly selected from the main corpus.

Ultimately, we achieved a 0.66 Cohen's kappa score for four-class annotation. According to (McHugh, 2012), it lies between a moderate and strong level of annotation agreement. Table 1 shows the counts of annotated tweets per label as well as information on the number of tweets marked as satire, using missing context, and media reports. We conclude that annotating social media content requires additional knowledge or the ability to follow satirical or slang language. This may hinder the learning process of the model and could negatively affect the outcomes.

Label	P	R	F1
Inducement	71%	52%	60%
Encouragement	66%	55%	60%
Voting turnout	70%	70%	70%
Normal	74%	86%	80%
Macro-average	**70%**	**66%**	**68%**

Table 2: Precision, Recall, and F1 score for each label of HerBERT model on the agitation data set.

3.3. Experiments

We trained a classifier based on a Polish Language Model called HerBERT (Rybak et al., 2020) that is dedicated to the Polish language. Finally, we achieved a 68% F1 score for the stratified train-test split in an 80/20 ratio. Table 2 presents the precision, recall and F1 score for each label. The data set and trained model are publicly available in the GitHub repository[1]. The outcome of our work is also available at `www.smart-wust.ml` in the section *Agitation*, where you can reach additional analysis and insights as well as examples of model usage including the scoring of your own entered text.

4. Polish Presidential Election - Use Case

The proposed data set makes it possible to discover electoral agitation in social media. The data set accompanied with the sample model we proposed can help electoral administration and non-governmental bodies to quantitatively analyze the magnitude of the agitation phenomenon. Thus, we performed a study over agitation during the 2020 Presidential Election (tweets classification) to take the share of agitation in the overall political discourse into account. We were interested in the last few weeks of the campaign, where the percentage of agitation tweets was at its highest and pre-election silence was in place, where agitation is prohibited by law.

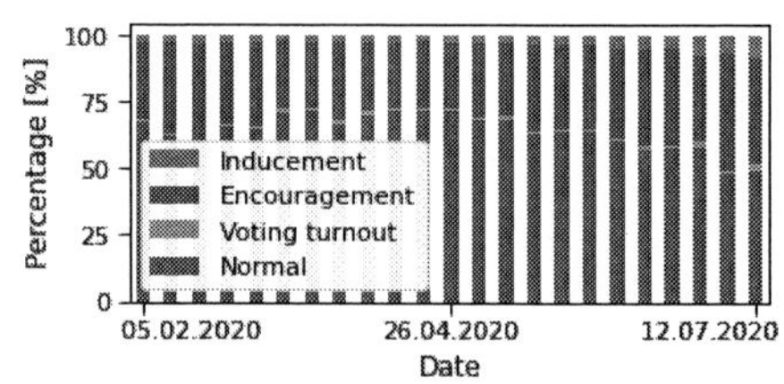

Figure 1: Percentage participation of tweets annotation categories in particular weeks during campaign.

We performed an experiment on a sample of 1,531,624 untagged tweets, where each tweet was classified using our trained model. The results shown in Figure 1 denote the final stage of the campaign being dominated

[1] https://github.com/mateuszbaransanok/e-agitation

by agitation (*inducement* and *encouragement* increased in total of 17 pp). More than a third of tweets contained agitation in the presidential election discourse. The encouragement to participate in voting increased in the weeks leading up to the day of the election, but nevertheless, they constituted a clear minority.

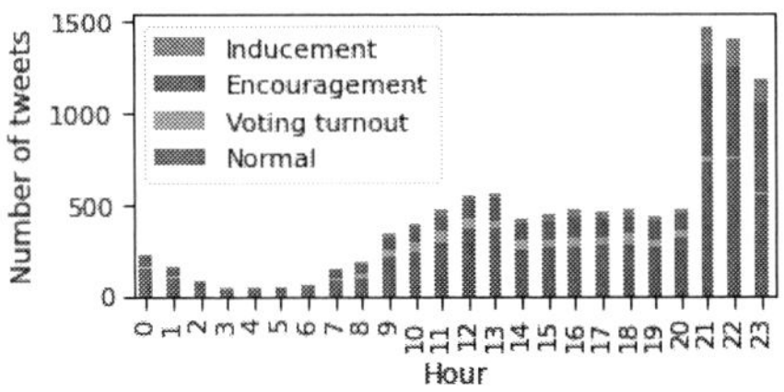

Figure 2: Number of tweets per hour during second round election day (12.07.2020). The pre-election silence ended at 9 p.m (21:00).

We also spotted the problem of electoral agitation on Twitter during pre-election silence, as shown in Figure 2. This also confirms (Musiał-Karg, 2018) the doubts whether the ban on campaigning during pre-election silence even exists, since so many Twitter users campaign for politicians during that time, violating the existing law. Even though the agitation decreases threefold in comparison to periods outside of pre-election silence, it still exists and may affect voters as a result. To the best of our knowledge, the result is a first attempt to automatically discover agitation in social media in Poland. Above all, further research and method development provide the prospect of supporting the judiciary in ensuring the fairness of the election campaign and freeing social media from political propaganda.

The data set we propose also enabled us to analyze sentiment polarity across categories. Figure 3 shows the estimated sentiment probability density function with respect to all metadata labels. The sentiment was assigned to a $[-1, 1]$ (negative to positive) range based on (Strzałka and Pokropiński, 2020). As we can see, even though *normal* content has mixed sentiment, it is mostly neutral. Posts of an agitating nature are completely different where sentiment is very negative, especially in the *encouragement* category. This proves that social media campaigns are mainly based on negative narration (Piontek, 2017) and frequently take the form of hate-speech. The least polarized class is the *voting turnout* where sentiment is uniformly balanced relative to all classes. As anticipated, media news falls mainly into the *normal* category and is characterized by a strictly neutral sentiment, which is the case even when media texts are classified as electoral agitation. Our analyses indicate that under election campaign conditions, the sentiment of a text itself can carry valuable information about the intentions behind it, something especially evident for unbiased media statements confronted with satirical content.

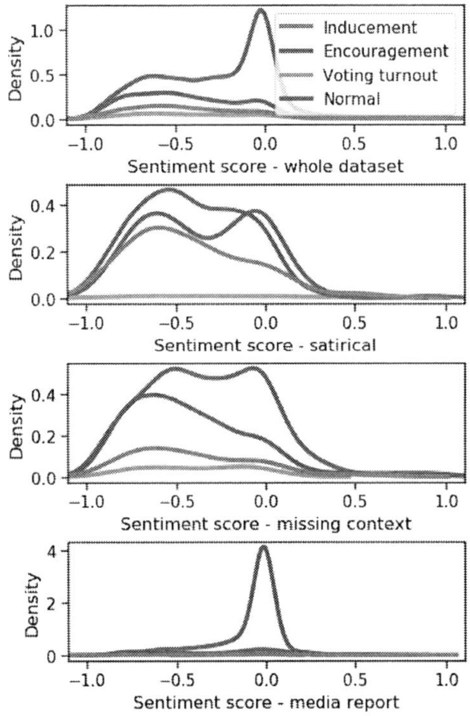

Figure 3: Sentiment score probability density function for all annotation classes with metadata classes distinction.

5. Conclusions and Future Work

The presented data set along with the model enables us to categorize social media posts in terms of electoral agitation and evaluate the number of posts campaigning in favor of candidates or the number of times pre-election silence was breached. This makes it suitable for the needs of a wide range of audiences, from researchers to journalists, electoral committees, and government authorities that care about the integrity of elections. The usefulness of studying this phenomenon is underlined by the presented case studies. Based on the collected data we can describe the studied election campaign as gaining in agitation intensity over time and highly offensive in the case of social media content. Publishing this data set makes it possible to train modern NLP models with various applications in the area of policy and law. We expect that the publication of this data set and its future use, in conjunction with machine learning techniques, will lead to increased fairness in election processes and will help reduce the spread of propaganda.

In this paper, we have identified promising areas of research using the composed data set. We plan to work on more data sets and models to ensure the integrity of the political campaigns, classify electoral agitation content, and widen natural language solutions in regards to the content in social media.

6. Bibliographical References

Aral, S. and Eckles, D. (2019). Protecting elections from social media manipulation. *Science*, 365(6456):858–861.

Augustyniak, L., Rajda, K., Kajdanowicz, T., and Bernaczyk, M. (2020). Political advertising dataset: the use case of the Polish 2020 presidential elections. In *Proceedings of the The Fourth Widening Natural Language Processing Workshop*, pages 110–114, Seattle, USA, July. Association for Computational Linguistics.

Kearney, M. W. (2013). Political Discussion on Facebook: an Analysis of Interpersonal Goals and Disagreement. Technical report, 12.

Lai, M., Patti, V., Ruffo, G., and Rosso, P. (2018). Stance evolution and twitter interactions in an italian political debate. *Lecture Notes in Computer Science (including subseries Lecture Notes in Artificial Intelligence and Lecture Notes in Bioinformatics)*, 10859 LNCS:15–27.

Lai, M. (2019). *On Language and Structure in Polarized Communities, https://riunet.upv.es/handle/10251/119116*. Ph.D. thesis, Universitat Politecnica de Valencia, 4.

McHugh, M. L. (2012). Interrater reliability: the kappa statistic. *Biochemia medica*, 22(3):276–282.

Musiał-Karg, M. (2018). The election silence in contemporary democracies. questions about the sense of election silence in the age of internet. *Przeglad Politologiczny*.

OSCE. (2019). Final Report on Parliamentary Elections. 13.10.2019, https://www.osce.org/files/f/documents/c/7/446371_1.pdf.

PEC. (2011). The Polish Election Code by means of the Act of 11 January 2018. 07.04.2022, https://pkw.gov.pl/uploaded_files/1640023078_kodeks-wyborczy-2021-grudzien.pdf.

Piontek, D. (2017). Reklama negatywna w polskich kampaniach wyborczych 2015 roku. *Środkowoeuropejskie Studia Polityczne*, page 71, 3.

Rashkin, H., Choi, E., Jang, J. Y., Volkova, S., and Choi, Y. (2017). Truth of varying shades: Analyzing language in fake news and political fact-checking. In *Proceedings of the 2017 conference on empirical methods in natural language processing*, pages 2931–2937.

Rosenfeld, M. (2003). Hate Speech in Constitutional Jurisprudence: A Comparative Analysis. *Cardozo Law Review*, 24, 1.

Rybak, P., Mroczkowski, R., Tracz, J., and Gawlik, I. (2020). Klej: Comprehensive benchmark for polish language understanding. Technical report.

Skogerbø, E. and Krumsvik, A. H. (2015). Newspapers, facebook and twitter: Intermedial agenda setting in local election campaigns. *Journalism Practice*, 9(3):350–366, 5.

Strzałka, F. and Pokropiński, M. (2020). sentimentpl: Pytorch models for polish language sentiment regression based on allegro/herbert and clarin-pl dataset. Technical report. https://github.com/philvec/sentimentPL.

Taulé, M., Rangel, F., Antònia Martí, M., and Rosso, P. (2018). Overview of the task on multimodal stance detection in Tweets on catalan #1Oct referendum. Technical report.

Proceedings of the First Workshop on Natural Language Processing for Political Sciences (PoliticalNLP), pages 37–45
Marseille, 24 June 2022

Enhancing Geocoding of Adjectival Toponyms with Heuristics

Breno Alef Dourado Sá, Ticiana L. Coelho da Silva, José Antônio Fernandes de Macêdo
Department of Computer Science
Federal University of Ceará, Fortaleza, Brazil
{brenoalef, ticianalc, jose.macedo}@insightlab.ufc.br

Abstract

Unstructured text documents such as news and blogs often present references to places. Those references, called toponyms, can be used in various applications like disaster warning and touristic planning. However, obtaining the correct coordinates for toponyms, called geocoding, is not easy since it's common for places to have the same name as other locations. The process becomes even more challenging when toponyms appear in adjectival form, as they are different from the place's actual name. This paper addresses the geocoding task and aims to improve, through a heuristic approach, the process for adjectival toponyms. So first, a baseline geocoder is defined through experimenting with a set of heuristics. After that, the baseline is enhanced by adding a normalization step to map adjectival toponyms to their noun form at the beginning of the geocoding process. The results show improved performance for the enhanced geocoder compared to the baseline and other geocoders.

Keywords: geocoding, toponyms, adjectival toponyms

1. Introduction

In everyday life, people often use place names to give directions, inform the location of events, and provide spatial information based on the shared knowledge of said names (Vasardani et al., 2013). These references to places, also called toponyms, are often present in documents with geographic content such as news, blogs, and even posts on social media. This geographic information can be used in many applications, such as disaster warning (Wu and Cui, 2018), emergency response (Singh et al., 2019), monitoring of epidemics (Lampos and Cristianini, 2012), crime prevention (Vomfell et al., 2018), news aggregation (Abdelkader et al., 2015), touristic planning (Colladon et al., 2019), among others.

The usage of geographic information embedded in unstructured text requires a process of toponyms extraction and resolution called geoparsing. Geoparsing comprises two steps: geotagging and geocoding.

Geotagging is a particular case of Named Entity Recognition (NER), a Natural Language Processing (NLP) task, which identifies named-entity mentions in texts and classifies them into predefined categories Person, Location, and Organization. For the task of geotagging, only entities corresponding to locations are relevant.

Geocoding is a process of disambiguating, and linking toponyms to geographic coordinates (Gritta et al., 2018b). This is not a trivial task, as it is common to see different locations sharing the same name around the world, for instance, *Springfield, Oregon*, and *Springfield, Queensland*. Moreover, toponyms sometimes appear in adjectival form, e.g., "*Spanish* sausages sales top €2M."

A geocoding technique can be defined as a model G_c such that for a given text T, $G_c(< t_1, t_2, \ldots, t_n >) =< p_1, p_2, \ldots, p_n >$, where t_i, $1 \leq i \leq n$, is a toponym extracted from T and p_i is its corresponding (latitude, longitude) tuple. The latitude and longitude are usually obtained from a gazetteer, a geographic dictionary containing place names and their coordinates.

The geographic information obtained using a geocoder can be used to automatically collect event information from news articles, which researchers may use to observe and extract information on politically relevant events as they occur (Lee et al., 2019). SPERG (Gunasekaran et al., 2018) is one of these initiatives. SPERG focuses primarily on archived newspaper reports on political events and aims to parse the exact event location with high accuracy of every place mentioned in a report. Political scientists require information from these reports for various study purposes, including the impact, attendee profile, and event location.

Another geocoding application relevant and related to political themes is built-in epidemiological early warning systems. First, epidemiological data typically requires time to be available due to time-consuming laboratory tests. Due to its prevalence, social media data, such as Twitter and Facebook, have been used for epidemiological studies on different infectious diseases such as Influenza (Allen et al., 2016), Dengue (Albinati et al., 2017), and COVID-19 (Jiang et al., 2021), among others. By geocoding such text data, the authorities can plan and act appropriately on effective interventions to control infectious diseases, reducing mortality and morbidity in human populations. Another application geared through the use of geocoding information for early conflict warning is ICEWS (O'brien, 2010).

Applications that use the geographic information of unstructured texts need a geocoder capable of assigning the best coordinates for the locations referenced in the text. This task can be a challenge when dealing with toponyms in adjectival form. For instance, considering the Geonames[1] gazetteer and the text "The *French* President and his foreign minister have been promoting a new course," the expected output of geocoding for the toponym is the tuple (lat=46, long=2), corresponding to the Republic of France. A simple lookup in the gazetteer is not enough to geocode correctly, as "French" is not the country's name, and other places are called in the same manner.

Figure 1 illustrates the problem with a map. Denoted by red markers are several locations named "French" in the gazetteer around the world, and indicated by a blue marker is the Republic of France. Although there is a possible location for the toponym inside France, it is not the entry corresponding to the country. Incorrectly geocoding the toponym could cause an application to treat the text as about a location in the United States of America instead of the French Republic. Thus, it is necessary to treat this kind of toponym somehow.

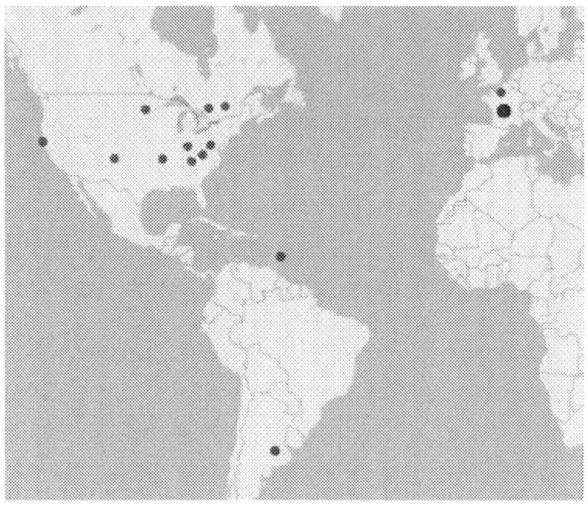

Figure 1: Possible locations for "French" in Geonames.

This paper addresses the geocoding task and aims to improve the process for adjectival toponyms, a type of toponym that other geocoders do not treat. Although adjectival toponyms have already been recognized and annotated in corpora(Kamalloo and Rafiei, 2018; Gritta et al., 2019), geocoders usually either ignore it like CLAVIN[2] or treat it as any other toponym in noun form like CamCoder (Gritta et al., 2018a).

The main contribution of this work is the proposal of a new heuristic to treat adjectival toponyms based on a dictionary of adjectival forms of places. A baseline geocoder is defined through experiments on a set of heuristics. It is further enhanced by adding a normalization step that maps adjectival toponyms to their noun form at the beginning of the process. The experiments confirm that the enhanced geocoder outperforms the baseline.

The structure of this paper is as follows. Section 2 gives a background of related works in the task of geocoding. Section 3 presents the data and methodology used in detail. Section 4 shows the results obtained and a comparison to other geocoders. Finally, Section 5 presents final thoughts and future work.

2. Related Work

Other works on geocoding have varied strategies depending on the focus of the application. Some geocoding plans assign a single location to an entire document, like the one proposed by (Rahimi et al., 2015) to geolocate Twitter users. The approach presented in this paper tries to assign a coordinate to every location referenced in a text. Current toponym resolution methods can be categorized as rule-based, statistical, and machine learning-based.

Several works propose rule-based approaches for geocoding tasks. (Rauch et al., 2003) and (Amitay et al., 2004) use population data as a disambiguation criterion. (Clough, 2005), on the other hand, prioritizes candidate locations with a higher administrative level. (Leidner, 2008) is one of the first comprehensive surveys on geocoding heuristics, addressing methods such as one sense per discourse and geometric minimality.

CLAVIN (Cartographic Location And Vicinity INdexer) is an open-source rule-based geocoder that gets candidates through Lucene[3] with score increments for some fields and values. It performs disambiguation by calculating a score for candidate combinations based on the commonality of countries and states. In other words, when there is more than one candidate for a location, priority is given to the candidate contained in the same administrative region as the precise locations. If the user specifies, CLAVIN also allows disambiguation based solely on population.

Approaches based on statistics seek to solve the problem through distribution models. This strategy is used in several works that focus on the geolocation of entire documents, as in (Butt and Hussain, 2013) and (Hulden et al., 2015), but it can also be applied to individual locations.

The *TopoCluster*, proposed by DeLozier et al. (2015) improves the work of Butt and Hussain (2013) and does the geocoding through pseudo-documents containing the toponym context, using windows of 15 words in each direction. Its resolution works by dividing the world into a grid with 0.5x0.5 degree cells and models the geographic distribution of context words over it. With its hot spots analysis, *TopoCluster* assigns toponyms to the most overlapping cells of the individual word distributions. In the same direction, there is an alternative version of *TopoCluster* called *TopoClusterGaz*. It uses a hybrid geographic dictionary of GeoNames and Natural Earth[4]. This solution searches on the gazetteer at the end of the process and assigns to the toponym the coordinates of the candidate closest to the predicted cell.

[1] https://www.GeoNames.org/

[2] https://github.com/Novetta/CLAVIN

[3] https://lucene.apache.org/

[4] https://www.naturalearthdata.com/

Strategies based on machine learning use trained models to predict the geographic coordinates for toponyms. Among current methods, the usage of bag-of-words representations combined with Support Vector Machines or Logistic Regression has achieved good results (Gritta et al., 2018b).
The CamCoder proposed by (Gritta et al., 2018a) divides the world into a grid. It uses a vector representation called MapVec to model the geographic distribution of the locations mentioned in the text. It uses a deep neural network to predict grid cells for toponyms. It then queries a Geonames database, choosing candidate places based on their population and distance to the predicted cell.
The strategy proposed in this paper also uses a Geonames based gazetteer and does the geocoding task using information such as population and alternate names. However, unlike the aforementioned works, the proposed geocoder in this work treats adjectival toponyms normalizing them to noun form at the beginning of the geocoding process. CLAVIN is the most similar geocoder to the one proposed in this work, but it filters out adjectival toponyms as it doesn't consider them references to places. TopoCluster addresses the same type of named entity but doesn't show effective results (DeLozier et al., 2015). CamCoder does not address adjectival toponyms.

3. Data and Methods

This section describes the methodology for the definition of the baseline geocoder and the enhanced version proposed in this paper.

3.1. Dataset and Metrics

This work uses the toponym taxonomy proposed by (Gritta et al., 2019), in which a toponym is classified based on the semantics of the noun phrase containing it and the context of the surrounding clause. For instance, in the phrase "A former *Russian* double agent was poisoned in the *English* city of *Salisbury*," there is an associative adjectival modifier (*"Russian"*), a literal adjectival modifier (*"English"*), and a literal toponym (*"Salisbury"*).
Due to the taxonomy used, GeoWebNews, a dataset also proposed by (Gritta et al., 2019), is used in the experiments. The dataset comprises 200 news articles from globally distributed news sites collected during the first eight days of April 2018. Table 1 presents the GeoWebNews toponym classes according to the taxonomy.
In this work, only the 2401 toponyms annotated with latitude, longitude, and an entry in Geonames are considered. The reason for that is to avoid the types of toponyms as languages and homonyms, which do not have ground truth coordinates as they are not locations, and the most difficult toponyms like festival venues, which do not have an entry in the gazetteer and would require additional resources specific to the domain to be geocoded.

Class	Category	Type
Literal	Literal	Literal
Coercion	Literal	Coercion
Mixed	Literal	Mixed
Embedded_Literal	Literal	Embedded Literal
Literal_Modifier	Literal	Noun Modifier Adjectival Modifier
Demonym	Associative	Demonym
Language	Associative	Language
Metonymic	Associative	Metonymy
Non_Literal_Modifier	Associative	Noun Modifier Adjectival Modifier
Embedded_Non_Lit	Associative	Embedded Associative
Homonym	Associative	Homonym

Table 1: Taxonomy of GeoWebNews classes

The following metrics are used for performance evaluation:

- **Mean Error Distance (MED)**: the mean of great-circle distances[5], in kilometers, between annotated locations and geocoder output locations;
- **Accuracy@X (Acc@X)**: the percentage of toponyms geolocated within X kilometers of the annotated locations. The chosen distance is 161 km (100 miles), previously used in other works such as (DeLozier et al., 2015; Gritta et al., 2019; Wang and Hu, 2019). The reason for that is the possible differences between gazetteer and annotated coordinates;
- **Area Under the Curve (AUC)**: a metric for the overall deviation between geolocated toponyms and ground-truth coordinates. Its value is calculated through the trapezoidal rule[6] using Equation 1, where x denotes the distances, $dim(x)$ is the number of elements in x, and 20039 is the approximated value of half the Earth's circumference in kilometers. The highest possible error is when the output location is diametrically opposed to the expected coordinates on the planet's surface. The better the geocoding, the closer the AUC must be

[5] https://geopy.readthedocs.io/en/stable/#geopy.distance.great_circle
[6] https://docs.scipy.org/doc/numpy/reference/generated/numpy.trapz.html

to 0.

$$AUC = \frac{\int_0^{dim(x)} ln(x)\,dx}{dim(x) * ln(20039)} \quad (1)$$

3.2. Baseline Heuristic Geocoder

The Heuristic Geocoder (HG) used as baseline breaks the task into two steps in which different heuristics can be used. The first step is to obtain the candidates by querying the gazetteer, and the second is the disambiguation. In the end, the geocoder outputs a gazetteer entry for the input toponym.

The geocoder receives a list of toponyms as input and outputs coordinates according to the following parameters:

- **Obtaining Candidates** :
  - **Search Type**: the type of search used for the toponym. "Filter" indicates exact matching, and "Full-text" indicates loose matching;
  - **Ordering**: tells the geocoder if candidates should be ordered by score, feature class, or population;
- **Candidate Disambiguation**:
  - **Top-K Geometric Minimality**: tells the geocoder how many candidates should be considered for disambiguation. If $K > 1$, chooses the candidate closest to previously geocoded locations.

The gazetteer is searched using ElasticSearch[7], a Lucene interface(Divya and Goyal, 2013) that has already shown effective results in geocoding applications due to its dynamic ranking (Clemens, 2015). Before the geocoder usage, an ElasticSearch index is created and populated with Geonames data, including information such as name, alternate names, feature class, and population. To allow filtering and full-text searches on name fields, those are created as text and keyword fields.

The geocoding process is done using the following heuristics:

- **Exact matching (H1)**: consider a place a candidate only when one of its names is exactly equal to the queried text. That means the entry for the *United States of America* is considered a candidate for "*United States*" or "*USA*", which are alternate names in the gazetteer, but not for "*States of America*";
- **Loose matching (H2)**: consider a place a candidate if there is a partial match between one of its names and the queried text. That means querying "*States of America*" will return *USA*'s entry as a candidate;
- **Order candidates by Score (H3)**: ranks candidates based on ElasticSearch default score. The score depends on the place's name and queried text;
- **Order candidates by Feature Class (H4)**: ranks candidates based on their Geonames' feature class. This means the country *Angola* will take precedence over the city *Angola, Indiana*;
- **Order by population (H5)**: ranks candidates based on their population. In this case, the entry for the *Republic of Korea* will take precedence over the one for the *Democratic People's Republic of Korea*;
- **Geometric Minimality (H6)**: minimizes the average distance between all geocoded toponyms. This is done by choosing candidates based on their mean distance to previously geocoded toponyms, assuming places mentioned in a text are as close as possible.

The parameter values for HG used as baseline are defined by evaluating combinations on GeoWebNews and comparing their performances. The one with the best result is chosen and later enhanced to treat adjectival toponyms. Table 2 shows the values for each parameter.

Parameter	Values
Search Type	Filter, Full-text
Ordering	Score, Feature Class, Population
Top-K Geometric Minimality	$K \in \{1, 5, 10\}$

Table 2: HG parameters values

3.3. Enhanced Heuristic Geocoder

When trying to geocode toponyms like *"Australian"* or *"Finnish"* using simple Geonames lookups, even though these words are references to places and can be classified as adjectival modifiers, they are not the places' names. Therefore, such terms are not included as the official names or alternative names on Geonames entries, meaning such toponyms must be normalized before geocoding. That means the usage of a new heuristic:

- **Adjectival Toponym Normalization (H7)**: normalize adjectival toponyms to their noun form at the beginning of geocoding. In this case, instead of querying "*Dutch*", the geocoder will get candidates for "*Kingdom of the Netherlands*".

To do so, an ElasticSearch index is created to be used as the dictionary. The index is then populated with a list of country names, as they appear in Geonames and their

[7] https://www.elastic.co/

adjectival and demonymic forms. For instance, the entry corresponding to the *Kingdom of Denmark* includes the adjectival form "*Danish*", which describes something as being from the country, and the demonymic form "*Danes*", which refers to its people. In this work, the adjectives are taken from Wikipedia's list of nationalities [8].

Thus, the strategy for geocoding adjectival toponyms involves adding a step before obtaining candidates. The toponyms are consulted in the dictionary index and replaced by a normalized version. That means the toponym *Danish* is normalized to *Kingdom of Denmark* before querying the gazetteer. The Heuristic Geocoder enhanced with this strategy is hereafter referred to as HG+.

4. Experimental Results

This section describes the results obtained for the baseline and enhanced geocoders.

4.1. HG Results

Table 3 shows the evaluation metrics for the 5 best parameter combinations ranked by AUC. The best result for every metric was obtained by using a more strict search method and population as the ordering criterion, that is, the combination of H1 and H5. Hence, that was the combination of parameters chosen for HG as the baseline for later improvement.

Geocoder Parameters	MED	Acc@161	AUC
Filter (H1) Pop. (H5) Top-1	**1162.74 ±1612.78**	**0.7713 ±0.2519**	**0.2036 ±0.1801**
Full-text (H2) Pop. (H5) Top-1	1228.28 ±1583.49	0.7187 ±0.2494	0.2729 ±0.1904
Filter (H1) Pop. (H5) Top-5 (H6)	1530.77 ±2106.15	0.6369 ±0.3515	0.3088 ±0.1922
Filter (H1) Pop. (H5) Top-10 (H6)	1613.80 ±2248.68	0.6210 ±0.3601	0.3239 ±0.2826
Full-text (H2) Pop. (H5) Top-5 (H6)	1252.69 ±1742.95	0.6262 ±0.3173	0.3472 ±0.2321

Table 3: Best results for the Heuristic Geocoder parameter combinations

Figure 2 presents the results for HG divided by GeoWebNews classes. Each bar shows the distribution of geocoding outputs for the toponym class, given by the y-axis. The color red indicates toponyms for which no candidates were found in the gazetteer, blue denotes places geocoded to the expected coordinates, and purple indicates location references geocoded to coordinates more than 161 km away from the expected ones. For toponyms of the "Literal" class, direct references to physical locations (e.g. "Harvests in *Australia*"), the geocoder shows a high number of correct predictions. However, for the ones of the "Non_Literal_Modifier" class, toponyms that modify a non-locational concept associated with a location (e.g. "*British* voters"), there are many cases in which no candidates were found or the geocoded coordinates were too far away from the expected.

4.2. HG+ Results

After the baseline geocoder was defined as the combination of H1 and H5, also called HG; it was improved to process adjectival toponyms. Table 4 shows the results for the HG+ in comparison to HG. The enhanced geocoder obtained the best performance in every metric.

Geocoder	MED	Acc@161	AUC
HG (H1 & H5)	1162.74 ±1612.78	0.7713 ±0.2519	0.2036 ±0.1801
HG+ (H1, H5 & H7)	**729.97 ±1340.19**	**0.8188 ±0.2412**	**0.1618 ±0.1669**

Table 4: Results for HG and HG+ on GeoWebNews

Figure 3 presents the results for HG+ split by GeoWebNews classes. Compared to the baseline performance, the geocoding has been improved for most types, increasing toponyms correctly geocoded. Associative modifier toponyms, indicated by the "Non_Literal_Modifier" class, are the ones with the most noticeable improvement.

This difference in performance is due to the new heuristic of processing adjectival toponyms. For instance, considering the sentence "They were found in the southern *English* city of *Salisbury*," HG would assign the coordinates for the town of *English, Indiana* instead of the ones for *England* regarding the adjectival toponym. HG+ can deal with this toponym because of the normalization step added, which makes it search for candidates matching "England."

4.3. Comparison to Other Proposals

HG+ was also compared to other works. The comparisons were done using the ground-truth files[9] provided by the EUPEG (Wang and Hu, 2019). The tests were done on GeoWebNews and TR-News, a dataset proposed by Kamalloo and Rafiei (2018) containing 118 human-annotated news articles from global and local news sources. Both datasets were chosen due to

[8] https://en.wikipedia.org/wiki/List_of_adjectival_and_demonymic_forms_for_countries_and_nations

[9] https://github.com/geoai-lab/EUPEG/

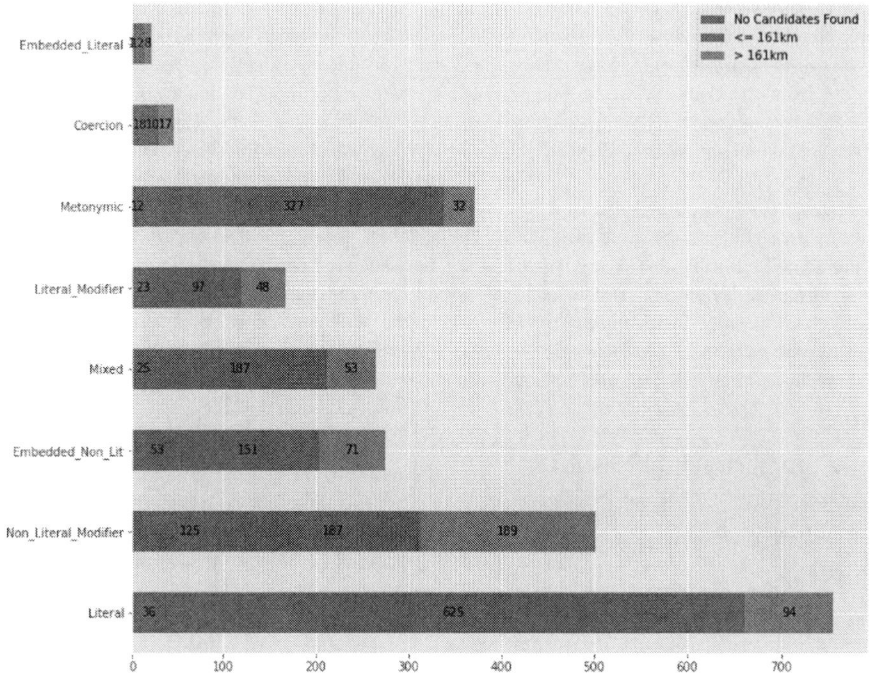

Figure 2: Results for HG on GeoWebNews by toponym type.

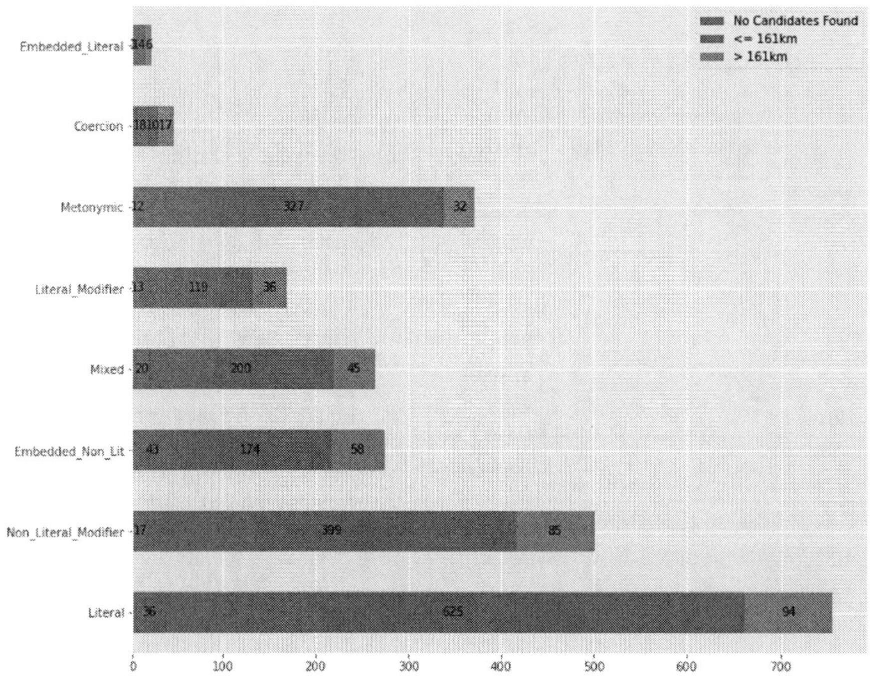

Figure 3: Results for HG+ on GeoWebNews by toponym type.

their coverage of adjectival toponyms[10]. Other well-known datasets, such as Geovirus (Gritta et al., 2018a), provide incomplete or no annotations of adjectival to-

[10]Approximately 14.9% of toponyms in GeoWebNews and 10.7% in TR-News are in adjectival form.

ponyms. Although LGL (Lieberman et al., 2010) also presents this type of toponym, the dataset was not used since its locations are highly region-specific, making them very difficult to disambiguate using the population heuristic with a global gazetteer.
For the CLAVIN geoparser, the REST version[11] was used in the comparison. Because CLAVIN doesn't allow isolated geocoding, HG+ was tested using the toponyms recognized by the geoparser, thus discarding any difference in performance caused by the geotagging process. Table 5 presents the results for CLAVIN and HG+ for GeoWebNews dataset, whilst Table 6 shows the results for TR-News. HG+ achieved the best result for all the evaluated metrics for both datasets.

Geocoder	MED	Acc@161	AUC
CLAVIN	790.18 ±1585.18	0.8100 ±0.3101	0.1268 ±0.2153
HG+ (H1, H5 & H7)	**392.85** **±1105.98**	**0.8432** **±0.2914**	**0.1086** **±0.1739**

Table 5: Comparison to CLAVIN geocoder on GeoWebNews

Geocoder	MED	Acc@161	AUC
CLAVIN	1570.10 ±2685.97	0.7687 ±0.3275	0.1889 ±0.2581
HG+ (H1, H5 & H7)	**1424.23** **±2644.26**	**0.7770** **±0.3346**	**0.1864** **±0.2592**

Table 6: Comparison to CLAVIN geocoder on TR-News

For the CamCoder geoparser, the code available on Github[12] was used. CamCoder allows the execution of its geocoder separately if provided with a formatted ground-truth file. Thus, the ground-truth files for GeoWebNews and TR-News, provided by EUPEG, were used to geocode annotated toponyms as they appear on each text.
Before the comparison, the CamCoder database was updated with the same Geonames dump used to populate the ElasticSearch index in which HG+ operates. CamCoder geocoding was then applied directly to the annotated toponyms, and the same was done for HG+. Table 7 presents the results for GeoWebNews, and Table 8 the results for TR-News. HG+ outperforms CamCoder on GeoWebNews for all three metrics. On TR-News the geocoder achieves better performance for Acc@161 and AUC.
When applied to both TR-News and GeoWebNews, HG+ showed a significant improvement for locations

Geocoder	MED	Acc@161	AUC
CamCoder	1033.53 ±1527.37	0.7536 ±0.2703	0.2007 ±0.1893
HG+ (H1, H5 & H7)	**729.98** **±1340.19**	**0.8188** **±0.2412**	**0.1617** **±0.1670**

Table 7: Comparison to CamCoder geocoder on GeoWebNews

Geocoder	MED	Acc@161	AUC
CamCoder	**1112.25** **±1566.50**	0.7933 ±0.2429	0.1966 ±0.2005
HG+ (H1, H5 & H7)	1250.09 ±1597.01	**0.8034** **±0.2380**	**0.1956** **±0.2068**

Table 8: Comparison to CamCoder geocoder on TR-News

of the A-class (e.g., countries, mountains, and islands) and the T-class (e.g., mountains, capes, and islands) on GeoNames. For instance, it correctly geocodes the toponyms in "The chancellor of a *Spanish* university [...]," which CLAVIN ignores, and CamCoder wrongfully geocodes to *Spanish, Ontario*. However, as expected of a geocoder based on the population heuristic, locations such as buildings, airports, parks, villages, and sections of populated places are still a problem, especially on TR-News, due to ambiguities like in the case of *Heathrow*, the airport in *London, England*, and *Heathrow*, the suburban community in *Florida, United States*.

5. Discussion and Future Work

This paper proposed the usage of a country adjectives dictionary as a heuristic to improve the geocoding of adjectival toponyms. The proposed geocoder uses ElasticSearch to query a Geonames gazetteer and a dictionary of country adjectives and demonyms. To disambiguate candidates, it uses the population heuristic.
The experiments carried out showed that the processing of adjectival toponyms improved the geocoding performance compared to the baseline. When tested against other known geocoders, it also improved results in both GeoWebNews and TR-News datasets.
For future work, more experiments can be carried out using other datasets to verify differences in performance. The normalization of adjectival toponyms could be improved by adding more adjectives related to other administrative regions such as provinces and cities. Furthermore, processing embedded adjectival toponyms could also improve geocoding.

Acknowledgment

The research reported in this work was supported by the Cearence Foundation for Support of Research (FUNCAP) project "Big Data Platform to Accelerate the

[11] https://hub.docker.com/r/novetta/clavin-rest

[12] https://github.com/milangritta/Geocoding-with-Map-Vector

Digital Transformation of Ceará State" under the number 04772551/2020 and "Citizen Platform" under the number 04772314/2020. The first author was partially funded by grant #133938/2019-0, Brazilian National Council for Scientific and Technological Development (CNPq).

6. Bibliographical References

Abdelkader, A., Hand, E., and Samet, H. (2015). Brands in newsstand: Spatio-temporal browsing of business news. In *Proceedings of the 23rd SIGSPATIAL International Conference on Advances in Geographic Information Systems*, pages 1–4.

Albinati, J., Meira Jr, W., Pappa, G. L., Teixeira, M., and Marques-Toledo, C. (2017). Enhancement of epidemiological models for dengue fever based on twitter data. In *Proceedings of the 2017 International Conference on Digital Health*, pages 109–118.

Allen, C., Tsou, M.-H., Aslam, A., Nagel, A., and Gawron, J.-M. (2016). Applying gis and machine learning methods to twitter data for multiscale surveillance of influenza. *PloS one*, 11(7):e0157734.

Amitay, E., Har'El, N., Sivan, R., and Soffer, A. (2004). Web-a-where: geotagging web content. In *Proceedings of the 27th annual international ACM SIGIR conference on Research and development in information retrieval*, pages 273–280.

Butt, M. and Hussain, S. (2013). Proceedings of the 51st annual meeting of the association for computational linguistics: System demonstrations. In *Proceedings of the 51st Annual Meeting of the Association for Computational Linguistics: System Demonstrations*.

Clemens, K. (2015). Geocoding with openstreetmap data. *GEOProcessing 2015*, page 10.

Clough, P. (2005). Extracting metadata for spatially-aware information retrieval on the internet. In *Proceedings of the 2005 workshop on Geographic information retrieval*, pages 25–30.

Colladon, A. F., Guardabascio, B., and Innarella, R. (2019). Using social network and semantic analysis to analyze online travel forums and forecast tourism demand. *Decision Support Systems*, 123:113075.

DeLozier, G., Baldridge, J., and London, L. (2015). Gazetteer-independent toponym resolution using geographic word profiles. In *Twenty-Ninth AAAI Conference on Artificial Intelligence*.

Divya, M. S. and Goyal, S. K. (2013). Elasticsearch: An advanced and quick search technique to handle voluminous data. *Compusoft*, 2(6):171.

Gritta, M., Pilehvar, M., and Collier, N. (2018a). Which melbourne? augmenting geocoding with maps.

Gritta, M., Pilehvar, M. T., Limsopatham, N., and Collier, N. (2018b). What's missing in geographical parsing? *Language Resources and Evaluation*, 52(2):603–623.

Gritta, M., Pilehvar, M. T., and Collier, N. (2019). A pragmatic guide to geoparsing evaluation. *Language Resources and Evaluation*, pages 1–30.

Gunasekaran, A. K., Imani, M. B., Khan, L., Grant, C., Brandt, P. T., and Holmes, J. S. (2018). Sperg: Scalable political event report geoparsing in big data. In *2018 IEEE International Conference on Intelligence and Security Informatics (ISI)*, pages 187–192. IEEE.

Hulden, M., Silfverberg, M., and Francom, J. (2015). Kernel density estimation for text-based geolocation. In *Proceedings of the AAAI Conference on Artificial Intelligence*, volume 29.

Jiang, Y., Huang, X., and Li, Z. (2021). Spatiotemporal patterns of human mobility and its association with land use types during covid-19 in new york city. *ISPRS International Journal of Geo-Information*, 10(5):344.

Kamalloo, E. and Rafiei, D. (2018). A coherent unsupervised model for toponym resolution. In *Proceedings of the 2018 World Wide Web Conference*, pages 1287–1296.

Lampos, V. and Cristianini, N. (2012). Nowcasting events from the social web with statistical learning. *ACM Transactions on Intelligent Systems and Technology (TIST)*, 3(4):1–22.

Lee, S. J., Liu, H., and Ward, M. D. (2019). Lost in space: Geolocation in event data. *Political science research and methods*, 7(4):871–888.

Leidner, J. L. (2008). *Toponym resolution in text: Annotation, evaluation and applications of spatial grounding of place names*. Universal-Publishers.

Lieberman, M. D., Samet, H., and Sankaranarayanan, J. (2010). Geotagging with local lexicons to build indexes for textually-specified spatial data. In *2010 IEEE 26th international conference on data engineering (ICDE 2010)*, pages 201–212. IEEE.

O'brien, S. P. (2010). Crisis early warning and decision support: Contemporary approaches and thoughts on future research. *International studies review*, 12(1):87–104.

Rahimi, A., Vu, D., Cohn, T., and Baldwin, T. (2015). Exploiting text and network context for geolocation of social media users. *arXiv preprint arXiv:1506.04803*.

Rauch, E., Bukatin, M., and Baker, K. (2003). A confidence-based framework for disambiguating geographic terms. In *Proceedings of the HLT-NAACL 2003 workshop on Analysis of geographic references*, pages 50–54.

Singh, J. P., Dwivedi, Y. K., Rana, N. P., Kumar, A., and Kapoor, K. K. (2019). Event classification and location prediction from tweets during disasters. *Annals of Operations Research*, 283(1):737–757.

Vasardani, M., Winter, S., and Richter, K.-F. (2013). Locating place names from place descriptions. *International Journal of Geographical Information Science*, 27(12):2509–2532.

Vomfell, L., Härdle, W. K., and Lessmann, S. (2018). Improving crime count forecasts using twitter and taxi data. *Decision Support Systems*, 113:73–85.

Wang, J. and Hu, Y. (2019). Enhancing spatial and textual analysis with eupeg: An extensible and unified platform for evaluating geoparsers. *Transactions in GIS*, 23(6):1393–1419.

Wu, D. and Cui, Y. (2018). Disaster early warning and damage assessment analysis using social media data and geo-location information. *Decision support systems*, 111:48–59.

Proceedings of the First Workshop on Natural Language Processing for Political Sciences (PoliticalNLP), pages 46–55
Marseille, 24 June 2022

Cause and Effect in Governmental Reports: Two Data Sets for Causality Detection in Swedish

Luise Dürlich[1,2], Sebastian Reimann[1,3], Gustav Finnveden[1], Joakim Nivre[1,2], and Sara Stymne[1]
[1]Department of Linguistics and Philology, Uppsala University, Sweden
[2]RISE Research Institutes of Sweden, Kista, Sweden
[3]Department for German Language and Literature, Ruhr-Universität Bochum, Germany
luise.durlich@ri.se, sebastian.reimann@ruhr-uni-bochum.de
gustav.finnveden@gmail.com, {joakim.nivre, sara.stymne}@lingfil.uu.se

Abstract

Causality detection is the task of extracting information about causal relations from text. It is an important task for different types of document analysis, including political impact assessment. We present two new data sets for causality detection in Swedish. The first data set is annotated with binary relevance judgments, indicating whether a sentence contains causality information or not. In the second data set, sentence pairs are ranked for relevance with respect to a causality query, containing a specific hypothesized cause and/or effect. Both data sets are carefully curated and mainly intended for use as test data. We describe the data sets and their annotation, including detailed annotation guidelines. In addition, we present pilot experiments on cross-lingual zero-shot and few-shot causality detection, using training data from English and German.

Keywords: test analysis, causality, causality detection, annotation, cross-lingual transfer

1. Introduction

The analysis of large volumes of text is an important task for political scientists and governmental agencies. In our project the end goal is to enable impact assessment of governmental reports, where the identification of causal relations is a key element. One scenario in this area is that a user wants to investigate potential causes and/or effects related to a specific concept, such as unemployment or pollution. In such a scenario we need a system that can rank matches mentioning a causal relationship with respect to a given concept. A more basic task is binary relevance classification of sentences with respect to causality, which can feed into a more advanced system. In this paper we focus on creating data sets for causality detection, enabling the development of methods for causality detection and ranking, which in turn can feed into more ambitious projects on impact assessment.

Our focus is on Swedish governmental reports. While these reports are publicly available, they are not available in a format directly suitable for text processing, since the focus is on page layout rather than document structure. We release a processed version of this corpus, with extracted texts. One additional obstacle faced in this project was the lack of annotated data for causality detection, since there were no previously available data sets for Swedish. We have addressed this lack of data by annotating two small data sets for Swedish causality detection, which we present in this paper. The data sets are carefully curated, with the main purpose to serve as test data. We focus on two different subtasks. The first is binary identification of sentences as causal or non-causal. The second is a ranking task with respect to a query sentence containing a given cause and/or effect, such as *traffic causes pollution* or *X causes cancer*, where the task is to decide which of a pair of extracted sentences is more relevant to the query. We focus on the sentence level, using sentences as the unit for identification and ranking. All data sets are based on sentences from the processed corpus of Swedish governmental reports and are publicly available under the CC BY 4.0 license.[1]

There are a few data sets available for other languages, like English (Mariko et al., 2020) and German (Rehbein and Ruppenhofer, 2020). However, these data sets were created for different purposes, with different label sets, granularity, and guidelines. Despite this, they are ideal to use for experiments on cross-lingual causality detection. We report results from pilot experiments on binary causality detection with zero-shot transfer into Swedish, showing how we can handle variations of the annotation schemes of these resources. In addition we investigate a few-shot scenario where we add a limited amount of Swedish training data. We leave experiments on ranking causal sentences to future work.

2. Related Work

As noted by Dunietz et al. (2015), causality is a complex topic, which has been discussed in many fields, including psychology and philosophy. In this work, we follow the approach of Dunietz et al. (2015) to focus only on causality which is explicitly expressed linguistically, by the use of some causal connective. A causal connective is any type of linguistic expression that is used to express a causal relation, for instance, verbs

[1]https://github.com/UppsalaNLP/Swedish-Causality-Datasets

like *cause*, conjunctions like *because*, nouns like *effect*, and different types of multi-word expressions like *be a result of*. This can be contrasted to some other annotation schemes, such as Girju (2003a), who rely on a common sense intuition of real-world causality.

There are some data sets annotated for causality available for other languages than Swedish. SemEval-2010 Task 8 (Hendrickx et al., 2010) focuses on classifying semantic relations between pairs of entities. It has nine different classes, of which cause-effect is one. Examples were collected using a pattern-based web search, with a high number of patterns per class. Each example was annotated by two annotators, followed by a consolidation phase. The data sets for the FinCausal 2020 shared task (Mariko et al., 2020) on the other hand concentrate exclusively on causal relations. They provide data sets for two subtasks: binary labelling of examples as causal or not, and extraction of causes and effects. The examples for both subtasks were taken from financial news. The annotation scheme only considers examples where the effect is a quantitative fact, which is a stricter definition than in other data sets. Examples were first annotated by a single annotator, then revised and discussed by two additional annotators until agreement.

Rehbein and Ruppenhofer (2020) provide a data set for causality in German. Their annotation scheme is an extension of Dunietz et al. (2015). They focus on causal language, only considering relations that are signaled by some causal connective. The annotations are on the token level according to the participant roles in a causal relation (cause, effect, actor, affected) and the types of causation (consequence, motivation, purpose). Each example was annotated by at least two annotators, and in a final phase all disagreements were resolved by two expert annotators. There are also other annotation efforts targeting causal relations among other types of relations. Mirza et al. (2014) annotate both temporal and causal relations between events in the TempEval-3 corpus. The Penn Discourse treebank includes annotations of causal discourse relations (Prasad et al., 2008). Mihăilă et al. (2016) describe an annotation effort for causal relations in biomedical texts.

While we are not aware of any work focusing on cross-lingual causality detection, there is some work on identifying discourse connectives based on parallel corpora and word alignments (Rehbein and Ruppenhofer, 2017; Versley, 2010). However, work on monolingual causality detection is more abundant, much of it focusing on English. Early work used rule-based methods (Garcia, 1997), decision trees (Girju, 2003b), and SVMs (Hendrickx et al., 2010). As for many other tasks, neural networks have recently become dominant. For the recent FinCausal shared task, the most common approach was based on pretrained language models. While the best models used ensembling architectures (Gordeev et al., 2020), also the simpler baseline model based on only an English BERT-based model had a strong performance (Mariko et al., 2020). While cross-lingual learning has not been used for causality detection, there has been much work on other tasks. A viable approach to many tasks is to fine-tune a pretrained language model on task data from some transfer language, which can then be applied in a zero-shot setting to some other language (Wu and Dredze, 2019; Conneau et al., 2020). Adding even a little bit of target language data, in a few-shot setting, can often improve the results considerably (Lauscher et al., 2020).

3. Data Processing

In this section we describe the creation of a corpus of Swedish governmental reports, which was the data source for the causality data sets. We describe the preprocessing and sentence segmentation of this corpus. We also describe the definition of a set of Swedish causality keywords, which were evaluated based on an initial annotation effort.

3.1. Governmental Report Corpus

The source of all our data sets is a subset of the Swedish Government Official Reports, *Statens offentliga utredningar* (SOU) in Swedish, a series of reports with the goal of introducing legislative proposals and investigating complicated matters in the legislative process. These are typically produced by either a committee or a single investigator appointed by the Swedish government. At the time of extraction, only a subset of the reports were available digitally in PDF and HTML format, covering mostly reports from 1994 to the present (fall 2020).[2]

We extracted the HTML versions with the intent of exploiting the structure of the markup. However, the HTML markup turned out to encode style elements focused on describing the page layout rather than document structure. Elements like titles, subtitles, headers, footers and larger structures such as tables of contents or lists were not identifiable as such through the HTML markup, although their font type and size were encoded through style attributes. This also meant that paragraphs of text were often split in half by headers and footers at page boundaries. Another issue with this representation was the formatting of running text in parallel columns in certain sections, where the text sections mainly appeared line by line from left to right rather than as blocks of text representing a column at a time. This type of formatting largely appeared in sections concerning legislative proposals and was used to present a revised wording of the law in one column, with the previous version for reference in the other column, and the two columns thus often contained two very similar pieces of text on the surface. Since this was challenging to process in a way that produced cohesive text and was also likely to introduce near duplicates in the data if it had worked as intended, such text was omitted from the final documents.

[2]https://riksdagen.se/sv/dokument-lagar/?doktyp=sou

To deal with this form of markup varying in layout and style between documents, we conducted a rule-based extraction to distinguish between running text and structural elements. In this process, only text and corresponding titles were kept and saved as HTML. Most documents[3] are preceded by a summary of their content, which we chose to split from the main document and save as a standalone file. These summaries could be written in English, simplified Swedish, or regular Swedish. Concerning the actual reports, some included sections written in other languages. The extraction script included a language detection part using langdetect[4], to verify that a given section was in Swedish. All text classified as non-Swedish was omitted. In some cases, the extracted text contained additional white space, which made it difficult to disambiguate hyphenation from cases of word-wrapping. The resulting corpus of 3,558 reports and 3,434 summaries is publicly available.[5] We refer to this corpus as the SOU corpus.

3.2. Sentence Extraction

From the SOU corpus, we sample individual sentences or sentence pairs to create the two data sets. To extract text samples for annotation, we split the text paragraphs from our cleaned HTML corpus into sentences. We segmented the text into sentences using a combination of SpaCy pipelines (Honnibal et al., 2019) for Swedish[6] and some rules to correct for frequent errors such as unrecognised sentence boundaries for abbreviations at the end of the sentence and issues with possessive or plural marking for acronyms, which are typically preceded by a colon (e.g. *SOU:er* 'SOUs') that were generally treated as a sentence boundary by the pipeline.

3.3. Causality Keywords

A first step was to define a set of causality keywords, to be used in the remainder of the project. Causality keywords correspond to causal connectives. We proposed a set of 21 causality keywords including single words and multi-word expressions that typically convey causal relations, shown in Table 1. To evaluate which of these expressions typically express causality, we performed a small annotation to investigate how often sentences containing these expressions were considered causal. This was a quick annotation effort by three annotators, without specific guidelines. This data set, which we call the binary trial data set, could then also be used as additional Swedish training data in a cross-lingual setting.

For each of the 21 keywords, we randomly extracted

[3]Some SOUs are divided into multiple parts and span multiple documents.

[4]https://pypi.org/project/langdetect/

[5]https://github.com/UppsalaNLP/SOU-corpus

[6]https://github.com/Kungbib/swedish-spacy

Causality keywords	English translations
bero på	depend on / be due to
bidra till	contribute to
leda till	lead to
på grund av	because of / due to
till följd av	due to / as a consequence of
vara ett resultat av	be a result of
framkalla	induce / evoke
förorsaka	cause
medföra	entail / involve
orsaka	cause
påverka	affect / influence
resultera	result
vålla	cause / inflict
därför	therefore / consequently
eftersom	because
effekt	effect
följd	consequence
orsak	cause
resultat	result
förklara	explain
rendera	render

Table 1: Causality keywords. The top 13 keywords were selected to be used in our main data sets.

10 sentences from the SOU corpus. Inflections of the terms were generated using the inflector provided by the Granska tool for Swedish grammar checking (Domeij et al., 2000). Multi-word terms were matched with at most two words in between each individual word.[7] Three experts annotated the sentences as causal, non-causal, or uncertain, without the use of any specific guidelines. The resulting data set contains 210 examples with annotations from three annotators.

The main purpose of this annotation was to identify a set of keywords that reliably expresses causal relations. We thus excluded keywords that either tended to be ambiguous or to refer to causality in a more abstract or hypothetical manner, for example, without really relating to any specific cause or effect. The final set of 13 keywords, the top 13 terms in Table 1, very frequently expressed causality. The remaining 8 keywords had a lower proportion of causal sentences. Note that all nouns are in this group. The selected 13 causality keywords are verbs (e.g. *orsaka* 'cause'), phrasal verbs (e.g. *leda till* 'lead to'), multi-word prepositions (e.g. *till följd av* 'due to'), and one verbal multiword expression (*vara ett resultat av* 'be a result of').

4. Causality Data Sets

In this section we describe the two curated data sets created in the project, which are briefly summarized in Table 2. For both data sets we watned to include some additional context to the annotators, and thus included

[7]We found that longer distances between the different parts of a term often did not match the correct structure but rather unrelated cases, where *till* and *på* acted as prepositions rather than verb particles.

Data set	Extraction	Annotators/ex	Size	%causal
Ranking	Causality keywords	2–3	800	–
Binary	Cause/effect pairs	2–3	330	48.5

Table 2: Overview of the causality data sets

Cause		Effect	
avskogning	deforestation	växthuseffekt	greenhouse effect
klimatanpassning	climate change adaptation	investeringsbehov	investment needs
klimatförändring	climate change	*investering*	investment
befolkningstillväxt	population growth	bostadsbrist	housing shortage
befolkningsmängd	population size	konsumtion	consumption
biltrafik	car traffic	luftförorening	air pollution
åskväder	thunderstorm	villabrand	house fire
regnväder	rainy weather		
reporäntan	bank rate	bolånekostnad	mortgage cost
arbetslöshet	unemployment	brottslighet	crime
utbildningsnivå	level of education	inkomst	income
rökning	smoking	blodtryck	blood pressure
droger	drugs	missbruk	abuse
radon	radon	cancer	cancer
luftföroreningar	air pollution	sjukdomar	diseases

Table 3: Cause and effect pairs. Terms marked with italics are alternatives to the original term above it, and 'rainy weather' was used only as a cause, not paired with an effect.

four context sentences, two before the target and two after. The annotators focused on the target sentences, but could use the context sentences for disambiguation when needed. The final data sets include the context sentences. The annotators are the authors of this paper, who are either native speakers of Swedish or native speakers of German with a good command of Swedish. For each data set, a subset of three annotators worked on it, always including two native Swedish speakers.

4.1. Binary Data Set

The binary data set is designed with the task of binary causality detection in mind. Specifically, the task is to decide on the sentence level, whether a given sentence contains a cause and effect related by some causal keyword.

Sentences were extracted from the SOU corpus based on a set of cause and effect terms, suggested by two political scientists, shown in Table 3. We extracted sentences containing both terms of a potential cause-effect pair, such as *cancer* and *radon*. The matching was done with stemmed versions of the terms. The motivation for this extraction method was that we wanted to allow other means of expressing causality than the limited set of causality keywords in Table 1. In the final annotation we did not require the sentences to express a causal relation with respect to the term pair used for extraction (which was not shown to annotators). A causal relation between any concepts was allowed.

The annotation was performed in three phases. In a first round, three annotators performed an annotation of 30 sentences without any guidelines. Based on this experience, initial guidelines were drawn up, which were used in a second phase. The guidelines were largely based on those for German by Dunietz et al. (2015), with the exception that we did not divide causality into different subtypes. This procedure increased the inter-annotator agreement from a Fleiss' kappa of 0.38 to 0.56. After this phase the guidelines were modified into the final version in Figure 1. In the final annotation phase, there were two annotators per sample, and a kappa score of 0.5. After the annotation, all examples from phase two and all disagreements from the final phase were consolidated by at least two annotators, to increase agreement. While unsure annotations were allowed, there were very few such annotations used, and they were all resolved to either positive or negative labels in the consolidation phase. In phase two, we used 10 sentences from 3 term pairs (the three bottom term pairs in Table 3), and in the final phase, we sampled 300 sentences equally from the remaining term pairs, filtering out duplicate and near duplicate sentences. The final data set contains 330 sentences, of which 48.5% are causal.

4.2. Ranking Data Set

We define the second task as ranking two sentences by their relevance to a causal query, where a query consists of either a single term specifying a cause or an effect, or a cause–effect term pair. Figure 2 gives an example of a ranking pair extracted for the prompt '[MASK] causes greenhouse effect'. In this example both of the sentences are relevant, but the second sentence is considered more relevant since it explicitly mentions *greenhouse effect* from the prompt. The motivation behind ranking pairs of sentences rather than ranking a longer list was that it is easier to define and create general guidelines for such a task.

A sentence S is said to contain a causal relation CR, if and only if:

- S contains a unit at word level, or above, a connective, which explicitly states a CR.
- This connective does not have any meaning other than causality (in S).
- S contains references to at least two entities for which the stated CR holds; a cause and an effect.
- Causes and effects are normally events or states of affairs, even though also an actor of a certain action can be metonymically considered to be a cause as well.

In addition:

- Modal causal sentences should be annotated (e.g. "X maybe causes Y").
- Negative causal statements should be annotated (e.g. "X does not cause Y").
- Causes and effects do not have to be explicit in S, they could instead be explicit in the context sentences (e.g. referred to by a pronoun).
- We require explicit causal connectives in the text; lexical causality like "kill" meaning "cause to die" should not be annotated.
- While the sentences are sampled based on "cause-effect word pairs", the annotation is not limited to causality with respect to this word pair, but a CR with respect to any two entities should be annotated as positive.

Annotation scheme

- **y**: yes, the sentence contains a CR
- **n**: no, the sentence does not contain a CR
- **?**: unsure/borderline case (avoid overusing)

Figure 1: Guidelines for the curated binary annotation.

Sentence 1	*Flera av teknikerna bedöms resultera i långsiktig inbindning av koldioxid.* 'Several of the techniques are considered to result in long-term sequestration of carbon dioxide.'
Sentence 2	*Exempelvis ger koldioxidutsläpp inga lokala skador, utan bidrar till växthuseffekten.* 'For example, carbon dioxide emissions do not cause local damage, but contribute to the greenhouse effect.'

Figure 2: Example of a ranking sentence pair for the prompt *[MASK] medför växthuseffekt* '[MASK] causes greenhouse effect'.

We extracted the ranking data set using the set of cause and effect pairs listed in Table 3. To find relevant text passages, we applied a semantic textual similarity model for Swedish, contrastive tension (Carlsson et al., 2021), based on the KB-BERT model for Swedish (Malmsten et al., 2020). The model was used to embed the subset of all sentences in the SOU corpus matching at least one of the 13 causal keywords in order to avoid matching too many sentences related in theme, but without explicit causal statements. For each query we also embedded a constructed prompt of the cause and/or effect using one of the causality keywords[8]. This prompt consisted of the causality keyword and either both cause and effect at the respective position around the keyword, or each of the two terms individually, with the other replaced by a MASK token. Among the embedded SOU sentences, we then selected the 500 nearest neighbours to the prompt embedding. To obtain pairs of sentences we randomly sampled the neighbours with replacement.

We conducted a first exploratory pilot annotation round on 9 prompts with 10 ranking examples each. Two to three annotators were tasked with determining out of a pair of two sentences the sentence that is the most relevant to a query consisting of a cause, an effect or both. In the course of this annotation round we observed almost no overlap in sentences between the ranking pairs, essentially providing us with mostly unconnected relevance judgments for each prompt. In order to increase the chances of observing the same sentence in multiple pairs, we randomly sampled a subset of 200 sentences out of the ranked list of neighbours that we then sampled pairs of sentences from. The goal of having the same sentence occur in multiple ranking pairs was to obtain a more connected ranking list in the end. Such a list allows us to verify that sentence annotations are consistent for connected sentences. Based on this pilot annotation, we created a set of guidelines.

Following another small pilot annotation round on a selection of the same 9 prompts with 10 new examples each, we observed that we were losing information in treating pairs where both sentences are relevant, but one more so than the other, the same as cases where only one sentence is relevant. To address this, we derived the final guidelines in Figure 3. According to the guidelines, the example in Figure 2 would be labeled as 5, i.e. both sentences are relevant, but the second sentence is more relevant to the query, since it uses a more specific term.

By following the guidelines on another annotation round with 30 more prompts inter-annotator, agreement improved from a Fleiss' kappa of 0.50 on the pilot data to 0.55 on the new examples. For the

[8]We tried applying each of the 13 keywords and ranking by relative frequency and rank of the match, but found that this did not really produce a better semantic ranking than just combining the term or terms with a single keyword. We picked *medföra* ('entail')

A sentence S is relevant in relation to a query Q with cause term C and/or effect term E if and only if the following two conditions hold:

1. At least one query term T in Q (T = C or T = E) is matched in S by a phrase M(T) that is either synonymous with or has a close semantic relation (hyponymy, hypernymy, meronymy) to T.
2. S can be understood as referring to (but not necessarily asserting) a causal relationship where M(C) is a cause or M(E) is an effect (or both).

When determining whether M(T) matches T (condition 1), the following heuristics may be applied:

1. More specific terms (hyponyms) always match more general terms. For example, "tea" and "herbal tea" both match "beverage". Added specificity may result from lexical hyponymy ("tea" – "beverage"), compounding ("herbal tea" – "tea") or modification ("tea with milk" – "tea").
2. More general terms (hypernyms) match more specific terms only if they are close in a semantic hierarchy. For example, "tea" and "beverage" match "herbal tea", but "liquid" does not. Added generality may result from lexical hypernymy ("beverage" – "tea"), decompounding ("tea" – "herbal tea") or dropped modification ("tea" – "tea with milk").
3. The interpretation of terms should be made in context, which means that contextual information may be used to, for example, resolve anaphoric reference, lexical ambiguity, or implicit modification. For example, a pronoun like "it" matches "beverage" if its antecedent matches "beverage", and "tea" matches "herbal tea" if the contextual information supports an inclusive interpretation but not if it makes clear that only "black tea" is relevant.

When ranking two relevant sentences in relation to a query Q with cause term C and/or effect term E, apply the following rules in order of decreasing priority:

1. Prefer sentences with a greater number of matching terms in the correct causal roles.
2. Prefer sentences with semantically closer matches of the query term(s). Specifically: exact match > synonym > hyponym > hypernym > meronym.
3. Prefer more specific and informative sentences. Specifically:
   (a) Prefer explicit statements of causality over implicit statements.
   (b) Prefer factual statements over modal statements.
   (c) Prefer positive statements over negative statements.
   (d) Prefer clausal statements over nominalizations.

Annotation Scheme:

0. both irrelevant
1. first sentence relevant, second sentence irrelevant
2. second sentence relevant, first sentence irrelevant
3. both sentences equally relevant
4. first sentence most relevant, second sentence also relevant
5. second sentence most relevant, first sentence also relevant

Figure 3: Guidelines for the ranking annotation.

30 prompts we chose to sample 20 sentence pairs per prompt. We found that some of the prompts — such as 'climate change adaptation entails investment needs', 'deforestation causes MASK" and 'thunderstorms cause MASK' — were overly specific and generated very few relevant matches with our extraction method. To account for this, we chose to re-rank them with respect to more thematically fitting prompts to the retrieved sentence pairs and added the climate change/investment and rainy weather terms. We also opted for adding the 90 pilot annotation examples (with the pairs: drugs/abuse, radon/cancer, air pollution/diseases). As these had been annotated with 4 instead of 6 labels, they were relabelled to fit the final annotation scheme. Each annotation with a disagreement was then consolidated by at least two annotators and checked for inconsistencies between overlapping pairs. The result is a set of 800 sentence pairs and their ranked relevance with respect to a specific causal prompt.

4.3. Comparison of Extraction Methods

In order to explore the connection between the two sentence extraction methods, where the ranking set was filtered based on causality keywords and the binary set was extracted based on term pairs, we investigated which causality keywords were used in the binary data set. To that end we automatically matched the causality keywords from Table 1, separating them into two groups, the selected group (top), and the filtered group (bottom). Half of the sentences, 80 sentences, had at least one such match, and in a few cases matched more than one keyword. We went through the remaining 80 sentences manually, marking the causal connective. Table 4 shows an overview of all connectives occurring at least four times. Both the selected and filtered causality keywords had a subset that occurred multiple times. For the remaining connectives, most of them were rare, with 49 connectives only occurring once. They are a mix of verbs, nouns, and different types of multi-word expressions. The most frequent keyword not on our keyword list is the verb *innebära* ('mean/imply'), which we could consider including in our set of causality keywords in future work. When we match our causality keywords towards the negative binary sentences, none of the selected 13 keywords match, which is a further validation that they can ex-

Type	Keyword	Translation	Frequency
Selected	påverka	to affect	18
	orsaka	to cause	9
	till följd av	due to	9
	leda till	to lead to	6
	bidra till	to contribute to	5
	på grund av	because of	5
	medföra	to entail	5
	bero på	to depend on	4
	Total		**64**
Filtered	effekt	effect	15
	följd	consequence	9
	därför	therefore	7
	eftersom	because	6
	orsak	cause	6
	Total		**49**
Other	innebära	to mean/imply	9
	om	if	4
	Total		**76**

Table 4: Causality keyword frequency in the curated binary data set, occurring at least 4 times. Totals also include less frequent keywords. Type refers to whether the causality keyword occurs in the list of causality keywords in Table 1.

tract causality with a high precision. Of the 8 filtered keywords, five of them occur in negative sentences, a total of eight times.

5. Pilot Experiments

In this section we report results on a pilot experiment on binary causality detection. Since we have no high-quality Swedish training data, we apply cross-lingual learning, using data in English and German. For testing we use the binary Swedish test set. We also apply few-shot learning, by adding the Swedish binary trial data set to the training set, showing that we need to address the imbalance of the data set in order for that approach to be useful.[9]

We base the cross-lingual experiments on the transformer-based, multilingual model XLM-Roberta (Conneau et al., 2020, XLM-R), using the architecture for sequence classification from the Transformer library (Wolf et al., 2020), with dropout and a linear layer for classification on top of it. We run our system for two epochs, with a learning rate of 2e-5, batch size 32, and maximum sequence length 256. The hyper-parameters were tuned by training on English data and testing on German development data (375 sentences provided by Rehbein and Ruppenhofer (2020)), which we believe is preferable to monolingual tuning.

We used both English and German source language training data. The English data is from the FinCausal data set by Mariko et al. (2020) and the SemEval-2010 data by Hendrickx et al. (2010), where the original multi-way annotations were transformed into binary annotations by considering all cause-effect relations to be positive examples and all other relations to be negative examples. For the German data, the annotations of Rehbein and Ruppenhofer (2020) were turned into binary annotations by considering all instances with both a cause and an effect to be causal. We noted in our experiments that the stricter guidelines of the FinCausal data, requiring quantifiable facts as effects, were problematic to us. Thus, we also opted to only use the positive examples from FinCausal, which we call FinCausal+. The size of these data sets are summarized in Table 5.

Data set	Train	%causal
SemEval	7,200	12.1
FinCausal	13,478	7.5
FinCausal+	1,010	100.0
German	3,104	50.5

Table 5: Size and proportion of causal examples for the English and German training data sets.

Data set	F1-macro	P	R
FinCausal	35.91	60.91	2.12
SemEval	63.11	69.01	50.38
SemEval +FinCausal	48.92	87.82	16.25
SemEval +FinCausal+	62.03	67.17	60.25
German	76.93	75,78	79.37
German +SemEval +FinCausal+	71.56	70.53	75,13

Table 6: F1-macro, and precision and recall for the causal class with different source language training data sets.

5.1. Zero-Shot Experiments

Table 6 presents the zero-shot results.[10] The results are averages over five runs with different random seeds. We show the F1-macro score, as well as precision and recall for the causal class. Here, the performance across different training data choices varies substantially. When looking at the F1-macro and the recall for the causal class of the models where a concatenation of the English source data or only the FinCausal data was used, we can see that the models failed to recognize many examples that actually expressed causality. This may be due to the strict annotation for the FinCausal data, since in the two experiments without the negative FinCausal examples the recall for the causal class and

[9]A subset of these experiments, and additional experiments with other embeddings, results for German, and additional analysis, are presented in Reimann (2021) and Reimann and Stymne (2022)

[10]As a further point of comparison, the monolingual performance of these systems when tested on a matching test set varies between 82.3 for German and 95.7 for FinCausal

		F1-macro	P	R
Consolidation by numerical scores	EN (SE + FC-c)	36.76	49.22	98.75
	DE	67.09	61.63	94.37
	EN + DE	53.90	54.70	98.12
Consolidation by majority vote	EN (SE + FC-c)	60.20	57.36	92.50
	DE	71.23	64.91	72.50
	EN + DE	71.86	66.83	84.83
Balanced Training Set	EN (SE + FC-c)	68.46	65.56	73.75
	DE	78.24	82.96	70.00
	EN + DE	77.46	79.45	72.50

Table 7: F1-macro and precision and recall for the causal class for the few-shot experiments.

the F1-macro were much higher.

Table 6 also demonstrates that finetuning on the German data clearly led to better results than doing so on the English data, even though the German training data contains substantially fewer examples. Combining German and English led to slightly worse results. A possible hypothesis for the superior performance with German may be that the underlying annotation guidelines for both the German data and the Swedish test data were relatively similar, which resulted in a notably better performance. Also, the German data, like the Swedish test data is balanced between positive and negative examples, unlike the English data. The findings of Turc et al. (2021), however, also hint that German in many cases may be generally more beneficial than English as a source language for cross-lingual NLP tasks. Both German and English are relatively closely related to Swedish, which might be a factor contributing to the reasonably good results, but further experiments would be required to investigate the effect of language relatedness.

5.2. Few-Shot Experiments

The evaluation of the causality keywords, described in section 3.3 led to the creation of the Swedish binary trial data set. We wanted to see if using this small and quickly annotated data set could improve results for Swedish. Since the trial data set contains separate annotations by three annotators, we needed to define ways of consolidating the three annotations. We applied three variants of consolidation. In the numerical scoring scheme, a positive annotation received a score of 0.2, an unclear annotation a score of 0.1 and a non-causal annotation a score of zero. We considered the causal label for examples that reach a score of 0.3 or more. The motivation for this scheme was that such sentences have at least some causal signal. This scheme led to 81% causal examples. A stricter alternative is a simple majority vote, where all sentences are considered causal if two of the three annotators agreed on that. However, even for consolidation through majority vote the distribution still is skewed towards the causal class, with 68% causal examples. Thus, we created a third, balanced, variation including all the negative examples as defined by majority vote plus a sample of positive examples from the training data, which has the same size. While this balanced the data set, it reduced the number of examples from 210 to 134.

Table 7 shows the results. For the target language data set, where annotations were calculated through the numerical scheme, the performance was surprisingly low. A clear overuse of the causal class can be observed. Interestingly, this problem seems to become less obvious when using the Swedish training data where the annotations were consolidated by majority vote, with fewer instances of the causal class. Note that neither of these two schemes led to any improvements over zero-shot learning. When we balance the Swedish training data, precision improved further, at some cost to recall, and we see the overall best scores. In all cases, the F1-macro scores are better than the corresponding zero-shot experiments. Again, there are clear differences between the transfer language choice, with German giving the best results in this setting as well, but with the gap to English somewhat reduced.

6. Conclusion

In this paper we present two curated data sets for Swedish causality detection. One data set is focused on binary identification of sentences containing causal expressions, whereas the second data set is focused on ranking of causal sentences with respect to a target cause and/or effect. These resources are mainly considered as test sets for Swedish causality detection. As such they enable the exploration and evaluation of causality detection and causality–theme ranking in Swedish. In addition we release a quickly annotated binary trial data set.

In a set of pilot experiments we explore cross-lingual causality detection, using training data from German and English and one of our new data sets for evaluation. We show that performance varies between three different training data sets in English and German. While we can get some improvements by adding our Swedish trial data set to the training data, this requires balancing the data in the trial set.

This work is a first step towards enabling impact assessment of Swedish governmental reports. The presented data sets will enable further work on both binary causality classification and ranking of causal sentences with respect to a theme, which could then feed into more advanced systems for impact assessment.

Acknowledgements

This work was funded by Vinnova in the project 2019-02252: Datalab for results in the public sector. We would like to thank Sven-Olof Junker and Martin Sparr at The Swedish National Financial Management Authority for valuable discussions and for providing the list of cause and effect pairs in Table 3. The computations were enabled by resources in project UPPMAX 2020/2-2 at the Uppsala Multidisciplinary Center for Advanced Computational Science.

7. Bibliographical References

Carlsson, F., Gyllensten, A. C., Gogoulou, E., Hellqvist, E. Y., and Sahlgren, M. (2021). Semantic re-tuning with contrastive tension. In *International Conference on Learning Representations*.

Conneau, A., Khandelwal, K., Goyal, N., Chaudhary, V., Wenzek, G., Guzmán, F., Grave, E., Ott, M., Zettlemoyer, L., and Stoyanov, V. (2020). Unsupervised cross-lingual representation learning at scale. In *Proceedings of the 58th Annual Meeting of the Association for Computational Linguistics*, pages 8440–8451, Online, July. Association for Computational Linguistics.

Domeij, R., Knutsson, O., Carlberger, J., and Kann, V. (2000). Granska–an efficient hybrid system for Swedish grammar checking. In *Proceedings of the 12th Nordic Conference of Computational Linguistics (NODALIDA 1999)*, pages 49–56, Trondheim, Norway, December. Department of Linguistics, Norwegian University of Science and Technology, Norway.

Dunietz, J., Levin, L., and Carbonell, J. (2015). Annotating causal language using corpus lexicography of constructions. In *Proceedings of The 9th Linguistic Annotation Workshop*, pages 188–196, Denver, Colorado, USA, June. Association for Computational Linguistics.

Garcia, D. (1997). Coatis, an nlp system to locate expressions of actions connected by causality links. In Enric Plaza et al., editors, *Knowledge Acquisition, Modeling and Management*, pages 347–352, Berlin, Heidelberg. Springer Berlin Heidelberg.

Girju, R. (2003a). Automatic detection of causal relations for question answering. In *Proceedings of the ACL 2003 Workshop on Multilingual Summarization and Question Answering*, pages 76–83, Sapporo, Japan, July. Association for Computational Linguistics.

Girju, R. (2003b). Automatic detection of causal relations for question answering. In *Proceedings of the ACL 2003 Workshop on Multilingual Summarization and Question Answering*, pages 76–83, Sapporo, Japan, July. Association for Computational Linguistics.

Gordeev, D., Davletov, A., Rey, A., and Arefiev, N. (2020). LIORI at the FinCausal 2020 shared task. In *Proceedings of the 1st Joint Workshop on Financial Narrative Processing and MultiLing Financial Summarisation*, pages 45–49, Barcelona, Spain (Online), December. COLING.

Hendrickx, I., Kim, S. N., Kozareva, Z., Nakov, P., Ó Séaghdha, D., Padó, S., Pennacchiotti, M., Romano, L., and Szpakowicz, S. (2010). SemEval-2010 task 8: Multi-way classification of semantic relations between pairs of nominals. In *Proceedings of the 5th International Workshop on Semantic Evaluation*, pages 33–38, Uppsala, Sweden, July. Association for Computational Linguistics.

Honnibal, M., Montani, I., Honnibal, M., Peters, H., Landeghem, S. V., Samsonov, M., Geovedi, J., Regan, J., Orosz, G., Kristiansen, S. L., McCann, P. O., Altinok, D., Roman, Howard, G., Bozek, S., Bot, E., Amery, M., Phatthiyaphaibun, W., Vogelsang, L. U., Böing, B., Tippa, P. K., jeannefukumaru, GregDubbin, Mazaev, V., Balakrishnan, R., Møllerhøj, J. D., wbwseeker, Burton, M., thomasO, and Patel, A. (2019). explosion/spaCy: v2.1.7: Improved evaluation, better language factories and bug fixes, August.

Lauscher, A., Ravishankar, V., Vulić, I., and Glavaš, G. (2020). From zero to hero: On the limitations of zero-shot language transfer with multilingual Transformers. In *Proceedings of the 2020 Conference on Empirical Methods in Natural Language Processing (EMNLP)*, pages 4483–4499, Online, November. Association for Computational Linguistics.

Malmsten, M., Börjeson, L., and Haffenden, C. (2020). Playing with words at the national library of sweden - making a swedish BERT. *CoRR*, abs/2007.01658.

Mariko, D., Abi-Akl, H., Labidurie, E., Durfort, S., De Mazancourt, H., and El-Haj, M. (2020). The financial document causality detection shared task (FinCausal 2020). In *Proceedings of the 1st Joint Workshop on Financial Narrative Processing and MultiLing Financial Summarisation*, pages 23–32, Barcelona, Spain (Online), December. COLING.

Mihăilă, C., Ohta, T., Pyysalo, S., and Ananiadou, S. (2016). BioCause: Annotating and analysing causality in the biomedical domain. *BMC Bioinformatics*, 14(2).

Mirza, P., Sprugnoli, R., Tonelli, S., and Speranza, M. (2014). Annotating causality in the TempEval-3 corpus. In *Proceedings of the EACL 2014 Workshop on Computational Approaches to Causality in Language (CAtoCL)*, pages 10–19, Gothenburg, Sweden, April. Association for Computational Linguistics.

Prasad, R., Dinesh, N., Lee, A., Miltsakaki, E., Robaldo, L., Joshi, A., and Webber, B. (2008). The Penn Discourse TreeBank 2.0. In *Proceedings of the Sixth International Conference on Language Resources and Evaluation (LREC'08)*, Marrakech, Morocco, May. European Language Resources Association (ELRA).

Rehbein, I. and Ruppenhofer, J. (2017). Catching the common cause: Extraction and annotation of causal relations and their participants. In *Proceedings of the 11th Linguistic Annotation Workshop*, pages 105–114, Valencia, Spain, April. Association for Computational Linguistics.

Rehbein, I. and Ruppenhofer, J. (2020). A new resource for German causal language. In *Proceedings of the 12th Language Resources and Evaluation Conference*, pages 5968–5977, Marseille, France, May. European Language Resources Association.

Reimann, S. and Stymne, S. (2022). Exploring cross-lingual transfer to counteract data scarcity for causality detection. In *Proceedings of the Web Conference 2022 (WWW '22 Companion); The 3rd International Workshop on Cross-lingual Event-centric Open Analytics (CLEOPATRA 2022)*, Virtual Event, Lyon, France.

Reimann, S. M. (2021). Multilingual zero-shot and few-shot causality detection. Master's thesis, Uppsala University, Sweden.

Turc, I., Lee, K., Eisenstein, J., Chang, M.-W., and Toutanova, K. (2021). Revisiting the primacy of english in zero-shot cross-lingual transfer.

Versley, Y. (2010). Discovery of ambiguous and unambiguous discourse connectives via annotation projection. In *Proceedings of the Workshop on Annotation and Exploitation of Parallel Corpora AEPC 2010.*, pages 83–92, Tartu, Estonia.

Wolf, T., Debut, L., Sanh, V., Chaumond, J., Delangue, C., Moi, A., Cistac, P., Rault, T., Louf, R., Funtowicz, M., Davison, J., Shleifer, S., von Platen, P., Ma, C., Jernite, Y., Plu, J., Xu, C., Le Scao, T., Gugger, S., Drame, M., Lhoest, Q., and Rush, A. (2020). Transformers: State-of-the-art natural language processing. In *Proceedings of the 2020 Conference on Empirical Methods in Natural Language Processing: System Demonstrations*, pages 38–45, Online, October. Association for Computational Linguistics.

Wu, S. and Dredze, M. (2019). Beto, bentz, becas: The surprising cross-lingual effectiveness of BERT. In *Proceedings of the 2019 Conference on Empirical Methods in Natural Language Processing and the 9th International Joint Conference on Natural Language Processing (EMNLP-IJCNLP)*, pages 833–844, Hong Kong, China, November. Association for Computational Linguistics.

Proceedings of the First Workshop on Natural Language Processing for Political Sciences (PoliticalNLP), pages 56–61
Marseille, 24 June 2022

Does Twitter know your political views? POLiTweets dataset and semi-automatic method for political leaning discovery

Joanna Baran, Michał Kajstura, Maciej Ziółkowski, Krzysztof Rajda
Wroclaw University of Science and Technology
Wyspiańskiego 27, 50-370 Wrocław, Poland
{joanna.baran, krzysztof.rajda}@pwr.edu.pl, {242491, 242475}@student.pwr.edu.pl

Abstract

Every day, the world is flooded by millions of messages and statements posted on Twitter or Facebook. Social media platforms try to protect users' personal data, but there still is a real risk of misuse, including elections manipulation. Did you know, that only 10 posts addressing important or controversial topics for society are enough to predict one's political affiliation with a 0.85 F1-score? To examine this phenomenon, we created a novel universal method of semi-automated political leaning discovery. It relies on a heuristical data annotation procedure, which was evaluated to achieve 0.95 agreement with human annotators (counted as an accuracy metric). We also present POLiTweets - the first publicly open Polish dataset for political affiliation discovery in a multi-party setup, consisting of over 147k tweets from almost 10k Polish-writing users annotated heuristically and almost 40k tweets from 166 users annotated manually as a test set. We used our data to study the aspects of domain shift in the context of topics and the type of content writers - ordinary citizens vs. professional politicians.

Keywords: political affiliation, political leaning, political profiling, Twitter dataset, political dataset

1. Introduction

Digital traces such as social media posts or interactions appear to be extremely powerful in gaining knowledge about our personal lives and predicting political beliefs (Kosinski et al., 2013). Automated analysis of electoral support on social media could effectively replace traditional surveys, being more cost-effective, allowing for examining a much larger portion of the population and giving more insights into voters' profiles. Unfortunately, as history has shown with the Cambridge Analytics example (Boldyreva, 2018), it is easy to misuse personal data, even to manipulate election results. Since then, social media companies have done a lot to strengthen the security of users' personal data (Hu, 2020). Have they done enough? Is it still possible to easily access enough personal data to model users' political affiliation?

To verify these questions, we propose a universal, semi-automatic political affiliation discovery method and a POLiTweets dataset - the novel political leaning discovery dataset, consisting of over 147k tweets from almost 10k Polish-writing users. As far as we know, this is the first published Polish dataset for predicting an individual's political orientation.

The main objective of this article is to answer the following Research Questions: (**RQ1**) Is it possible to determine one's political affiliation using one's social media activity? (**RQ2**) How many social media posts are needed to accurately determine one's political leaning? (**RQ3**) Do professional politicians use the same language as their party supporters?

Our main contribution includes 3 points. Firstly, we designed a novel method of semi-automatic annotation of political leaning data. Secondly, we used so to collect the first Polish publicly open dataset for predicting political affiliation in a multi-party setup. Finally, we performed an analysis of the current political polarization in the Polish Twitter community.

2. Related Work

Assessing political affiliation - which party a given user is a supporter - is the main challenge of constructing political affiliation detection dataset. There have been several works on labelling political orientation using Twitter or Facebook.

Manual annotation. Probably the most accurate method is to survey volunteers willing to declare their political opinion (Kosinski et al., 2013; Preotiuc-Pietro et al., 2017) or manual annotation by a group of specialists who have access to publicly available user account information (Cohen and Ruths, 2013; Samih and Darwish, 2020). Unfortunately, both approaches are very time-consuming and practically unattainable for a large amount of data. For this reason, many automatic annotation methods have been proposed.

Annotation by relations. This approach assumes that the majority of the politicians we observe on Twitter reflect our views to some extent. The most popular method is to propagate party labels through analysis of followers and following users of politician accounts. (King et al., 2016; Golbeck and Hansen, 2014; Sylwester and Purver, 2015; Barberá, 2015). However, the follower relationship can introduce some noise, given the existence of users observing opposing politicians (eg. to get a balanced opinion). An et al. (2012) provided annotation by exploiting the political bias of popular news media provider accounts in the USA and their mutual followers' group.

Annotation by keywords. The use of hashtags or keywords in tweets has been explored in some work as an indicator of user's affiliation, as exemplified by the Scottish Independence Referendum study of social media public opinions (Fang et al., 2015). Similarly, Tatman (2017) focused only on specific electoral slogans in users' bios or usernames.

Annotations by interactions. These methods take advantage of users' interactions with the content they view. Rajadesingan and Liu (2014) introduced a semi-supervised retweet-based label propagation algorithm, based on the belief that retweeting a tweet may indicate endorsement of its content. Nevertheless, one can easily find tweets shared with a negative comment, retweeted to show disapproval. A more reliable premise is a user's "like" (Papakyriakopoulos et al., 2018). Analysis of the likes distribution towards political parties' posts has proven to be very effective in this task and was verified by a manual survey in Kristensen et al. (2017). Like is a very strong signal of support towards the post creator and, in our opinion, the best choice to develop heuristics for assigning political labels to users' social media profiles.

Finally, we need to point out that most of the published collections have focused on the two-party system, as is present in the USA (Conover et al., 2011; Yan et al., 2017) (binary classification setup). The multi-party prediction problem is far more challenging and yet still underestimated in research works, even though the majority of democratic countries are characterized by a diverse political arena. This highlights the importance of creating multi-party datasets for a more complex study of social media users.

3. Political Afiliation Discovery Method

In this section, we describe the proposed semi-automatic method of political leaning discovery and test its quality.

3.1. Method Steps

Our approach to detect one's political affiliation goes as follows (Figure 1):

(1) Manually create the list of prominent political figures and their Twitter accounts in examined country/culture. Assign them a party label according to the politician's affiliation.

(2) Aquire tweets posted from those accounts (we used an official Twitter API).

(3) Save a list of social media users that liked collected politicians' tweets.

(4) Filter out individuals with less than 10 likes to reduce the noise in acquired labels.

(5) Count and group each users' likes by a political party. Choose the most frequent one as a label. Exclude inconclusive users with an equal number of likes for different parties for training purposes. For testing purposes, they could be manually annotated and included in the test set.

(6) Collect selected users' tweets. Each scraped entry had to contain at least one predefined hashtag or keyword related to controversial topics - a post addressing

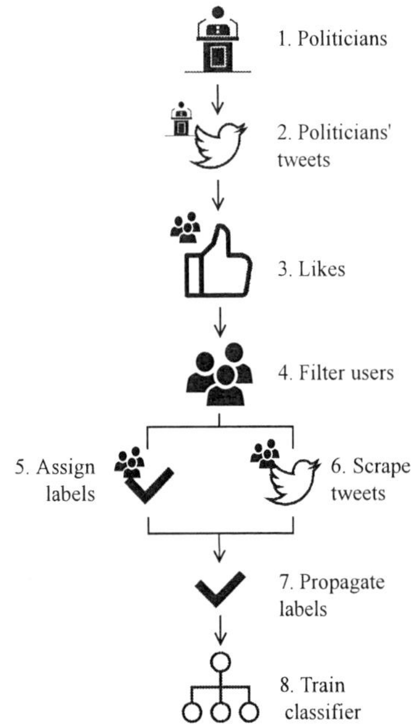

Figure 1: An illustration of the data acquisition pipeline

this kind of politically loaded and divisive subject is more likely to reflect the political views of a person writing it Bail et al. (2018).

(7) Propagate obtained users' labels to all users' tweets, resulting in a heuristically annotated text classification dataset.

(8) Train a text classifier, which can be then used for analysing the political affiliation of any provided text. It can be also applied to a user-level classification, aggregating individual posts' labels for each user, further increasing the accuracy of the method.

3.2. Heuristic Quality Evaluation

As the proposed method relies on a heuristic approach to data annotation, we ensured its performance by comparing it with human annotators. All users present in the test set were manually verified and labelled by three independent annotators using all available public data, such as posts, bio, followers network and uploaded images. When a discrepancy occurred, a majority vote was taken to select a party name. Determining a person's political preferences based on social media posts is a highly subjective task, but annotators scored a high inter-annotator agreement of 0.74 Krippendorff's alpha coefficient. In total, we had 29 960 posts from 133 users for which we had human annotations.

Labels obtained using the proposed automatic labelling scheme matched the manual annotations with a **0.95 accuracy**, which confirms heuristics reliability.

4. POLiTweets Dataset Summary

We used our proposed political leaning discovery method to collect a dataset consisting of **186 868**

tweets in Polish language, written by 9 837 Twitter users. Description and full hashtag list of controversial topics selected in method Step 6 are presented in Section 9.2. Data were posted between March 2021 and January 2022. As labels set, we have chosen five main political groups with the greatest impact on the current Polish political scene - our selection was based on Parliament representation and election polls, more details in Section 9.1.

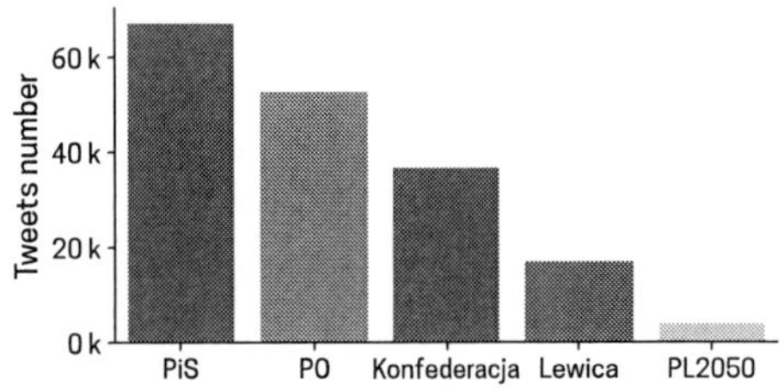

Figure 2: POLiTweets party label distribution

The distribution of assigned labels was unbalanced (Figure 2), which is quite consistent with the Polish political reality.
The previously manually annotated users and their tweets were taken as a test set (see Section 3.2). It contained only profiles with at least 15 posts per each. The rest of the data (over 147k tweets) was randomly split in a 9:1 ratio creating a training and validation split. We ensured that each entry has a minimum of 5 words that are not a hashtag, user mention or URL. The dataset is available in CSV files containing TweetID instead of explicit text, according to Twitter's guidelines about redistributing their content for scientific purposes. Test collection file appears twice due to different annotation sources - from heuristics method (*heuristics-test*) and human annotators (*manual-test*). We provide also a file with posts of the Polish parties' official Twitter accounts and their active politicians' list. Additionally, we prepared an *ambiguous test set* of manually annotated tweets of 33 users for whom we skipped filtering by the ratio of likes in Step 5 of our method (Section 3.1). We will refer to them as *ambiguous* because discovering their political views is a much more difficult task even for a human annotator due to a more uniform distribution of those users' likes across political parties. All filed are publicly available in the GitHub repository [1].

5. Experiments and Results

The final step of our method was to train a classifier on the acquired tweets' textual data, without using any additional knowledge. We used it for analysis of current political polarization among the Polish Twitter community.
Experimental setup. As a classifier, we finetuned the base version of HerBERT - a BERT-based language model dedicated to Polish language (Mroczkowski et al., 2021) - with a sequence classification head. The choice of this architecture was justified by its numerous effective applications in the NLP field. We considered it a good starting point for obtaining preliminary results on our dataset. The training took maximally 50 epochs with an early stopping patience parameter equal to 15 epochs. The batch size was set to 32 and the model was optimized using AdamW with a learning rate of 1e-5 along with a warmup linear scheduler. The preprocessing stage included the removal of hashtags, user mentions and URLs from posts to prevent data leakage. Due to the large imbalance of classes in the dataset, we applied a weighted sampler.
Model performace. The text classifier achieved 0.64 micro F1-score on the *manual-test* split. More detailed results are presented in Table 1.

Party name	Precision	Recall	F1-score
PiS	0.78	0.75	0.76
PO	0.64	0.67	0.65
Konfederacja	0.35	0.36	0.36
Lewica	0.18	0.26	0.21
PL2050	0.31	0.07	0.12
Total	-	-	0.64

Table 1: Scores for particular classes

Classifier errors as Polish political scene descriptor. The confusion matrix, presented in Figure 3, reveals differences between political parties in Poland. Rows and columns are ordered by the place in political spectrum, *Lewica* being the furthest to the left and *Konfederacja* on the rightmost side (Kosowska-Gastoł, 2021). The text classifier makes most errors between political groups with similar social and economic views. The lowest score is achieved for the centrist party - *Polska2050*, which can be explained mostly by a strong class imbalance and hard to distinguish political opinions.

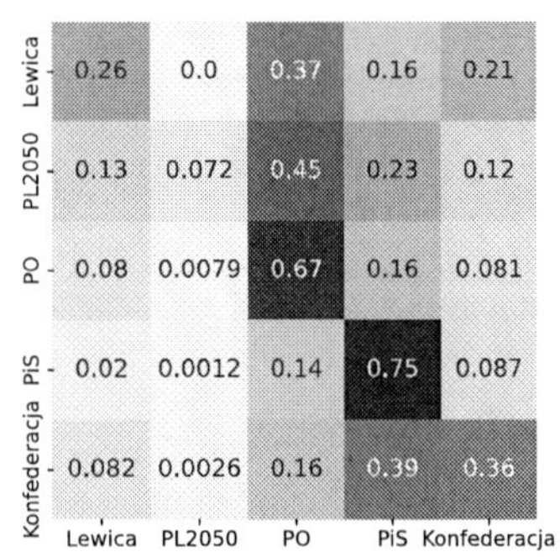

Figure 3: F1-score confusion matrix

Effects of Domain Shift. We investigated the effect of domain shift on our classifier by considering it from two perspectives. To examine writers' shift, the clas-

[1] https://github.com/Joanna065/politweets

sifier trained previously on tweets from regular Twitter users (ordinary citizens) was used to predict party labels on professional politicians' posts, which were obtained in Step 2 of our method (Section 3). To study domain shift among topics, the training was carried out using the same experimental setup as stated above, but with a training set containing posts from 3 topics, leaving the last topic's posts as a test set.

Domain-out	F1-score
Politicians	0.35
Topic - abortion	0.40
Topic - lexTVN	0.45
Topic - EU & CJEU	0.48
Topic - The Polish Order	0.46

Table 2: Results for domain shift study. Each row states test set used

Results shown in the Table 2 prove that the model's performance under domain shift is severely affected. The model tested on politicians' tweets achieved only 0.35 of micro averaged profile-level F1-score. A similar situation occurred for the experiment on topics - the highest result was 0.48 F1-score, compared to 0.65 without the domain shift scenario (Table 1).

6. Discussion

RQ1: Is it possible to determine one's political affiliation using one social media activity? Yes, but we have to take into account the quality and balance of the input data. The research showed that the underrepresented parties were less recognizable by the classifier - model performance was the highest for more frequent political labels (like *PiS* or *PO* in the Polish case).

RQ2: How many social media posts are needed to accurately determine one's political leaning? To answer that question, we tested the classifier incrementally by increasing a subset of users' posts (from 1 to 15), choosing the most common label for the profile. We conducted evaluations on all 3 available test sets. The experiment was repeated 30 times with different tweet selection orders. Basing final predictions on more tweets drastically improves the performance of our method, which is presented in Figure 4. Accumulated predictions for well-defined users, for whom the number of collected likes was significantly higher for one party than the others, allowed to achieve a micro-averaged F1-score of 0.85 when used on 10 posts. For the more difficult user cases, the classifier scored significantly lower, but still above 0.7 F1-score.

RQ3: Do professional politicians use the same language as their party supporters? Unfortunately, no. The classifier we chose proved to be sensitive to any changes in test data compared to training examples. It occurs not only in writer shift but also in the aspect of topic shift. This leads to the conclusion that despite the impressive results on in-domain texts, the deployment of such models should be carried out with special care.

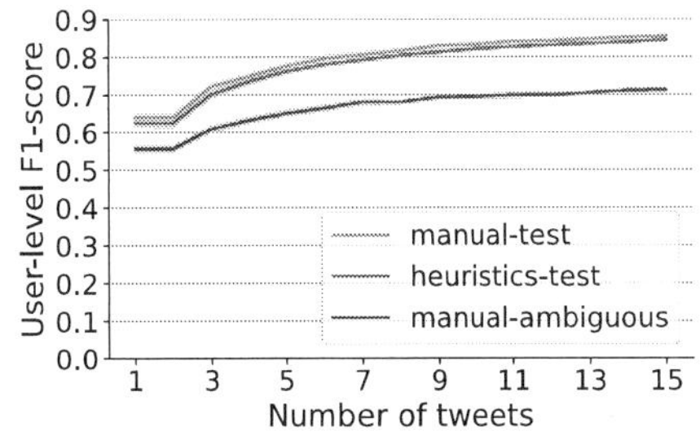

Figure 4: Impact of the number of posts on model performance

Method advantages. The main advantage of our method is resource and time savings, compared to manual dataset annotation or traditional political affiliation surveying. Such surveys typically last for days to acquire a representative population, while our method can perform in only a few hours. It is also quite general - the data collection scheme can be applied to other social media platforms and any country or culture, due manual selection of controversial topics and seed profiles. Moreover, models trained on such data can also generalize to any kind of in-domain text, even those from users not actively liking any content produced by politicians.

Method limitations. We assessed political leaning in a semi-automatic way. It requires choosing an initial set of politicians' accounts to scrape tweets from. It also needs a selection of some controversial, politically-loaded topics to filter out the discussion. Such topics depend mostly on country culture and current political debate and need to be chosen with care.

7. Conclusions and Future Works

In this work, we proposed a semi-automatic, universal schema for political affiliation discovery, based on the heuristic method of data acquisition and annotation. Our approach proved to be highly effective, achieving a 0.95 user-level accuracy agreement when compared with the manually annotated dataset. We also introduce POLiTweets - the first publicly available dataset for political leaning analysis in Polish, with almost 187k tweets from nearly 10k users. We proved that using tweets from popular and controversial topics, it is possible to associate Twitter users with political parties they support with sufficient confidence. Such knowledge may be exploited for microtargeting purposes, similar to how it was in the Cambridge Analytica scandal (Boldyreva, 2018). Publishing even a few personal opinions on such topics may uncover users' political views - as our experiments showed, 10 posts are enough to classify political affiliation with a 0.85 F1-score.

Being aware of the high dependency on the data domain - topics and writers' type - we'd like to apply the domain adaptation techniques (eg. Ma et al. (2019)) to support classifier stability. Also, more model architectures are needed to examine. We find it a good start for the follow-up work we tend to perform.

8. Bibliographical References

An, J., Cha, M., Gummadi, K. P., Crowcroft, J., and Quercia, D. (2012). Visualizing media bias through twitter. In *ICWSM 2012*.

Bail, C. A., Argyle, L. P., Brown, T. W., Bumpus, J. P., Chen, H., Hunzaker, M. B. F., Lee, J., Mann, M., Merhout, F., and Volfovsky, A. (2018). Exposure to opposing views on social media can increase political polarization. *Proceedings of the National Academy of Sciences*, 115(37):9216–9221.

Barberá, P. (2015). Birds of the same feather tweet together: Bayesian ideal point estimation using twitter data. *Political Analysis*, 23:76 – 91.

Boldyreva, E. (2018). Cambridge analytica: Ethics and online manipulation with decision-making process. pages 91–102, 12.

Cohen, R. and Ruths, D. (2013). Classifying political orientation on twitter: It's not easy! *Proceedings of the 7th International Conference on Weblogs and Social Media, ICWSM 2013*, pages 91–99, 01.

Conover, M. D., Goncalves, B., Ratkiewicz, J., Flammini, A., and Menczer, F. (2011). Predicting the political alignment of twitter users. In *2011 IEEE Third International Conference on Privacy, Security, Risk and Trust and 2011 IEEE Third International Conference on Social Computing*, pages 192–199.

Fang et al. (2015). Topic-centric classification of twitter user's political orientation. In *Proceedings of the 38th International ACM SIGIR Conference on Research and Development in Information Retrieval*, SIGIR '15, page 791–794, New York, NY, USA. Association for Computing Machinery.

Golbeck, J. and Hansen, D. (2014). A method for computing political preference among twitter followers. *Social Networks*, 36:177–184. Special Issue on Political Networks.

Hu, M. (2020). Cambridge analytica's black box. *Big Data & Society*, 7(2):2053951720938091.

King, A. S., Orlando, F. J., and Sparks, D. B. (2016). Ideological extremity and success in primary elections: Drawing inferences from the twitter network. *Social Science Computer Review*, 34(4):395–415.

Kosinski, M., Stillwell, D., and Graepel, T. (2013). Private traits and attributes are predictable from digital records of human behavior. *Proceedings of the National Academy of Sciences of the United States of America*, 110, 03.

Kosowska-Gastoł, B. (2021). Te same, ale czy takie same? : analiza oblicza ideowo-programowego polskich partii politycznych - różne perspektywy metodologiczne. In Aleksandra Kruk, editor, *Postulaty polityczne i wyborcze partii politycznych*, pages 17–35. Oficyna Wydawnicza UZ, Zielona Góra.

Kristensen, J., Albrechtsen, T., Dahlgaard, E., Jensen, M., Pedersen, M. S., and Bornakke, T. (2017). Parsimonious data: How a single facebook like predicts voting behaviour in multiparty systems. *PLOS ONE*, 12, 04.

Ma, X., Xu, P., Wang, Z., Nallapati, R., and Xiang, B. (2019). Domain adaptation with BERT-based domain classification and data selection. In *Proceedings of the 2nd Workshop on Deep Learning Approaches for Low-Resource NLP (DeepLo 2019)*, pages 76–83, Hong Kong, China, November. Association for Computational Linguistics.

Mroczkowski, R., Rybak, P., Wróblewska, A., and Gawlik, I. (2021). Herbert: Efficiently pretrained transformer-based language model for polish. *CoRR*, abs/2105.01735.

Papakyriakopoulos, O., Hegelich, S., Shahrezaye, M., and Medina Serrano, J. C. (2018). Social media and microtargeting: Political data processing and the consequences for germany. *Big Data Society*, 5:205395171881184, 07.

Preotiuc-Pietro, D., Liu, Y., Hopkins, D. J., and Ungar, L. H. (2017). Beyond binary labels: Political ideology prediction of twitter users. In *ACL*.

Rajadesingan, A. and Liu, H. (2014). Identifying users with opposing opinions in twitter debates. 02.

Samih, Y. and Darwish, K. (2020). A few topical tweets are enough for effective user-level stance detection. *ArXiv*, abs/2004.03485.

Sylwester, K. and Purver, M. (2015). Twitter language use reflects psychological differences between democrats and republicans. *PLOS ONE*, 10(9):1–18, 09.

Tatman, R. (2017). #maga or #theresistance: Classifying twitter users' political affiliation without looking at their words or friends.

WNP.PL. (2021). Rośnie poparcie dla pis, ko i polski 2050.

Yan, H., Lavoie, A., and Das, S. (2017). The perils of classifying political orientation from text. In *LINK-DEM@IJCAI*.

9. Appendix

9.1. Used electoral polls

Our selection of political parties to label POLiTweets dataset was based on the results of the September 24-27, 2021 CAWI survey conducted on a nationwide and representative group of Polen (WNP.PL, 2021), which are as follows: Prawo i Sprawiedliwość (PiS, *eng. Law and Justice*) - 38%, Platforma Obywatelska (PO, *eng. Civic Platform*) - 26%, Polska 2050 (PL2050, *eng. Poland 2050*) - 14%, Konfederacja (*eng. Confederation*) - 9%, Lewica (*eng. The Left*) - 8%.

9.2. Controversial topic selection

The period of data acquisition and conduction of our research was in 2021 and early 2022. At that time, the most divisive topics in Polish society with political overtones were:

1. Abortion (*pol. aborcja*) - due to the tightening of the abortion law and the resulting numerous strikes in the country,

Topic	Keywords list	No. tweets
Abortion	aborcja, strajkkobiet, godek, czarnyprotest, AniJednejWiecej, prolife, BabiesLivesMatter, LegalnaAborcja, AborcjaJestOk	40 116
EU & CJEU	tsue, turów, polexit, konstytucja, zostajeMYwUE, MyZostajemy, NieWygasiciePolski, TrybunałKonstytucyjny, trybunał, UniaToMy, ZostajewUnii, PolexitNow, ZostajemyWEuropie	73 733
LexTVN	lextvn, tvn	63 609
The Polish Order	PolskiŁad, Polski Ład, PolskiLad, Polski Lad	5 277

Table 3: Topics with descriptive keywords along with their number in the dataset

2. European Union, EU & Court of Justice of the European Union, CJEU (*pol. Unia Europejska, UE & Trybunał Sprawiedliwości Unii Europejskiej, TSUE*) - in connection with the penalties imposed on Poland resulting from the extension of active mining in Turów and the expansion of anti-EU sentiments by the ruling party PiS,

3. LexTVN - an amendment to the Broadcasting Act concerning the granting of broadcasting licenses to foreign entities,

4. The Polish Order (*pol. Polski Ład*) - the plan for the recovery of the Polish economy after the COVID-19 pandemic proposed from 2022, including new changes in tax law.

Topic distribution. It is worth mentioning that in the POLiTweets dataset we obtained there were posts concerning several topics at the same time. We present detailed statistics in Table 3 along with a list of keywords we used to collect tweets via the API. Most of the data were acquired on *EU & CJEU* and *LexTVN* - these were the main highlights of the 2021 year in Poland. The least amount of data comes from *The Polish Order* topic, as the law came into effect in early 2022 when the collection of the dataset has ended.

Proceedings of the First Workshop on Natural Language Processing for Political Sciences (PoliticalNLP), pages 62–71
Marseille, 24 June 2022

Political Communities on Twitter: Case Study of the 2022 French Presidential Election

Hadi Abdine[1*], **Yanzhu Guo**[1*], **Virgile Rennard**[1,2*], **Michalis Vazirgiannis**[1,3]
[1]Ecole Polytechnique, [2]Linagora, [3]AUEB

{hadi.abdine, yanzhu.guo, virgile.rennard}@polytechnique.edu
mvazirg@lix.polytechnique.fr

Abstract

With the significant increase in users on social media platforms, a new means of political campaigning has appeared. Twitter and Facebook are now notable campaigning tools during elections. Indeed, the candidates and their parties now take to the internet to interact and spread their ideas. In this paper, we aim to identify political communities formed on Twitter during the 2022 French presidential election and analyze each respective community. We create a large-scale Twitter dataset containing 1.2 million users and 62.6 million tweets that mention keywords relevant to the election. We perform community detection on a retweet graph of users and propose an in-depth analysis of the stance of each community. Finally, we attempt to detect offensive tweets and automatic bots, comparing across communities in order to gain insight into each candidate's supporter demographics and online campaign strategy.

Keywords: French Presidential Election 2022, Natural Language Processing, Political Community Detection, Social Media

1. Introduction

Social media has created a forum for everyone to express themselves, bringing disputes to a wide audience and playing an increasingly crucial part in today's information economy. With the 2008 U.S. presidential election, a relatively new paradigm was observed, where a large part of the political campaign was held on either Facebook or Twitter. The extensive outreach of these platforms has been shown to bring multiple benefits to politicians, such as increases in donations (Petrova et al., 2021), or an amplified impact on the politically inattentive youth (Utz, 2009). The tremendous amount of data provided by social media platforms gives us insight into the inner workings of the online political horizon.

This paper aims to present an in-depth study on the Twitter landscape of the 2022 French elections. We start by creating a Twitter dataset containing more than 60 million tweets from more than a million users. The tweets are extracted based on keywords related to the election. We use this dataset to build a retweet graph among the users and run a graph-based algorithm for community detection. By analyzing the top hashtags and word clouds of tweets posted by users of each community, we are able to interpret which candidate they each support. We go on to visualize the geographical distribution of each candidate's online supporters across different regions, making comparisons between communities. Eventually, we perform offensiveness detection and bot detection in all the communities. The detection of offensive tweets reveals that supporters of certain candidates are more likely to post offensive contents. The results of bot detection also indicates that there are higher levels of bot activities in certain online communities than in others. However, we would like to emphasize that the results of both offensiveness detection and bot detection are produced by automatic classification models reflecting patterns of the datasets they were trained on. Such models are subject to various limitations and by no means reflect our personal opinions.

The rest of this paper is organized as follows. Section 2 provides an overview of the related work. Section 3 describes our the dataset we use and how we collected it. Section 4 supplies a detailed description of the graph-based communities. Section 5 detects offensive tweets in each community while section 6 studies the use of automated bot accounts. Finally, section 7 summarizes our research and presents potential future work.

2. Related Work

Early work on Twitter analysis of political elections dates back to when Twitter was founded. An example is a study on the 2008 U.S. presidential election (Diakopoulos and Shamma, 2010) where the debate performance of presidential candidates is characterized by aggregated Twitter sentiment. This initiated a branch of research centered around monitoring online public reactions during election periods. Relevant studies have been carried out on a wide range of elections in different countries, including the 2012 South Korea presidential election (Bae et al., 2013), the 2013 German parliamentary election (Rill et al., 2014), and the 2017 UK general election (Yaqub et al., 2020).

Another popular branch of research aims at forecasting election results based on Twitter data. For example, a study on the 2009 German federal election (Tumasjan et al., 2010) claims that the respective shares of Twitter volume can accurately reflect the distribution of electoral votes for the six main parties. However, another

*These authors contributed equally to this work

study on the 2011 Singapore presidential election using Twitter sentiment succeeded in picking out the top two candidates but failed to predict the final ranking (Choy et al., 2011). It is generally agreed upon that Twitter analysis for election outcome prediction cannot substitute traditional polling approaches (Bermingham and Smeaton, 2011), and that explainable models should accompany the predictive results (Gayo-Avello et al., 2011).

More recently, attention has been drawn to the diffusion of misinformation and toxicity during online campaigns. Relevant topics include the detection of fake news (Cinelli et al., 2020), social bots (Pastor-Galindo et al., 2020), political trolls (Badawy et al., 2018) as well as hate speech (Siegel et al., 2021) and offensive language (Grimminger and Klinger, 2021). Our work is closely related to this field of study while also drawing upon graph-based analysis of Twitter network structures (Radicioni et al., 2021).

3. Dataset

We create a novel Twitter dataset with the 2022 French presidential election as the central topic. The tweets used for building this dataset date from February 14, 2022 to April 5, 2022. This dataset corresponds to a large and coherent corpus consisting of small pieces of text related to the election candidates and major events during their campaigns. In our case, we focus on tweets that include tokens such as "présidentielle" and "élection", as well as the names of candidates and their parties. We extract tweets in the French language containing the keywords mentioned above through Twitter's public streaming API. The public streaming API is able to extract a subset of the real-time Twitter stream. The resulting dataset consists of 62.6 million tweets and 1.2 million users. Our dataset of Tweet IDs is available upon request. We adhere to Twitter's Developer Agreement and Policy * and therefore can only distribute up to a total of 1,500,000 Tweet IDs to a single entity within a 30 day period.

4. Graph-based Community Detection

Given that the election has been at the center of attention in France since the beginning of 2022, daily campaigns, scandals, and debates are widespread through social media. We believe that there would be detectable online communities related to the different candidates and that each community will contain important information about each party's campaign. Therefore, we construct a retweet graph of Twitter users based on our dataset.

4.1. Graph Creation

With our set of extracted tweets, their authors, and the users who retweet these tweets, we create a directed weighted graph $G = (V, E)$ where $n = |V|$ denotes the number of nodes. Specifically, each node represents a user on Twitter, and a weighted edge connects two nodes if one user retweets the other. For instance, the weight $A_{u,v}$ of the edge (u, v) from vertex v to vertex u notes the number of times that the user u retweeted the user v. We believe that a normal retweet indicates approval of the tweet's content, unlike the quote retweets and the replies. Therefore, the graph does not model the textual similarity of the tweets but only the relation between users. Note that the obtained graph G might contain self-loops that correspond to self-retweets. The obtained graph contains 1.2M nodes and 12.4M edges.

To avoid small, non-dense clusters formed from few numbers of users with few retweets, we decided to work on a dense subset of the graph that we obtained using the k-core decomposition algorithm instead of working on a full graph. The k-core decomposition algorithm (Seidman, 1983) aims to find subsets of a graph G. The subsets are called k-cores of G and are obtained by a recursive pruning strategy. Each node inside a k-core is connected to at least k other nodes inside this subset. The hyperparameter k is chosen so that we do not get a cluster with less than ten users. The final used k-core graph has 47,578 nodes and 8.2M edges. Seven communities are found in our dataset through applying this approach.

4.2. Community Detection

In graph mining, community detection helps to reveal the hidden relations among the nodes in a graph. Hence, to discern opinion groups inside the k-core graph, we apply the Louvain community detection method (Blondel et al., 2008) on an undirected version of our graph without self-loops. The Louvain method is chosen as it has reasonable computation costs while maximizing modularity. Moreover, it does not require fine-tuning of hyperparameters. It is therefore the only applicable method for finding communities in large graphs.

Seven communities were found after applying this approach to the user-based k-core graph. To get a general overview of the communities, we compute the frequencies of hashtags used by the users inside each community. We define the frequency of a hashtag as the number of users using this hashtag inside a community. We notice that first six out of these seven communities have remarkable hashtags with high frequencies that relate each community to a candidate in the election. For example, in one community with 16,190 users, the top three hashtags are `#melenchonvagagner`, `#melenchonsecondtour` and `#jevotemelenchon` with respectively 16,073, 14,378 and 10,127 users. In contrast, no other hashtags supporting other candidates appear in this community's 50 most frequent hashtags. Thus, we label this community with "Mélenchon". Finally, the seventh and last community only holds keywords against the current President of France in the top 50 hashtags

* `https://developer.twitter.com/en/developer-terms/agreement-and-policy`

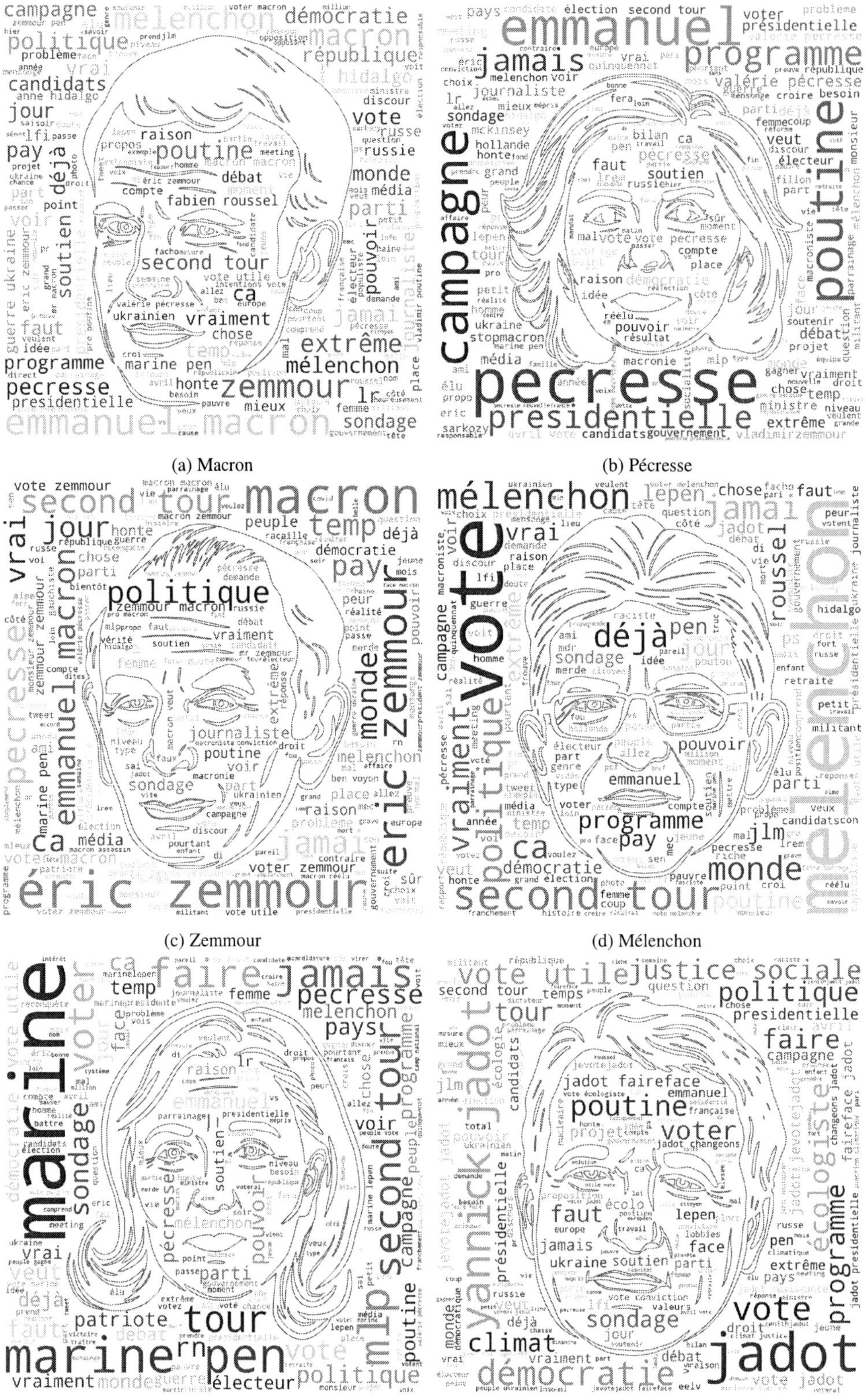

(a) Macron

(b) Pécresse

(c) Zemmour

(d) Mélenchon

(e) Le Pen

(f) Jadot

Figure 1: Word clouds generated from tweets posted by users in each community.

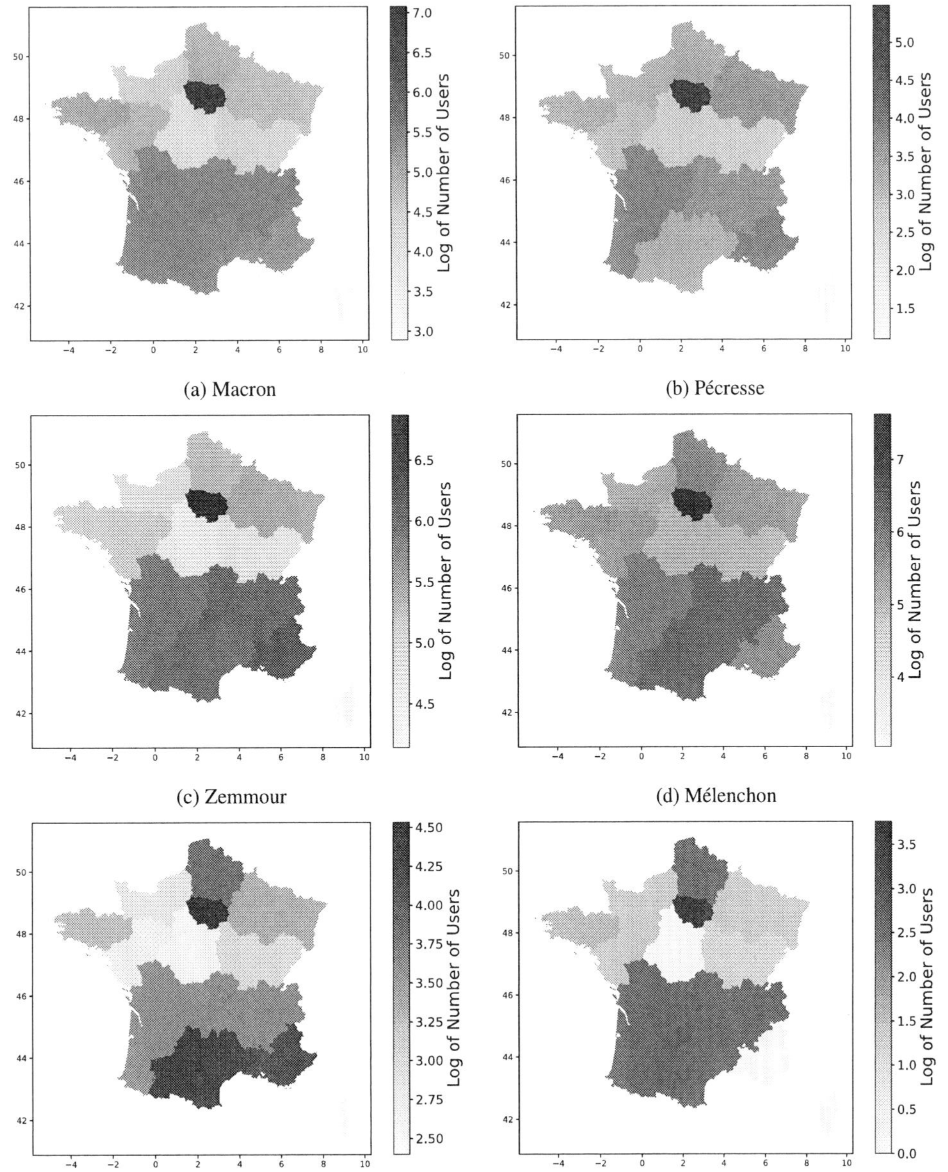

(a) Macron

(b) Pécresse

(c) Zemmour

(d) Mélenchon

(e) Le Pen

(f) Jadot

Figure 2: Choropleth map of users in each community.

Community	# Accounts	Frequent hashtags
Mélenchon	15,001	#melenchonvagagner, #melenchonsecondtour, #jevotemelenchon
Anti-Macron	12,428	#macrondehors, #toutsaufmacron, #macrondegage
Zemmour	12,101	#zemmourpresident, #jevotezemmour, #zemmourpresident2022
Macron	5,816	#avecvous, #macron2022, #5ansdeplus
Pécresse	1,035	#valeriepresidente, #pecresse2022, #nouvellefrance
Le Pen	1,001	#marinepresidente, #dimanchejevotemarine, #jevotemarine
Jadot	196	#jadot2022, #jevotejadot, #totalsoutienàjadot

Table 1: Statistics of different communities.

as we can see in the second row in table 1. We thus label it as the "Anti-Macron" community. In table 1 we detail the labels, the number of users, as well as the most biased and frequent hashtags for each community.

4.3. Word Cloud Analysis

To further analyze the political stances of the seven communities, we group the tweets posted by users of each community and generate a word cloud for each group of tweets. The resulting word clouds assemble the set of the most frequent unigrams and bigrams (after removing stop words) in each group of tweets, with their sizes proportional to their frequencies. Our analysis shows that except for the community with the "Anti-Macron" theme, all the other communities are distinctively composed of users who support one of the candidates among Emmanuel Macron, Valérie Pécresse, Éric Zemmour, Jean-Luc Mélenchon, Marine Le Pen and Yannick Jadot. The word clouds for each of these communities are shown in Figure 1. In addition to identifying which candidate each community of users supports, we can also use the word clouds to obtain a general idea of each candidate's campaign program. For example, the word cloud for Jadot's community contains words such as "justice social (social justice)" and "écologiste (ecologist)" with significant weights, and these concepts precisely lie at the center of his campaign program.

4.4. Geolocation Analysis

For each community of users, we plot the distribution of their geolocations within different regions of Metropolitan France. We select users with geolocation information and feed the declared locations into the geolocator from geopy* to obtain the region each area belongs to. We only consider users who are located within Metropolitan France. Although this limits our analysis to a subset of users from the dataset, the distribution can still reflect the overall situation.

Given that users are remarkably concentrated in the Île de France region for all the communities, we plot the choropleth map with the number of users scaled by logarithm to visualize the variations for the other areas more clearly. The choropleth map is shown in Figure 2. Through observing these maps, we can gain insights into each candidate's respective heartland. For instance, Le Pen has a much higher proportion of supporters in Occitanie, Provence-Alpes-Côte d'Azur and Hauts-de-France than all the other candidates. We also find that the supporters of Macron, Pécresse and Mélenchon are more evenly distributed among different regions outside of Île de France than the other three candidates. Zemmour and Le Pen both lack Twitter supporters in the middle and northwestern areas, while Jadot lacks supporters in the whole northern half of France except the region Hauts-de-France.

*https://github.com/geopy/geopy

Our study was carried out right before the first turn of the election. We later did a follow-up of the actual results and found that the choropleth map of votes* bear a striking resemblance to our choropleth maps of communities.

5. Detection of Offensive Tweets

Along with the growing popularity of social media and online platforms, the use of offensive online language has become a significant problem. Under such circumstances, automatic detection of offensive language has received much research attention (Risch et al., 2020). With presidential elections being such a controversial topic, relevant tweets are bound to contain offensive language. It is expected that online supporters of a given candidate would make offensive comments towards other candidates and their supporters. However, supporters of the more extreme candidates might also be more inclined to use offensive language. The targets of offensive tweets might include other public groups in addition to opposing candidates and their supporters. We build an automatic classification model to detect offensive tweets in each political community and eventually compare the results across communities.

5.1. Detection Model

We initialize our model using BERTweetFR (Guo et al., 2021) and fine-tune it on the MLMA Hate Speech Dataset (Ousidhoum et al., 2019). BERTweetFR is a French RoBERTa model (Liu et al., 2019), initialized using the general-domain French language model CamemBERT (Martin et al., 2020) and further fine-tuned on 16GB of French tweets. It achieves the state-of-the-art performance on French Twitter tasks. The MLMA Hate Speech Dataset is a multilingual multi-aspect Twitter dataset for hate speech analysis. We take a subset of this dataset selecting only French tweets labeled as either "normal" or "offensive". The resulting subset contains 821 normal tweets and 1690 offensive tweets. After fine-tuning for 3 epochs, our classification model achieves a f1 score of 83.96% on a 80/20 train-test split.

5.2. Detection Results

We run our classification model for tweets posted by users in each political community. We only consider unique tweets, discarding retweets by deduplicating them based on the text content. This choice is made because we aim to detect the origination of offensive language rather than to analyze its propagation pattern. The detection results are shown in Table 2. A key observation is that users from the Anti-Macron and Zemmour communities are the most likely to post offensive tweets, reaching respective proportions of 0.307 and 0.305. This is in line with our expectations: the Anti-Macron community is naturally supposed to be more offensive as the main goal is to oppose and defy; as for

*https://tinyurl.com/ycxya5dx

Community	# Unique Tweets	# Offensive Tweets	Proportion of Offensive Tweets
Mélenchon	756,318	208,178	0.275
Anti-Macron	549,138	168,685	**0.307**
Zemmour	1,034,538	316,214	**0.305**
Macron	468,138	126,122	0.269
Pécresse	80,365	19,487	0.242
Le Pen	86,272	25,368	0.294
Jadot	12,340	1,632	0.132

Table 2: Offensive Tweets in Each Community

Zemmour, he is a far-right candidate who has been personally fined €10,000 for hate speech by a Paris court [*]. We also observe that the communities of right-wing candidates tend to have more offensive content in general, with the only exception being Pécresse's who is a more moderate candidate. A possible explanation is the employment of automatic bots in her community. We will further elaborate on the topic of bots in the following section.

6. Detection of Automatic Bots

It has come to light in recent years that a significant amount of Twitter accounts are controlled, at least partly, by software. Some research estimate that between 9% to 15% of all twitter accounts are somewhat automated (Varol et al., 2017). Bots are an important tool for opinion manipulation (Subrahmanian et al., 2016), and are being used to influence important subjects such as political elections ((Ferrara, 2017),(Deb et al., 2019)). Bots also help spread misinformation ((Shao et al., 2017)), and have impacted the online debate on vaccination (Broniatowski et al., 2018), with an estimated 45% of COVID-19 related Twitter accounts exhibiting bot-like behavior ((Memon and Carley, 2020)). This section proposes to estimate the role bots are playing in the 2022 French election by comparing their relative use within each community.

6.1. Detection model

There is a multitude of available Twitter bot detection models ((Lee et al., 2021), (Kudugunta and Ferrara, 2018), (Miller et al., 2014), (Ali Alhosseini et al., 2019)), and APIs ((Davis et al., 2016)) that use semantic, statistical or neighborhood properties to evaluate the likelihood of an account being a bot. However, due to the large amount of data we have to process, we need to use a scalable and generalizable models. This study is therefore going to rely on statistical features available in the user metadata object given by the Twitter API. Our employed model is similar to the one presented in (Yang et al., 2019b), which is scalable and yields adequate generalization results on the task of bot detection (Feng et al., 2021) in different scenarios.

[*] `https://www.bbc.com/news/world-europe-60022996`

6.1.1. Feature Selection

The list of available user metadata features relevant to bot detection is listed as below:

- STATUSES COUNT
- FOLLOWERS COUNT
- FRIENDS COUNT
- FAVOURITES COUNT
- LISTED COUNT
- DEFAULT PROFILE
- VERIFIED
- GEOGRAPHICAL LOCATION ENABLED

These available features give other interesting statistical information that we compute as additional derived features for the model. Such features include the frequency of tweets (statuses count/user age), the respective growth rate of followers, friends, favorites and listed accounts (respective counts/user age). We also take into account information from the username, such as its length and the number of digits it contains. The length of user description is also proven to be a relevant feature (Yang et al., 2019b).

We choose random forest as our classifier, as it yields near-perfect results on any individually labeled dataset.

6.1.2. Training Data

The choice of training data for such a task is crucial. There are many different types of bots for different domains, and there is generally poor classification generalization across datasets (Echeverría et al., 2018). Considering the task at hand which is the classification of politically oriented Twitter users into bots or human labels, we decided to train our model on a concatenation of multiple available datasets: **Political-bots-2019** (Yang et al., 2019a) (a compendium of political bots), **midterm-2018** (Yang et al., 2019b) (a hand-labeled dataset of users and bots during the 2018 American midterm elections), **botwiki** (Yang et al., 2019b) (a collection of self identified Twitter bots), **verified-2019** (Yang et al., 2019b) (a collection of verified Twitter users), **Cresci 2019-2018** ((Mazza et al., 2019), (Cresci et al., 2018)) (datasets of manually annotated bots), and finally **Twibot-20** (Feng et al., 2021) (a comprehensive hand labeled dataset of Twitter bots). The statistics of each dataset is shown in Table 4.

Community	# Accounts	# Bots	Proportion of bots in community	# Tweets	# Automated Tweets	proportion Automated tweets
Mélenchon	15,001	2,507	0.167	5,755,664	1,273,656	0.284
Anti-Macron	12,428	2,181	0.175	5,435,820	1,268,240	0.304
Zemmour	12,101	2,217	0.183	**6,160,153**	1,501,207	0.322
Macron	5,816	1,001	0.172	2,219,491	514,820	0.302
Pécresse	1,035	208	**0.200**	408,319	134,373	**0.490**
Le Pen	1001	184	0.184	463,290	127,633	0.380
Jadot	196	30	0.153	66,541	19,876	0.426

Table 3: Bots statistics of different communities

Datasets	# human	# bots
POLITICAL-BOTS-2019	0	62
MIDTERM-2018	8,092	42,446
BOTWIKI	0	698
VERIFIED-2019	1,987	0
TWIBOT-20	5,237	6,589
CRESCI-18/19	6,514	7,455
TOTAL	21,830	57,250

Table 4: Statistics of training datasets.

6.1.3. Training results

Correlation It is crucial to consider the most discriminative features when attempting a task like bot detection, the model should be interpretable. For example, as we see in Figure 3, there is a strong correlation between the automation of an account and the age of the account, whether or not the account is verified or geolocalisation enabled. Another strong indicator of automation is the presence of a default-profile, which means an account with a lack of personalization (i.e. custom banner or profile picture).

Feature importance By studying the importance of each feature, we find that the number of statuses, the information of followers (such as its raw count and growth rate) and the age of the user are the most critical features for the classifier.

Results Our random forest classifier achieves a 95.0% f1 score with 10-fold cross validation.

6.2. Bot Detection Results

From our experiments, we observe that there is a significant amount of automated accounts in our dataset – with an estimation of at least 15%, with a conservative labeling threshold, of accounts partaking in the debate coming from bots. We have tuned the classification threshold, which is usually at 50% certainty to 75%, considering the importance of precision in the case of bot classification.

As shown in Table 3, while the number of users in each community is significantly different, we find a similar proportion of bots for each cluster. Therefore, we conjecture that there has not been any large-scale operation to influence the election with bots from any side.

Another insight we can get from Table 3 is the campaigning approach of each community. We do not deduplicate tweets to remove retweets, considering the importance of retweeting in automated accounts. For example, the cluster supporting Zemmour, while being smaller than some of the others, has significantly more tweets, including retweets per person, showing the particular engagement Zemmour supporters seem to offer online. Similarly, we can see that it is the only large cluster with the most considerable bot activity, albeit by a small margin. On the other side, we can see that the Pécresse cluster, smaller in scale, has heavy activities from bots. This difference in bot activity for the three smallest communities may come from factors such as some very dynamic automated news pages.

6.2.1. Limitations of Automatic Bot Detection

It is important to keep in mind that bot detection, while being effective, is a limited approach, especially in the case of political elections. While a lot of bots can be found, a nuance is to be made, as bots in a cluster are not necessarily promoting the candidate. Some of the more basic bots that promote cryptocurrency or fishing sites usually simply post the same messages repeatedly, along with all the popular hashtag at a time t. Such a behavior artificially inflates the number of bots we find in the community of candidates that are naturally more active on twitter. The same goes for "automatized behavior", as we see in figure 3 and in our feature importance section. While algorithms are accurate, their most discriminative features are the number of statuses, followers, and the age of the user. The situation can be more complicated in the case of politics, as there are actual people who are willing to tweet with the hashtag #MélenchonPrésident one hundred times a day simply because they are extremely passionate about the campaign.

7. Conclusion and Future Work

In this paper, we have leveraged graph-based community detection methods to gather insights into each of the most significant candidates' online campaigns for the 2022 French presidential election. We have been able to build a portrait of the average voter for each can-

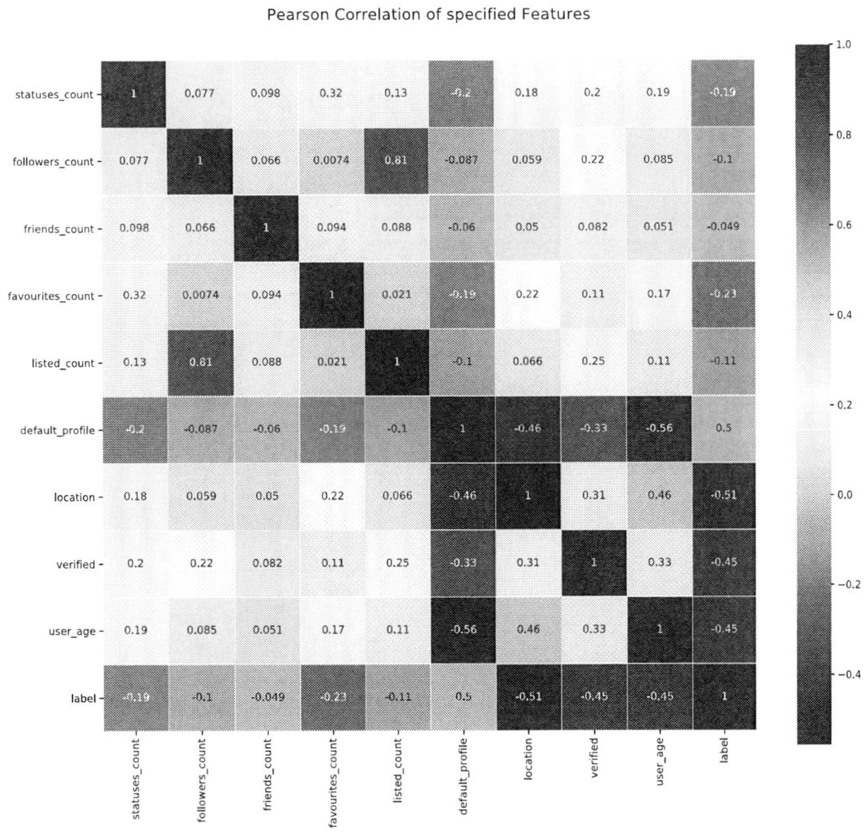

Figure 3: Heatmap of Pearson correlation between features and labels.)

didate, the interest they carry in different political subjects, their geolocalization, and their language habits. We have also presented results on the usage of automated accounts, or the lack thereof, in each community.

Many future tasks are possible to be performed on this dataset. Based on the community detection of political communities, a relevant study could be to analyze of the impact of major political events or debates. Considering that we have collected tweets from February to April on a daily basis, we could quantify the shift in the communities after debates between two candidates or how the start of the Ukraine war influenced electors. In the same way, we could also investigate the shift between the two turn of votes. French elections are based on a two-turn system, with the first turn aiming at narrowing down the the list of candidates and only keeping the two largest ones. The continued gathering of data and community detection could show us which communities turn to which candidate during the period between the two turns and how their language habits evolve.

Acknowledgment

This research was supported by the ANR chair AML/HELAS (ANR-CHIA-0020-01).

8. Bibliographical References

Ali Alhosseini, S., Bin Tareaf, R., Najafi, P., and Meinel, C. (2019). Detect me if you can: Spam bot detection using inductive representation learning. In *Companion Proceedings of The 2019 World Wide Web Conference*, WWW '19, page 148–153, New York, NY, USA. Association for Computing Machinery.

Badawy, A., Ferrara, E., and Lerman, K. (2018). Analyzing the digital traces of political manipulation: The 2016 russian interference twitter campaign. In *2018 IEEE/ACM international conference on advances in social networks analysis and mining (ASONAM)*, pages 258–265. IEEE.

Bae, J.-h., Son, J.-e., and Song, M. (2013). Analysis of twitter for 2012 south korea presidential election by text mining techniques. *Journal of Intelligence and Information Systems*, 19(3):141–156.

Bermingham, A. and Smeaton, A. (2011). On using twitter to monitor political sentiment and predict election results. In *Proceedings of the Workshop on Sentiment Analysis where AI meets Psychology (SAAIP 2011)*, pages 2–10.

Blondel, V. D., Guillaume, J.-L., Lambiotte, R., and Lefebvre, E. (2008). Fast unfolding of communities in large networks. *Journal of Statistical Mechanics: Theory and Experiment*, 2008(10):P10008, oct.

Broniatowski, D. A., Jamison, A. M., Qi, S., AlKulaib, L., Chen, T., Benton, A., Quinn, S. C., and Dredze, M. (2018). Weaponized health communication: Twitter bots and russian trolls amplify the vaccine debate. *American Journal of Public Health*, 108(10):1378–1384. PMID: 30138075.

Choy, M., Cheong, M. L., Laik, M. N., and Shung, K. P. (2011). A sentiment analysis of singapore presidential election 2011 using twitter data with census correction. *arXiv preprint arXiv:1108.5520*.

Cinelli, M., Cresci, S., Galeazzi, A., Quattrociocchi, W., and Tesconi, M. (2020). The limited reach of fake news on twitter during 2019 european elections. *PloS one*, 15(6):e0234689.

Cresci, S., Lillo, F., Regoli, D., Tardelli, S., and Tesconi, M. (2018). Cashtag piggybacking: uncovering spam and bot activity in stock microblogs on twitter. *CoRR*, abs/1804.04406.

Davis, C. A., Varol, O., Ferrara, E., Flammini, A., and Menczer, F. (2016). Botornot: A system to evaluate social bots. *CoRR*, abs/1602.00975.

Deb, A., Luceri, L., Badawy, A., and Ferrara, E. (2019). Perils and challenges of social media and election manipulation analysis: The 2018 US midterms. *CoRR*, abs/1902.00043.

Diakopoulos, N. A. and Shamma, D. A. (2010). Characterizing debate performance via aggregated twitter sentiment. In *Proceedings of the SIGCHI conference on human factors in computing systems*, pages 1195–1198.

Echeverría, J., Cristofaro, E. D., Kourtellis, N., Leontiadis, I., Stringhini, G., and Zhou, S. (2018). LOBO - evaluation of generalization deficiencies in twitter bot classifiers. *CoRR*, abs/1809.09684.

Feng, S., Wan, H., Wang, N., Li, J., and Luo, M. (2021). Twibot-20: A comprehensive twitter bot detection benchmark. *CoRR*, abs/2106.13088.

Ferrara, E. (2017). Disinformation and social bot operations in the run up to the 2017 french presidential election. *CoRR*, abs/1707.00086.

Gayo-Avello, D., Metaxas, P., and Mustafaraj, E. (2011). Limits of electoral predictions using twitter. In *Proceedings of the International AAAI Conference on Web and Social Media*, volume 5, pages 490–493.

Grimminger, L. and Klinger, R. (2021). Hate towards the political opponent: A twitter corpus study of the 2020 us elections on the basis of offensive speech and stance detection. In *Proceedings of the Eleventh Workshop on Computational Approaches to Subjectivity, Sentiment and Social Media Analysis*, pages 171–180.

Guo, Y., Rennard, V., Xypolopoulos, C., and Vazirgiannis, M. (2021). BERTweetFR : Domain adaptation of pre-trained language models for French tweets. In *Proceedings of the Seventh Workshop on Noisy User-generated Text (W-NUT 2021)*, pages 445–450, Online, November. Association for Computational Linguistics.

Kudugunta, S. and Ferrara, E. (2018). Deep neural networks for bot detection. *CoRR*, abs/1802.04289.

Lee, K., Eoff, B., and Caverlee, J. (2021). Seven months with the devils: A long-term study of content polluters on twitter. *Proceedings of the International AAAI Conference on Web and Social Media*, 5(1):185–192, Aug.

Liu, Y., Ott, M., Goyal, N., Du, J., Joshi, M., Chen, D., Levy, O., Lewis, M., Zettlemoyer, L., and Stoyanov, V. (2019). Roberta: A robustly optimized bert pretraining approach. *arXiv preprint arXiv:1907.11692*.

Martin, L., Muller, B., Ortiz Suárez, P. J., Dupont, Y., Romary, L., de la Clergerie, É., Seddah, D., and Sagot, B. (2020). CamemBERT: a tasty French language model. In *Proceedings of the 58th Annual Meeting of the Association for Computational Linguistics*, pages 7203–7219, Online, July. Association for Computational Linguistics.

Mazza, M., Cresci, S., Avvenuti, M., Quattrociocchi, W., and Tesconi, M. (2019). Rtbust: Exploiting temporal patterns for botnet detection on twitter. *CoRR*, abs/1902.04506.

Memon, S. A. and Carley, K. M. (2020). Characterizing COVID-19 misinformation communities using a novel twitter dataset. *CoRR*, abs/2008.00791.

Miller, Z., Dickinson, B., Deitrick, W., Hu, W., and Wang, A. (2014). Twitter spammer detection using data stream clustering. *Information Sciences*, 260:64–73, 03.

Ousidhoum, N., Lin, Z., Zhang, H., Song, Y., and Yeung, D.-Y. (2019). Multilingual and multi-aspect hate speech analysis. In *Proceedings of the 2019 Conference on Empirical Methods in Natural Language Processing and the 9th International Joint Conference on Natural Language Processing (EMNLP-IJCNLP)*, pages 4675–4684, Hong Kong, China, November. Association for Computational Linguistics.

Pastor-Galindo, J., Zago, M., Nespoli, P., Bernal, S. L., Celdrán, A. H., Pérez, M. G., Ruipérez-Valiente, J. A., Pérez, G. M., and Mármol, F. G. (2020). Spotting political social bots in twitter: A use case of the 2019 spanish general election. *IEEE Transactions on Network and Service Management*, 17(4):2156–2170.

Petrova, M., Sen, A., and Yildirim, P. (2021). Social media and political contributions: The impact of new technology on political competition. *Manag. Sci.*, 67:2997–3021.

Radicioni, T., Saracco, F., Pavan, E., and Squartini, T. (2021). Analysing twitter semantic networks: the case of 2018 italian elections. *Scientific Reports*, 11(1):1–22.

Rill, S., Reinel, D., Scheidt, J., and Zicari, R. V. (2014). Politwi: Early detection of emerging political topics on twitter and the impact on concept-level sentiment analysis. *Knowledge-Based Systems*, 69:24–33.

Risch, J., Ruff, R., and Krestel, R. (2020). Offensive language detection explained. In *Proceedings of the Second Workshop on Trolling, Aggression and Cyberbullying*, pages 137–143, Marseille, France, May. European Language Resources Association (ELRA).

Seidman, S. (1983). Network structure and minimum degree.soc netw 5:269-287. *Social Networks*, 5:269–287, 09.

Shao, C., Ciampaglia, G. L., Varol, O., Flammini, A., and Menczer, F. (2017). The spread of fake news by social bots. *CoRR*, abs/1707.07592.

Siegel, A. A., Nikitin, E., Barberá, P., Sterling, J., Pullen, B., Bonneau, R., Nagler, J., Tucker, J. A., et al. (2021). Trumping hate on twitter? online hate speech in the 2016 us election campaign and its aftermath. *Quarterly Journal of Political Science*, 16(1):71–104.

Subrahmanian, V. S., Azaria, A., Durst, S., Kagan, V., Galstyan, A., Lerman, K., Zhu, L., Ferrara, E., Flammini, A., Menczer, F., Waltzman, R., Stevens, A., Dekhtyar, A., Gao, S., Hogg, T., Kooti, F., Liu, Y., Varol, O., Shiralkar, P., Vydiswaran, V. G. V., Mei, Q., and Huang, T. (2016). The DARPA twitter bot challenge. *CoRR*, abs/1601.05140.

Tumasjan, A., Sprenger, T., Sandner, P., and Welpe, I. (2010). Predicting elections with twitter: What 140 characters reveal about political sentiment. In *Proceedings of the International AAAI Conference on Web and Social Media*, volume 4, pages 178–185.

Utz, S. (2009). The (Potential) Benefits of Campaigning via Social Network Sites. *Journal of Computer-Mediated Communication*, 14(2):221–243, 01.

Varol, O., Ferrara, E., Davis, C. A., Menczer, F., and Flammini, A. (2017). Online human-bot interactions: Detection, estimation, and characterization. *CoRR*, abs/1703.03107.

Yang, K., Varol, O., Davis, C. A., Ferrara, E., Flammini, A., and Menczer, F. (2019a). Arming the public with AI to counter social bots. *CoRR*, abs/1901.00912.

Yang, K., Varol, O., Hui, P., and Menczer, F. (2019b). Scalable and generalizable social bot detection through data selection. *CoRR*, abs/1911.09179.

Yaqub, U., Sharma, N., Pabreja, R., Chun, S. A., Atluri, V., and Vaidya, J. (2020). Location-based sentiment analyses and visualization of twitter election data. *Digit. Gov.: Res. Pract.*, 1(2), apr.

Proceedings of the First Workshop on Natural Language Processing for Political Sciences (PoliticalNLP), pages 72–78
Marseille, 24 June 2022

What Does the Indian Parliament Discuss? An Exploratory Analysis of the Question Hour in the Lok Sabha

Suman Adhya, Debarshi Kumar Sanyal
Indian Association for the Cultivation of Science
Jadavpur, Kolkata – 700032, India
adhyasuman30@gmail.com, debarshisanyal@gmail.com

Abstract

The TCPD-IPD dataset is a collection of questions and answers discussed in the Lower House of the Parliament of India during the Question Hour between 1999 and 2019. Although it is difficult to analyze such a huge collection manually, modern text analysis tools can provide a powerful means to navigate it. In this paper, we perform an exploratory analysis of the dataset. In particular, we present insightful corpus-level statistics and a detailed analysis of three subsets of the dataset. In the latter analysis, the focus is on understanding the temporal evolution of topics using a dynamic topic model. We observe that the parliamentary conversation indeed mirrors the political and socio-economic tensions of each period.

Keywords: Parliament of India, dynamic topic model, latent Dirichlet allocation, TCPD-IPD, political data

1. Introduction

The Parliament of India is the highest legislative body of India. The members of its Lower House or the Lok Sabha are directly elected by the people while its Upper House comprises representatives elected by the members of all State Legislative Assemblies. Although parliamentary proceedings are immensely useful to a political scientist, they are too large to be manually analyzed. This motivates the use of algorithmic tools to explore them. In this paper, we analyze the TCPD-IPD dataset (Trivedi Centre for Political Data, 2019) of around 298K pairs of questions and answers (QA) in English discussed in the Lok Sabha during the Question Hour – the first hour of every business day of the Parliament – from 1999 to 2019 spanning four Lok Sabha terms (13th term: 1999-2004, 14th: 2004-09, 15th: 2009-14, 16th: 2014-19). During the Question Hour, any Member of Parliament in the Lok Sabha (abbreviated: MP) may ask any question to the ministers related to the administrative activity of the government, and thus, hold it accountable for its actions (Sanyal, 2016; Tripathi and Kumar, 2021). Question time is also an integral part in many other parliamentary democracies like those of Canada, Australia and UK (Martin and Rozenberg, 2014).

Technical specification of the TCPD-IPD dataset appears in (Bhogale, 2019). But the dataset has not been explored, except in (Sen et al., 2019) where the authors aim to identify, for a few chosen themes, whether the questions asked by MPs echo the trend in mass media and social media. Topic modeling has been used to analyze the parliamentary proceedings of various countries, see, e.g., (Greene and Cross, 2017; Gkoumas et al., 2018; Ishima, 2020). In this paper, we study TCPD-IPD using the following pipeline. First, a static topic model of the entire dataset is built and the top topics identified. Then a subset of the dataset is selected for further analysis as follows: (a) A dynamic topic model is built on it; (b) The temporal evolution of topics and words in a topic are plotted; (c) The top-ranking documents at a given time in each of these plots are analyzed. We obtain interesting insights from this analysis. This demonstrates the effectiveness of our technique. Our specific contributions are:

1. We describe important high-level statistical features of the dataset and bias in the participation of MPs (Sec. 2.).

2. We identify the top topics in the entire dataset (Sec. 3.).

3. We make a more nuanced study of the QA pertaining to three specific ministries – Finance, Railways, and Health and Family Welfare — by building a dynamic topic model in each case (Sec. 4.).

4. For each ministry mentioned above, we identify words that showed significant variation in their probability in a topic over time (Sec. 4.) and the major events to which they relate. Thus, word choreography in a dynamic topic model is used to reconstruct events in political history. We hope the insights and lessons from the past will help inform future responses to critical national issues.

2. High-Level Features of TCPD-IPD

We enumerate below some interesting insights we obtained from the dataset.

2.1. Ministry-wise data distribution

TCPD-IPD contains questions related to 85 different ministries. Fig. 1 shows the data distribution for the top ten ministries (comprising almost 50% of the full dataset). Clearly, *Finance*, *Railways* and *Health and Family Welfare* are the top three ministries.

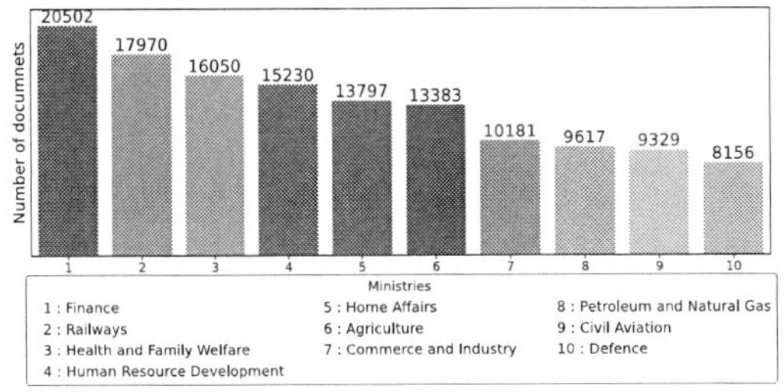

Figure 1: Ministry-wise data distribution.

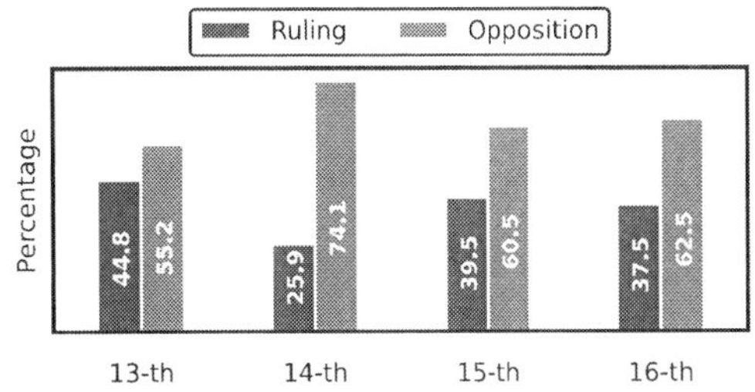

Figure 2: Participation of ruling alliance vis-a-vis that of the opposition.

2.2. Term-wise data distribution

Among a total of 298,292 questions, the number of questions asked in each term of the Lok Sabha is as follows: 13th: 73,531; 14th: 66,371; 15th: 79,401; 16th: 78,989. We found out that over the span covered in this dataset, Lok Sabha always met for more than 50 sittings in a year, except in 2004 (48 sittings) and 2008 (46 sittings). This correlates with the lowest number of questions asked in 2004 (9398 questions) and 2008 (9851 questions). Two of the three sessions in 2004 and all sessions in 2008 are included in the 14th Lok Sabha. Although the fewer sittings are highlighted in many news reports (Anuja, 25 Nov 2020), we did not find mention of its impact on the Question Hour, that we clearly identified above.

2.3. Participation of MPs

Unlike the previous Lok Sabha terms, in the 16th the ruling alliance asked more questions than the opposition. In that term, they had a historic 65% share of the House. Since the numeric strength of the ruling alliance is, by rule, higher than that of the opposition, we normalize them to get an idea of participation from each side *had the number of representatives from either side been equal.* We believe this will afford a fairer comparison between their participation. Let R_n and O_n be the number of members of the ruling alliance and the opposition, respectively, and R_q and O_q be the number of number of questions asked by the ruling alliance and the opposition, respectively. Then $R_{pp} = \left(R_q \times \frac{O_n}{R_n+O_n}\right)$, $O_{pp} = \left(O_q \times \frac{R_n}{R_n+O_n}\right)$. As seen in Figure 2, in the transformed space, the opposition still asks more questions than the ruling alliance, matching the expectations from a healthy democracy.

2.4. Gender and caste bias in participation

Over the four Lok Sabha terms covered by the dataset, 91.6% questions were asked by men while 8.4% questions were raised by women. The average gender ratio of men to women was 8.3:1 over the same four terms. Thus the the skewed gender ratio correlates with the distribution of questions. It is noteworthy here that the Women's Reservation Bill proposing the reservation of one-third of the seats in the Lok Sabha for women has been pending since 2010 (Marwah, 2019), thus, allowing the bias to continue. As regards the caste distribution, 80.6% questions were raised by MPs from the general caste while the rest come from the reserved categories. Note that 24.03% of Lok Sabha seats are reserved for the reserved categories while the rest belong to the general caste. Figure 3 shows the number of questions on gender and caste-related issues asked in the Parliament; Appendix 6.5. lists the keywords we used for this analysis.

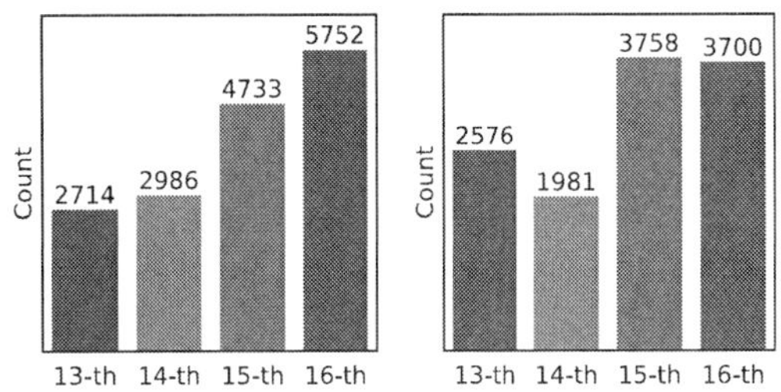

(a) *Gender*-related. (b) *Caste*-related.

Figure 3: *Gender* and *caste* related discussions in each Lok Sabha term.

3. Topic Model for TCPD-IPD

We used topic modeling to get a thematic view of the TCPD-IPD dataset. Researchers have observed that Latent Dirichlet Allocation (LDA) ((Blei et al., 2003)), which employs Gibbs sampling for inference, often produces superior topics than those from modern variational inference-based topic models; see, e.g., (Blei et al., 2017; Lisena et al., 2020). This motivated us to use LDA instead of neural topic models. We pre-processed the entire TCPD-IPD corpus, used LDA to extract 50 topics, and manually labeled them (See Appendix 6.1.-6.3.). We filtered out a few noisy, heterogeneous topics and among the rest plotted the top ten topics in Fig. 4. Clearly, there is a huge emphasis on growth in economy and science, at the state and national levels.

4. Ministry-wise Analysis

We have selected three ministries – Finance, Railways, and Health and Family Welfare – for further analysis.

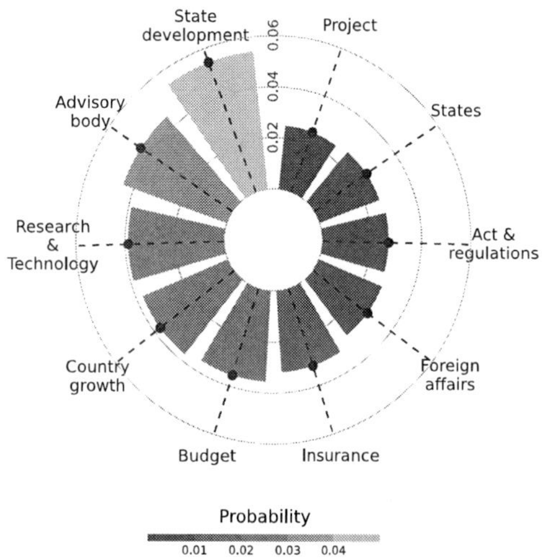

Figure 4: Hot topics discussed in the Indian parliamentary QA sessions.

We set the topic count to 20 for all the three ministries. To model the temporal variation in topics, we had to make a choice between the classical Dynamic Topic Model ((Blei and Lafferty, 2006)) which is essentially an adaptation of LDA for sequential data (hereafter, called LDAseq) and the more modern Dynamic Embedded Topic Model (D-ETM) ((Dieng et al., 2019)), both developed by David Blei and collaborators. In our experiments, we found LDAseq produced better topics (see Appendix 6.4.). Similar observation is reported made in (Dieng et al., 2019).

Using LDAseq, we obtained the temporal evolution of the probabilities of five topics for each ministry, as shown in Fig. 5. In Finance, the peaks in 'agricultural loan' in 2008 and 2014 relate to the debt waivers announced at that time, though farmers' loans remain a perennially important topic. The focus on 'rural development' slowly reduces while other topics like 'banking', 'economic growth' (more questions asked when GDP change is unexpectedly high or low) and 'pension schemes' remain more stable. In Railways, the early 2000's witnessed many new government projects and associated parliamentary QA, but the focus gradually shifted to 'infrastructure development' and 'passenger amenity', where questions veered around the increasing private participation. The announcement of many projects on rail safety in the last Lok Sabha term is indicated by increased presence of the topic 'railway safety'. The steep price hike in passenger and freight fare in 2014 sparked intense deliberation in the Parliament. In the Ministry of Health and Family Welfare, discussions on women and child care and rural medical infrastructure increased after the National Health Mission was launched in 2005. The focus on medical research in the early part of the decade led to the establishment of many premier medical institutions throughout the country but gradually the interest waned.

The *rare* words in a topic were often more informative and captured specific events or issues. So in the following sub-sections, we choose a few representative topics from each ministry and show the temporal evolution of the probability of the rare words in the selected topics. In each plot, we also annotate one of the dominant words with example questions asked during the Question Hour.

4.1. Finance

We have selected two topics, *'banking'* and *'pension reforms'*, and plotted the probability of a few selected tokens in them as a function of time in Figure 6. In the topic 'banking' shown in Figure 6a, we find that the word 'credit_card' peaks in 2007. Our analysis shows that most of the questions around this time are related to the growing credit card frauds in India and the sudden rise in credit card interest rates by some banks, coinciding with reports in mass media. Another aspect in credit card-related discussion is *Kisan Credit Card* (KCC) – a low-interest credit card for farmers, which was introduced in 1998 and significantly improved in 2004. The steady rise in discussion on debit cards correlates with the increasing adoption of debit cards (that avoided the debt trap of credit cards) in India. With demonetization and increased government emphasis on end-to-end digital – as opposed to cash – transactions, terms like 'atm', 'digital_transaction', and 'cyber_security' gain prominence while the popularity of more traditional mediums like 'cheque' reduces.

Figure 6b shows the topic on pension reforms. In late 2003, Government of India notified that it was abolishing the then existing government-funded pension system for all its new employees and that they would come under the National Pension System (NPS) to be administered through the new Interim Pension Fund Regulatory and Development Authority (PFRDA). NPS enabled subscribers to make planned savings for post-retirement income. NPS was extended to all Indian citizens in 2009. Being a monumental change, NPS provoked a number of questions that peaked around 2011; MPs wanted to know the details of the scheme, including its performance, implementation challenges, extension to unorganized sectors, and even its security. The government introduced the Voluntary Retirement Scheme (VRS) in nationalized banks in early 2000's to reduce the financial load on the public exchequer. Thousands of employees across various organizations accepted VRS in 2000-2001. Given the high unemployment rate in the country, VRS generated a lot of panic among people and pointed questions in the Parliament on the the government's future plans about its workforce. The other visible terms 'apy' 'dbt' and 'jan_dhan' refer to recent financial inclusion programs.

4.2. Railways

Here, we highlight only one topic, namely, 'infrastructure development' which is displayed in Fig. 7. Ob-

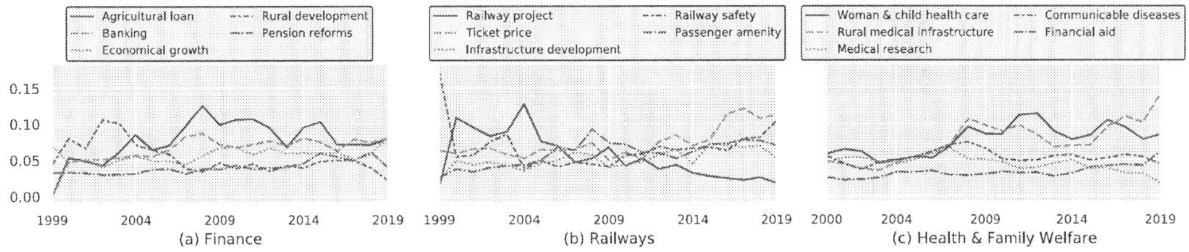

Figure 5: Temporal evolution of topics in 3 subsets of TCPD-IPD using LDAseq.

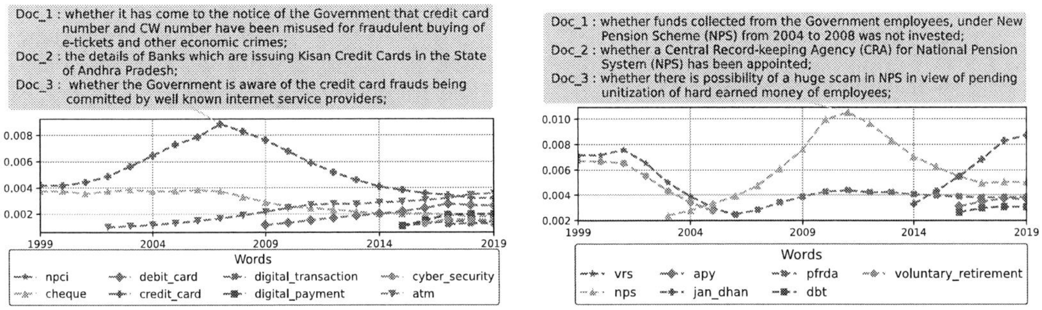

(a) Topic: *Banking*

(b) Topic: *Pension Reforms*

Figure 6: Selected topics obtained by running LDAseq on the Finance subset of TCPD-IPD.

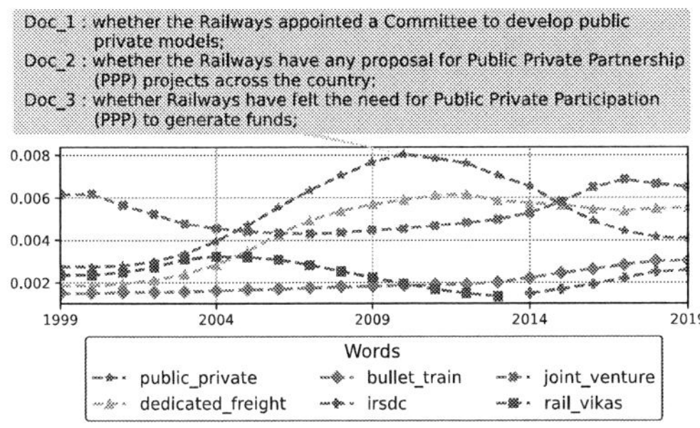

Figure 7: Topic *Infrastructure Development* in Railways.

serve the peak of the term 'public_private' around 2010 when the Railways ministry introduced a new model for public-private partnership to modernize the Indian Railways. Indeed, there has always been questions and panic in the Lok Sabha on the public-private models as privatization of the economy could increase fares, job loss, and casualization of labor (Makhija, 2006; Reddy, 2019). A related term 'joint_venture' was a part of many discussions. While early uses of it (in 2000's) focused on joint ventures of Indian Railways with other public sector companies, the recent focus (since 2015) has been on the increasing role of private players. Indeed similar exchanges occurred between the MPs and the Civil Aviation ministry on the privatization of airlines. Terms like 'rail_vikas' and 'irsdc' refer to companies owned by Indian Railways and entrusted with maintenance of Railways. The rise in freight volumes led to the ideation of Dedicated Freight Corridors (DFC) in 2005 and generated a number of questions ('dedicated_freight') related to their cost, progress, and expansion. Discussions on the introduction of bullet trains have been present for a long time but they gathered momentum when a vision document was tabled by the government in December, 2009 and the construction of the Mumbai-Ahmedabad high-speed rail corridor started in 2017.

4.3. Health and Family Welfare

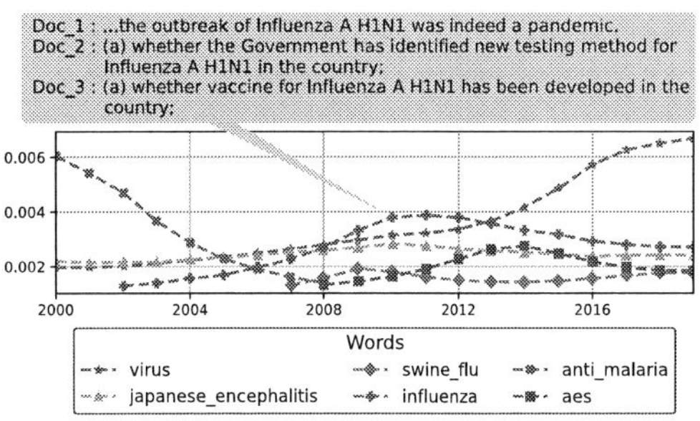

Figure 8: Topic *Communicable Diseases* in Health and Family Welfare.

Here, we have chosen the topic 'Communicable Diseases'. Fig. 8 shows the evolution of word probabilities in this topic. Clearly, we find an increasing focus on the word 'virus' because India has been repeatedly hit by the Swine influenza virus (such as H1N1), including in 2009 when swine-flu turned into a pandemic and in 2014-15 (Kshatriya et al., 2018). MPs in the Lok Sabha enquired about the number of cases, test adminstration, government interventions, vaccination drives, the role of WHO, and the effort to develop indigenous vaccines. Another major disease in India has been malaria but a response in Lok Sabha informs us that malarial death reduced steadily over the years, and that is attested to by the steady decline on its focus in the Parliament. India recorded thousands of deaths due to Acute Encephalitis Syndrome (AES) in 2008-14 (Ghosh and Basu, 2016) and Japanese Encephalitis in 2005-11 (Adhya et al., 2013). During these unfortunate occurrences, the Lok Sabha witnessed intense discussions on the diseases.

5. Conclusion and Future Work

We identified the salient features of TCPD-IPD and then illustrated the temporal evolution of topics in three important subsets of the data. In future, we will attempt to automatically detect topical change points, annotate them with trigger events (e.g., VRS announcement), auto-summarize the top documents containing a specific topic or word at a given time, and motivate investigative reporting or research on the impact of the most sensitive topics discussed in the Parliament (e.g., the effect of VRS on mid-age employees). We hope our study will help construct more probing parliamentary questions and formulate better national policies.

6. Appendix

6.1. Data preprocessing for topic modeling

We have removed the punctuation from the dataset, then lowercased and lemmatized the words. We have also removed the stopwords, and filtered out the remaining words having document frequency lower than 0.001 and higher than 0.95. We have only kept the words that have at least 3 characters. Finally, we removed the documents with less than 3 words in them. After preprocessing, we created bigrams to better capture word co-occurrence statistics.

6.2. Configuration for topic models

We used the following hyperparameters to run LDA, LDAseq and D-ETM.

1. **LDA** (Blei et al., 2003): We use Gensim's implementation of LDA model[1]. To enable reproducibility, we use a fixed random seed, i.e., set the `random_state` = 2021. We set `passes` to 20 and use the default values for the remaining hyperparameters.

2. **LDAseq** (Blei and Lafferty, 2006): We use the Gensim implementation[2]. We set the `random_state` value as 2021 and `passes` as 20. For the rest of the hyperparameters, we use the defaults.

3. **D-ETM** (Dieng et al., 2019): We use the original implementation[3] with `batch_size` = 64 and `epochs` = 100, and keep the default values for the rest of the hyperparameters.

6.3. Topics in TCPD-IPD

We used LDA to extract 50 topics from the entire TCPD-IPD dataset as it achieved the highest coherence score (see Fig 9) when topic count was varied from 25 to 200 in steps of 25. The topics with their manual labels are shown in Table 1. Note that we could not run LDAseq because it was taking too much time. It did not terminate even after running for 72 hours. We could not run D-ETM as it experienced posterior collapse, which could not be resolved even after changing the hyperparameters.

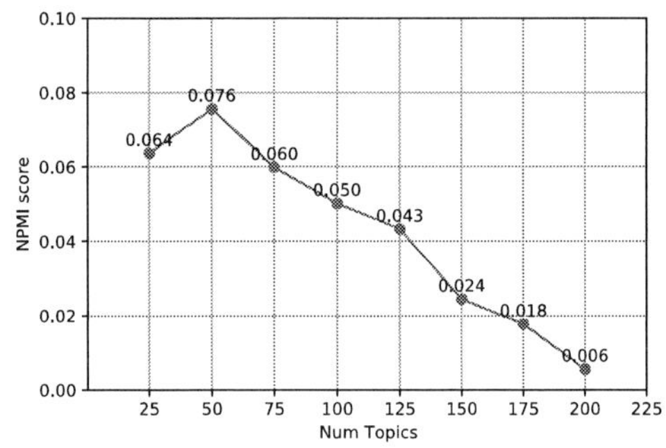

Figure 9: NPMI values for different number of topics in LDA over the full TCPD-IPD dataset.

6.4. Topics in subsets of TCPD-IPD

We have carried out a pilot study on dynamic topic modeling with data subsets for the three ministries (Finance, Railways, and Health and Family Welfare). We set the topic count to 20. We have divided each data subset into year-wise slices, partitioned each slice into train:validation:test as 8:1:1, and run LDAseq and D-ETM on them. Then we calculated the coherence (NPMI), diversity, and topic quality ($= NPMI \times Diversity$) for each model by averaging them over the time slices. Table 2 shows that LDAseq performs best and hence we choose it to extract topics from the ministry-specific datasets. The topics that appear in Fig. 5 in the main text have been manually labeled by looking at their top five words. Table 3 shows these topic compositions.

6.5. Keyword extraction for gender and caste-related discussions

To generate keywords for the analysis of gender and caste-related discussions, we have applied SkipGram,

[1] https://radimrehurek.com/gensim/models/ldamodel.html

[2] https://radimrehurek.com/gensim/models/ldaseqmodel.html

[3] https://github.com/adjidieng/DETM

Top-5 words in topic	Manual label
country, foreign, agreement, international, sign	*Foreign affairs*
standard, quality, safety, use, pollution	*Pollution*
urban, city, housing, delhi, construction	*Urban development*
security, state, police, home, affair	*Law & order*
road, highway, national, construction, state	*Road construction*
bank, loan, rbi, credit, account	*Banking*
committee, state, review, recommendation, report	*Advisory body*
state, andhra_pradesh, uttar_pradesh, maharashtra, tamil_nadu	*States*
fund, crore, release, year, state	*Budget*
gas, oil, milk, production, natural_gas	*Petroleum*
air, airport, defence, civil_aviation, airline	*Civil aviation*
post, employee, central, office, officer	*Central Employee*
export, import, product, trade, textile	*Market overview*
project, complete, work, cost, sanction	*Project*
case, court, high_court, person, disability	*Judicial system*
solar, renewable_energy, energy, system, power	*Renewable energy*
act, state, provision, section, rule	*Act & regulations*
service, information, provide, telecom, network	*Information technology*
payment, tax, pay, revenue, amount	*Tax*
power, plant, capacity, supply, state	*Electricity plant*
sport, fertilizer, ltd, limit, corporation	*Fertilizer plant*
madam, action, complaint, case, report	*Grievance*
water, river, state, resource, drinking_water	*Water resources*
education, school, university, student, human_resource	*HR in Education*
scheme, state, development, provide, implement	*State development*
coal, mine, production, mineral, mining	*Coal mining*
rural, district, area, village, functional	*Rural issues*
delhi, mumbai, city, gujarat, chennai	*Metropolitan areas*
health, state, family_welfare, drug, medical	*Health services*
answer, lok_sabha, reply, statement, lay	*Parliament*
farmer, agriculture, crop, agricultural, production	*Agriculture*
china, bangladesh, island, nepal, disaster	*Natural disaster*
increase, year, rate, country, reduce	*Country growth*
steel, port, connectivity, capacity, major	*Ports shipping*
tribal, schedule, minority, scholarship, tribe	*Tribal affairs*
food, price, consumer, state, foodgrain	*Food price*
sector, private, policy, public, investment	*Private sector*
woman, child, employment, worker, labour	*Woman & child labour*
ngo, bihar, society, organisation, organization	*NGO*
tourism, culture, site, tourist, development	*Tourism*
industry, development, infrastructure, unit, scheme	*Industry*
company, issue, guideline, application, insurance	*Insurance*
research, technology, centre, training, national	*Research & Technology*
railway, train, station, passenger, rail	*Railway*
land, forest, area, environment_forest, state	*Wildlife conservation*
state, proposal, set, chhattisgarh, propose	Miscellaneous
vehicle, procurement, website, award, contract	Miscellaneous
year, wise, state, last_three, number	Miscellaneous
due, pleased, loss, reason, affect	Miscellaneous
thereto, reaction, chaudhary, manoj, true	Miscellaneous

Table 1: Topics in the entire TCPD-IPD dataset.

Dataset	Coherence		Diversity		Topic Quality	
	LDAseq	D-ETM	LDAseq	D-ETM	LDAseq	D-ETM
Finance	0.088	0.078	0.652	0.496	0.057	0.039
Railways	0.129	0.094	0.686	0.558	0.088	0.052
Health	0.103	0.096	0.617	0.571	0.064	0.055

Table 2: Topic quality analysis.

which is one of the models used in the neural network-based word2vec algorithm to generate word embeddings (Mikolov et al., 2013). We have run SkipGram on the entire TCPD-IPD dataset and taken the top twenty neighbors (based on cosine similarity of the generated word vectors) of each of the keywords 'gender' and 'caste'. The words are shown in Table 4. Then, we have counted the documents that contain those words. We have ignored the words shown in italics in the table as they introduced many irrelevant documents into the count.

6.6. Explanation of certain terms

Words in the main text that are difficult to understand outside the Indian context are explained below.

1. 'npci': National Payments Corporation of India, created by the Reserve Bank of India under the

Year	Top-5 words in topic	Manual label
	Ministry of Finance	
1999	rate, growth, cent, increase, year	*Economical growth*
2009	rate, cent, growth, increase, year	
2019	growth, cent, rate, economy, sector	
1999	bank, rbi, reserve, issue, guideline	*Banking*
2009	bank, rbi, issue, guideline, reserve	
2019	bank, rbi, fraud, issue, transaction	
1999	project, state, world, development, bank	*Rural development*
2009	project, state, development, infrastructure, rural	
2019	project, development, state, infrastructure, fund	
1999	bank, loan, credit, nabard, state	*Agricultural loan*
2009	bank, loan, credit, farmer, year	
2019	loan, bank, farmer, credit, scheme	
1999	scheme, employee, pension, interest, deposit	*Pension reforms*
2009	scheme, pension, fund, deposit, interest	
2019	scheme, account, pension, state, pradhan_mantri	
	Ministry of Railways	
1999	work, complete, progress, project, line	*Railway project*
2009	work, complete, section, line, gauge_conversion	
2019	work, section, complete, line, gauge_conversion	
1999	freight, traffic, passenger, good, ticket	*Ticket price*
2009	ticket, passenger, freight, increase, scheme	
2019	passenger, ticket, fare, freight, train	
1999	system, safety, track, committee, report	*Railway safety*
2009	system, track, safety, committee, signal	
2019	system, track, safety, train, committee	
1999	project, corporation, rail, development, company	*Infrastructure development*
2009	project, development, corridor, rail, identify	
2019	development, project, corridor, rail, high_speed	
1999	station, facility, provide, platform, provision	*Passenger amenity*
2009	station, facility, provide, platform, work	
2019	station, provide, facility, platform, scheme	
	Ministry of Health and Family Welfare	
2000	research, institute, study, council, develop	*Medical research*
2009	research, study, clinical_trial, institute, council	
2019	research, medical, study, clinical_trial, council	
2000	child, population, programme, national, reproductive	*Woman & child healthcare*
2009	child, programme, national, care, woman	
2019	child, care, woman, national, provide	
2000	disease, malaria, control, case, death	*Communicable diseases*
2009	disease, control, case, report, malaria	
2019	patient, treatment, provide, free, scheme	
2000	centre, care, area, service, rural	*Rural Medical Infrastructure*
2009	patient, treatment, provide, free, hospital	
2019	national, public, healthcare, provide, include	
2000	patient, treatment, provide, hospital, free	*Financial aid*
2009	project, crore, fund, expenditure, cost	
2019	project, fund, crore, cost, completion	

Table 3: Temporal topics for each ministry in TCPD-IPD dataset.

Word	Top 20 neighbors
gender	**gender, gender_equality, gender_disparity, women, woman, gender_sensitivity, gender_sensitization, gender_gap, gender_parity, girl, gender_sensitive, female_literacy, sex, male_female, disparity, child_sex, child, girl_child, literacy_rate, sex_selective**
caste	**caste, tribe, scs, obcs, obc,** *schedule,* **caste_tribe, scheduled_tribe, dalit, social_justice, scs_sts, scheduled_caste,** *vijay_sampla, empowerment_napoleon, belong, subbulakshmi_jagadeesan,* **atrocity, minority,** *pal_gurjar, empowerment_smt*

Table 4: Top 20 neighbors (using `Word2Vec`) for each keyword.

Ministry of Finance, to enable digital payments and settlement systems in India.

2. 'nabard': National Bank for Agriculture and Rural Development, operating under the Ministry of Finance. It regulates the institutions that supply financial help to the rural society.
3. Kisan Credit Card (KCC): Farmers' Credit Card.
4. 'apy': Atal Pension Yojana. 'Yojana' means scheme.
5. 'dbt': Direct Benefit Transfer.
6. 'jan_dhan': Pradhan Mantri Jan Dhan Yojana. Translates to 'Prime Minister's People's Wealth Scheme'.
7. 'rail_vikas': Railway Vikas Nigam Limited is owned by the Ministry of Railways involved in building rail infrastructure.
8. 'irsdc': Indian Railway Station Development Corporation.
9. 'scs', 'obc', 'obcs', 'scs_sts', 'scheduled_tribe', 'scheduled_caste': These words denote historically disadvantaged communities in India. Scheduled Castes, Scheduled Tribes, and Other Backward Classes are abbreviated as SC, ST, OBC, respectively.

7. Bibliographical References

Adhya, D., Dutta, K., and Basu, A. (2013). Japanese Encephalitis in India: risk of an epidemic in the National Capital Region. *International Health*, 5(3):166–168.

Anuja, G. V. (25 Nov 2020). Parliament may see historically low number of sittings this year. *Mint*.

Bhogale, S. (2019). TPCD-IPD: TCPD Indian Parliament codebook (question hour). *Trivedi Centre for Political Data, Ashoka University*.

Blei, D. M. and Lafferty, J. D. (2006). Dynamic topic models. In *Proceedings of the 23rd International Conference on Machine Learning*, pages 113–120.

Blei, D. M., Ng, A. Y., and Jordan, M. I. (2003). Latent Dirichlet allocation. *Journal of Machine Learning Research*, 3:993–1022.

Blei, D. M., Kucukelbir, A., and McAuliffe, J. D. (2017). Variational inference: A review for statisticians. *Journal of the American Statistical Association*, 112(518):859–877.

Dieng, A. B., Ruiz, F. J. R., and Blei, D. M. (2019). The dynamic embedded topic model. *CoRR*, abs/1907.05545.

Ghosh, S. and Basu, A. (2016). Acute encephalitis syndrome in India: the changing scenario. *Annals of Neurosciences*, 23(3):131.

Gkoumas, D., Pontiki, M., Papanikolaou, K., and Papageorgiou, H. (2018). Exploring the political agenda of the Greek Parliament plenary sessions. In *Proceedings of the LREC 2018 Workshop ParlaCLARIN: Creating and Using Parliamentary Corpora*.

Greene, D. and Cross, J. P. (2017). Exploring the political agenda of the European Parliament using a dynamic topic modeling approach. *Political Analysis*, 25(1):77–94.

Ishima, H. (2020). How electoral reform alters legislative speech: Evidence from the parliament of Victoria, Australia 1992–2017. *Electoral Studies*, 67:102192.

Kshatriya, R., Khara, N., Ganjiwale, J., Lote, S., Patel, S., and Paliwal, R. (2018). Lessons learnt from the Indian H1N1 (swine flu) epidemic: Predictors of outcome based on epidemiological and clinical profile. *Journal of Family Medicine and Primary Care*, 7(6):1506.

Lisena, P., Harrando, I., Kandakji, O., and Troncy, R. (2020). ToModAPI: A topic modeling API to train, use and compare topic models. In *Proceedings of Second Workshop for NLP Open Source Software (NLP-OSS)*, pages 132–140.

Makhija, A. K. (2006). Privatisation in India. *Economic and Political Weekly*, pages 1947–1951.

Martin, S. and Rozenberg, O. (2014). *The roles and function of parliamentary questions*. Routledge.

Marwah, V. (2019). Gender, caste and indian feminism: The case of the women's reservation bill. In *Women's and Gender Studies in India*, pages 151–163. Routledge India.

Mikolov, T., Sutskever, I., Chen, K., Corrado, G. S., and Dean, J. (2013). Distributed representations of words and phrases and their compositionality. *Advances in Neural Information Processing Systems*, 26.

Reddy, V. Y. (2019). Privatisation in India. *Privatisation in Developing Countries*, pages 178–198.

Sanyal, K. (2016). Regulating the regulators: Role of Parliament. *Economic and Political Weekly*, 51(13):16–19.

Sen, A., Ghatak, D., Kumar, K., Khanuja, G., Bansal, D., Gupta, M., Rekha, K., Bhogale, S., Trivedi, P., and Seth, A. (2019). Studying the discourse on economic policies in India using mass media, social media, and the parliamentary question hour data. In *Proceedings of the 2nd ACM SIGCAS Conference on Computing and Sustainable Societies*, pages 234–247.

Tripathi, V. and Kumar, R. (2021). Parliament amidst pandemic: Situating the opposition. *Economic and Political Weekly*, 56(33):16–19.

8. Language Resource References

Trivedi Centre for Political Data, Ashoka University. (2019). *TPCD-IPD: TCPD Indian Parliament Dataset (Question Hour) 1.0*.

Proceedings of the First Workshop on Natural Language Processing for Political Sciences (PoliticalNLP), pages 79–85
Marseille, 24 June 2022

Don't Burst Blindly: For a Better Use of Natural Language Processing to Fight Opinion Bubbles in News Recommendations

Evan Dufraisse[†*], **Célina Treuillier**[*], **Armelle Brun**[*],
Julien Tourille[†], **Sylvain Castagnos**[*], **Adrian Popescu**[†]
[†] Université Paris-Saclay, CEA, List, F-91120, Palaiseau, France
[*] Université de Lorraine - CNRS - Loria, Vandoeuvre les Nancy Cedex, France
{evan.dufraisse, julien.tourille, adrian.popescu}@cea.fr
{celina.treuillier, armelle.brun, sylvain.castagnos}@loria.fr

Abstract

Online news consumption plays an important role in shaping the political opinions of citizens. The news is often served by recommendation algorithms, which adapt content to users' preferences. Such algorithms can lead to political polarization as the societal effects of the recommended content and recommendation design are disregarded. We posit that biases appear, at least in part, due to a weak entanglement between natural language processing and recommender systems, both processes yet at work in the diffusion and personalization of online information. We assume that both diversity and acceptability of recommended content would benefit from such a synergy. We discuss the limitations of current approaches as well as promising leads of opinion-mining integration for the political news recommendation process.
Keywords: Political polarization, News processing, Recommender systems, Opinion bubbles

1. Introduction

The ubiquitous use of social media has revolutionized the way people consume news and get exposed to information. Social media give users access to a huge amount of news, and opportunities to engage with diverse opinions. However, the access to such a rich information landscape comes with important challenges. In particular, personalization tools, designed to help users access content they are interested in, filter and hide information, offering only news in line with a user's opinion. This selective exposure limits the presentation of contrasting viewpoints, leading to the creation of opinion bubbles (Pariser, 2011; Bozdag and van den Hoven, 2015). In the political domain, such an exposure tends to polarize citizens' opinions (Pariser, 2011; Zuiderveen Borgesius et al., 2016), often drifting them towards extreme viewpoints (Sunstein, 2009). On the long run, polarization is detrimental to the political debate and ultimately to democratic societies. The High Level Expert Group on Media Diversity and Pluralism highlights that people need to confront opinions that differ from their own to develop themselves fully[1].

In this context, opinion bubbles are a growing concern for researchers from different disciplines (e.g. political science, economics, computer science or media), with interests ranging from assessing the real impact of personalization (Zuiderveen Borgesius et al., 2016) to bursting these bubbles (Burbach et al., 2019). In this work, we focus on computer science research on opinion bubbles in two distinct but related domains. The News Recommender System (NRS) community has a long-term interest in designing recommendation algorithms that broaden users' view about a given topic. To this end, researchers focus on forming a diversified set of news articles to make sure that users can access diversified opinions. These research efforts mainly differ in the way they measure diversity and how they use it (Kunaver and Požrl, 2017; Raza and Ding, 2021; Möller et al., 2018). However, as we will show, the news content analysis and the way diversity is managed are not adapted to the specificity of political NRS, which limits the impact of diversification.

For its part, the Natural Language Processing (NLP) community focuses on news content understanding through different tasks such as topic modeling, opinion mining or argument mining (Hemmatian and Sohrabi, 2019 10; Lawrence and Reed, 2020). The most effective strategies in those fields are supervised and heavily rely on annotated data. This makes the elaboration of solutions even more challenging considering the highly dynamic nature of news in terms of topics and opinions.

In this paper, we discuss the importance of a fine-grained analysis of the opinions expressed in the news, combined with a NRS that handles these opinions, and not only topics, to create personalized sets of recommendations and efficiently burst bubbles. From an ethical point of view, the NRS should not favor any specific opinion but should guarantee that the recommendations are representative of the diversity of the opinions expressed about the topic (Helberger, 2019).

The rest of the paper is organized as follows. After presenting a review of the literature of NRS (Section 2), we focus on news content analysis in NLP (Section 3). In Section 4 we present our view of the characteristics that a system designed to burst bubbles should have, as well as the way it should be designed.

2. News Recommender Systems

Online platforms offer access to a vast amount of content, which needs to be ranked according to the preferences of each reader. In this context, NRS are designed to help readers find relevant information among the large quantity of news available (Raza and Ding, 2021). The news recommendation task has three main characteristics that distinguish it from other recommendation tasks: news articles quickly become obsolete (1) and are characterized by a high turnover (2) as a large number of news articles is published every second (Lunardi et al., 2020). This induces the need for recommendation models that can be updated on the fly and that do not require many interactions between news and readers. Besides, news consumption tends to influence users' opinion (3) (Helberger, 2019). This is highly critical when it comes to politics, as NRS have been shown to contribute to the creation of opinion bubbles, representing a threat to democracy (Pariser, 2011).

As a consequence, sets of recommendations have to be properly balanced to ensure that users can access news that convey diverse opinions. This refers to the accuracy-diversity dilemma (Zhou et al., 2010), which refers to the search of an optimal balance between a high level of accuracy, to keep users' trust, and a sufficient diversification among recommendations. In the news domain, diversity is often viewed as mandatory since it represents a core principle for the development of a democratic society (Helberger, 2019). However, the literature does not offer a unique way to represent the news, to evaluate the diversity, nor to recommend diversified sets of news articles.

2.1. News representation

Before measuring their diversity, news articles are often pre-processed in order to build a representation of their content (e.g. body, title, preamble or keywords). This representation must be designed to precisely characterize news. Recent models in NRS use deep-learning approaches such as named entity recognition, entity-linking, or knowledge-graph to provide a complete representation of news (Wang et al., 2018; Joseph and Jiang, 2019; Zhang et al., 2021). These representations are optimized for high accuracy but do not meet the needs for a precise control of recommendation diversification. Moreover, NRS mainly promote diversity through the use of topic modeling, and rely on simple bag-of-words representation. For instance, they represent the discriminating power of each word in the news using TF-IDF (Gao et al., 2020) or build topic representation using LDA (Tintarev et al., 2018). Few studies focus on Sentiment Analysis (Wu et al., 2020) by identifying and representing positive and negative sentiments in the news. The authors hypothesize that topic and sentiment analysis can increase the diversity of recommended opinions, but no empirical evidence is provided. Models that focus on topic diversification and coarse sentiment diversification can barely capture opinions, even less their nuances. Their use to foster opinion diversity in NRS is thus limited. Apart from topics and opinions, particularities of textual content such as the style of the authors or the use of irony, are not processed by NRS either.

2.2. Diversity measures in NRS

NRS differ in their definition of diversity and its associated metrics. For the simplest cases, diversity is considered as the opposite of similarity. The similarity measure can be instantiated by cosine similarity or based on distance (e.g. Jaccard or Euclidean) (Möller et al., 2018; Lunardi et al., 2020). In rare cases, other metrics are used, such as entropy (Shannon index, Rao's quadratic entropy) (Möller et al., 2018).

Generally, diversity metrics are derived from other fields, but the literature rarely adapt them to the news domain, which may result in meaningless values. More importantly, as mentioned above, diversities computed from simple representations of news can hinder even more their accuracy.

2.3. Diversification processes

Diversity measures constitute the basis for diversification processes. Diversification is often implemented as a post-processing step which re-ranks a list of recommended contents by prioritizing contents with a high variety of topics (Lunardi et al., 2020; Ziegler et al., 2005). An important downside of this approach is that diversity cannot be improved if the initial list is homogeneous. To answer this limitation, researchers propose to incorporate diversity into the core of the recommendation algorithm. (Raza and Ding, 2020) presents a recommendation algorithm that weights both diversity and accuracy in a personalized way, and tries to answer the accuracy-diversity dilemma. As a result, diversification among recommendations is not simply based on the re-ranking of the news, but relies on the prior parameter optimization of the recommendation model. To summarize, existing diversification processes are interesting, but their potential is limited by the use of simplistic news representations. Representations which are more adapted to the specificity of news – in particular political news – and diversification are needed. They can be obtained by applying advanced NLP techniques.

3. Natural Language Processing

Diversifying news content opinions requires a fine-grained understanding of articles' stances. Several NLP sub-fields have developed approaches to meet this end. In the following, we distinguish proxy measures, that extract opinion cues, from finer-grained strategies.

3.1. Proxy strategies to stance detection

A system able to extract fine-grained opinions from arbitrary textual contents is still an object of research. Facing this challenge, proxy measures that are easier to obtain can serve as coarse opinion indicators. The methods presented in this subsection are often gathered under the umbrella term of "media bias detection". We refer the reader to (Nakov et al., 2021) for a complete survey of the subject.

3.1.1. Content-based strategies

Media biases can take several forms: (i) a subjective stylometry, (ii) a coverage restricted to a subset of topics (topic diversity), (iii) an unequal attention paid to certain aspects or facts in events (framing), or (iv) a constant leaning towards a political group.

Stylometry-based detection approaches revolve around the detection of subjective expressions using dictionaries. The latter are usually gathered using an unsupervised strategy (Riloff and Wiebe, 2003). Recently, (Patankar et al., 2019) used (Recasens et al., 2013) lexicon to make a bias-aware NRS. However, this strategy only detects a lack of stylometric neutrality but cannot help determine an article's stance. Topic diversity bias is already discussed in the NRS literature, we redirect to Section 2 for further information.

Framing (Entman, 1993) implies a consistent focus on some aspects of an issue that leads to its partial comprehension and biased interpretation by the reader. An early NRS strategy implemented to counter this bias used keyword extraction and unsupervised clustering of articles (Park et al., 2009). Later, automatic approaches for framing identification have been developed around the detection of so-called frames, which are characteristic aspects of a particular issue. Considering a representative set of articles that address a same topic, the aim is to detect significant deviations in aspects distribution as an indicator of bias. However, the issue-specificity of aspects prevent their widespread computational use. (Boydstun et al., 2014) solves this issue by developing a set of 15 generic frames that are pervasive in most subjects. This approach was later consolidated with a dataset (Card et al., 2015). More recently, (Kwak et al., 2021) offered a new approach around the use of "micro-frames". They construct semantic axes based on the Glove embeddings (Pennington et al., 2014) of 1,621 antonyms selected from WordNet (Miller, 1995). Using the Glove embeddings of words within a text, they compute their cosine distances to the semantic axes, and derive bias indicators from the score distribution. Nonetheless, frame identification for stance detection is limited, as two articles could defend opposite views over the same set of aspects but with the same polarities.

If one can derive clues on a source's political leaning using its topic diversity and framing, other cues based on semantically loaded expressions have proved their efficiency. Several methods use the U.S congressman's speeches as source data to extract politically differentiating expressions (Groseclose and Milyo, 2005; Gentzkow and Shapiro, 2010; Bayram et al., 2019). Recently, (D'Alonzo and Tegmark, 2021) led a comparative study over several media, solely using articles to extract such expressions.

3.1.2. Audience-based strategies

Stance detection through audience analysis is a complementary approach to text-based methods that stems from the homophily principle, which postulates that users principally interact with content they agree with. The overall political stance of a media can be derived by analyzing those interactions. Most research in this field revolves around the use of Twitter follow/retweet interactions to map media or entities in the political spectrum (Wong et al., 2016; Stefanov et al., 2020; Darwish et al., 2020). Other approaches use readily available media bias analyses from News Guard[2], AllSides[3], or Media Bias/Fact Check[4] to consolidate supervised datasets of articles (Baly et al., 2020).

The derived political stances could be used to diversify opinions through the diversification of news sources. Two underlying assumptions could preclude the success of such an approach, namely, that "News articles follow the political leaning of their source outlet" and that "Political leanings of news outlets do not change across topics". (Ganguly et al., 2020) has recently shown that both of these assumptions are often violated on an article basis. To fully grasp the political stance of an article, one needs to rely on the content itself.

3.2. Opinion-Mining for stance detection

In computer science, "Opinion Mining" and "Sentiment Analysis" are often used interchangeably. Nonetheless, in everyday language, an opinion is rather defined as a "judgment formed about something". Choices of subjective and sentimentally expressive words are indicative of such judgments, and form the basis of stance detection.

Among the three levels of sentiment-analysis usually distinguished (document, sentence and entity), only the finer-grained one is suitable for stance detection, as the document and sentence levels of analyses are too coarse to be informative of a writer's stance. A document or a sentence could contain several entities upon which opinions are expressed.

3.2.1. Aspect-Level Opinion Mining

(Liu, 2010) defines opinions as quintuples $(e_i, a_{ij}, s_{ijkl}, h_k, t_l)$, where e_i is the ith entity considered, a_{ij} is the jth aspect of that entity, and s_{ijkl} is the sentiment that the opinion holder h_k expresses towards the aspect a_{ij} at time t_l. Opinion mining at the aspect level is interested in extracting, sometimes partially, those quintuples. The two most studied extraction frames are "product aspect mining", with the extraction of (e_i, a_{ij}, s_{ij}) triplets, and "stance detection" with the extraction of (e_i, s_i) tuples. These frames can be split into two steps: Aspect-Extraction (AE), and Aspect-Based Sentiment Classification (ABSC). Aspect-based Opinion Mining has mostly been applied to product reviews datasets (Pontiki et al., 2014; Pontiki et al., 2015; Pontiki et al., 2016), but also to financial (Jangid et al., 2018; Gaillat et al., 2018) , and more recently, news datasets (Steinberger et al., 2017; Hamborg and Donnay,).

Aspect-Extraction (AE) Given an opinionated-text content as input, AE aims at extracting the targets and aspects ((a_{ij},e_i) or e_i) towards which a sentiment might be expressed. Approaches can be grouped into four types. Frequency-based approaches extract most frequent nouns and noun phrases after Part-of-Speech (PoS) tagging, notably missing less frequent aspects, and generating a large number of noisy targets. Other approaches such as (Qiu et al., 2011) extract domain-specific opinion words and targets using syntactic relationships. They alternatively expand both an opinion word lexicon and a set of candidate targets in a bootstrapping fashion. Supervised methods, by formalizing AE as a sequence-labeling task have also been implemented. Finally, non-lexicon-based unsupervised methods make use of topic-modeling approaches (e.g. LDA, PLSA). An example of such an approach is (Titov and McDonald, 2008), which models a document as a mixture of both local and global topics, local topics are derived at a window scale to capture target aspects. The above approaches assume explicitly mentioned aspects, however, aspects can also be implicit. We refer the reader to literature surveys (Hemmatian and Sohrabi, 2019 10; Nazir et al., 2020) for further information on the topic.

Aspect-Based Sentiment Classification (ABSC) Once extracted aspects and entities, we need to determine the sentiment expressed towards them. In this context, machine learning methods are often distinguished from rule-based ones. Rule-based methods mostly rely on PoS tagging and the adjective-noun proximity heuristic to associate adjectives to aspects. These methods have been supplanted by machine learning methods, among which Deep-Learning recently took the lead. Most approaches are supervised but getting annotated data is expensive. This lack of annotated datasets is often balanced using hybrid approaches that integrate external knowledge using sentiment lexicons, ontologies, or discourse parser features. Datasets are scarce in the news domain, and a recently (Hamborg and Donnay,) supplied a high-quality dataset for the task. A challenge in the field, as in many, is the development of frugal approaches that require less or no annotations, especially regarding the difficulty of transferring ABSC capabilities between domains (Nazir et al., 2020).

If aspect-based opinion mining can help derive an article's stance, it cannot explain its underlying reasons. Argument Mining (see the survey (Lawrence and Reed, 2020)) fills this gap by extracting argumentation structures in texts. Improvements in irony and sarcasm detection, or even negation handling could also be of use.

4. Towards a NLP-RS Hand-to-Hand Approach for Political NRS

We highlighted some limits in both NRS and NLP fields, that show existing approaches to be unsuitable to reduce the impact or to burst filter bubbles, by ensuring a diversity of themes and opinions in NRS. First, the diversity measures used in RS mostly evaluate the news content differences, only ensuring that the set of recommendations are not too similar. This is due to the simple representations of articles used, which do not allow accurate representation of opinions, and are thus inadequate to ensure fair recommendations by inclusively representing diverse opinions. Recent lines of thought promote the plurality of opinions in NRS using representation metrics (Vrijenhoek et al., 2021). Nevertheless, the notion of opinion is still treated basically in the form of a positive, negative or neutral but intangible opinion on a statement. A step further, we support the idea of a temporal diversification to adapt to the shifts in opinion and the evolving needs of users during the recommendation process.

Second, due to the highly dynamic nature of news, opinion mining techniques must be generic and adaptable to new sources and opinions. State-of-the-art aspect-based opinion analysis systems implement supervised machine learning algorithms and need annotated data to be trained. This hinders the capabilities of such systems to adapt quickly on new topics and their associated aspects. Semi-supervised approaches need to be further investigated to remedy this issue and to cope with the dynamic nature of news.

These limitations show the need for a stronger cooperation between RS and NLP communities. News opinion mining tasks have to be driven by the need of a specific diversity/similarity temporal evaluation. Recommendation tasks have to rely on precise opinion representations to enable content diversification.

Future developments resulting from such a cooperation need to be extensively evaluated. However, NRS evaluation is a difficult and sensitive task. Especially when it comes to opinionated content diversification. Evaluation protocols should include both qualitative and quantitative metrics to build a complete view of the NRS performances. Quantitatively, topic and aspect-based opinion extraction models need to be evaluated through standard benchmarks available in the NLP community (Hamborg et al., 2021). This step guarantees that news representations contain all necessary information for diversification. If several RS benchmarks exist in the community, none has been developed to quantitatively evaluate diversification as defined in this paper.

Qualitatively, effectiveness of NRS in bursting opinion bubbles must be evaluated. Longitudinal studies, enrolling several groups of people with different social and cultural backgrounds, could shed light on the performance and acceptability of such a system through time, but also on the evolution of the opinions of people. However, these questions are not discussed in either domain and requires an expansion of collaboration with political science researchers in the study.

5. Acknowledgements

This work has been funded by the BOOM ANR Project - ANR-20-CE23-0024.

6. Bibliographical References

Baly, R., Da San Martino, G., Glass, J., and Nakov, P. (2020). We can detect your bias: Predicting the political ideology of news articles. In *Proceedings of the 2020 Conference on Empirical Methods in Natural Language Processing (EMNLP)*, pages 4982–4991. Association for Computational Linguistics.

Bayram, U., Pestian, J., Santel, D., and Minai, A. A. (2019). What's in a word? detecting partisan affiliation from word use in congressional speeches. In *2019 International Joint Conference on Neural Networks (IJCNN)*, pages 1–8. IEEE.

Boydstun, A. E., Card, D., Gross, J. H., Resnik, P., and Smith, N. A. (2014). Tracking the development of media frames. *Work. Pap.*, pages 1–25.

Bozdag, E. and van den Hoven, J. (2015). Breaking the filter bubble: democracy and design. *Ethics and Information Technology*, 17(4):249–265.

Burbach, L., Halbach, P., Ziefle, M., and Calero Valdez, A. (2019). Bubble trouble: Strategies against filter bubbles in online social networks. In *Digital Human Modeling and Applications in Health, Safety, Ergonomics and Risk Management. Healthcare Applications*, volume 11582, pages 441–456. Springer International Publishing.

D'Alonzo, S. and Tegmark, M. (2021). Machine-learning media bias. *arXiv:2109.00024 [cs]*.

Darwish, K., Stefanov, P., Aupetit, M., and Nakov, P. (2020). Unsupervised user stance detection on twitter. *Proceedings of the International AAAI Conference on Web and Social Media*, 14(1):141–152.

Entman, R. M. (1993). Framing: Toward clarification of a fractured paradigm. *Journal of Communication*, 43(4):51–58.

Ganguly, S., Kulshrestha, J., An, J., and Kwak, H. (2020). Empirical evaluation of three common assumptions in building political media bias datasets. *Proceedings of the International AAAI Conference on Web and Social Media*, 14(1):939–943.

Gao, Y., Zhao, H., Zhou, Q., Qiu, M., and Liu, M. (2020). An improved news recommendation algorithm based on text similarity. In *2020 3rd International Conference on Smart BlockChain (SmartBlock)*, pages 132–136. IEEE.

Gentzkow, M. and Shapiro, J. M. (2010). What drives media slant? evidence from u.s. daily newspapers. *Econometrica*.

Groseclose, T. and Milyo, J. (2005). A measure of media bias. *The Quarterly Journal of Economics*, 120(4):1191–1237.

Hamborg, F., Donnay, K., and Gipp, B. (2021). Towards target-dependent sentiment classification in news articles. In *Diversity, Divergence, Dialogue*, volume 12646, pages 156–166. Springer International Publishing.

Helberger, N. (2019). On the democratic role of news recommenders. *Digital Journalism*, 7(8):993–1012.

Hemmatian, F. and Sohrabi, M. K. (2019-10). A survey on classification techniques for opinion mining and sentiment analysis. *Artificial Intelligence Review*, 52(3):1495–1545.

Joseph, K. and Jiang, H. (2019). Content based news recommendation via shortest entity distance over knowledge graphs. In *Companion Proceedings of The 2019 World Wide Web Conference*, pages 690–699. ACM.

Kunaver, M. and Požrl, T. (2017). Diversity in recommender systems – a survey. *Knowledge-Based Systems*, 123:154–162.

Kwak, H., An, J., Jing, E., and Ahn, Y.-Y. (2021). FrameAxis: characterizing microframe bias and intensity with word embedding. *PeerJ Computer Science*, 7.

Lawrence, J. and Reed, C. (2020). Argument mining: A survey. *Computational Linguistics*, 45(4):765–818.

Liu, B. (2010). Sentiment analysis and subjectivity. In *Handbook of Natural Language Processing*, pages 627–666.

Lunardi, G. M., Machado, G. M., Maran, V., and de Oliveira, J. P. M. (2020). A metric for filter bubble measurement in recommender algorithms considering the news domain. *Applied Soft Computing*, 97.

Möller, J., Trilling, D., Helberger, N., and van Es, B. (2018). Do not blame it on the algorithm: an empirical assessment of multiple recommender systems and their impact on content diversity. *Information, Communication & Society*, 21(7):959–977.

Nakov, P., Sencar, H. T., An, J., and Kwak, H. (2021). A survey on predicting the factuality and the bias of news media. *arXiv:2103.12506 [cs]*.

Nazir, A., Rao, Y., Wu, L., and Sun, L. (2020). Issues and challenges of aspect-based sentiment analysis: A comprehensive survey. *IEEE Transactions on Affective Computing*.

Pariser, E. (2011). *The filter bubble: what the Internet is hiding from you*. Penguin Press.

Park, S., Kang, S., Chung, S., and Song, J. (2009). NewsCube: delivering multiple aspects of news to mitigate media bias. In *Proceedings of the SIGCHI Conference on Human Factors in Computing Systems*, pages 443–452. ACM.

Patankar, A., Bose, J., and Khanna, H. (2019). A bias aware news recommendation system. In *2019 IEEE 13th International Conference on Semantic Computing (ICSC)*, pages 232–238. IEEE.

Qiu, G., Liu, B., Bu, J., and Chen, C. (2011). Opinion word expansion and target extraction through double propagation. *Computational Linguistics*, 37(1):9–27.

Raza, S. and Ding, C. (2020). A regularized model to trade-off between accuracy and diversity in a news recommender system. In *2020 IEEE International*

Conference on Big Data (Big Data), pages 551–560. IEEE.

Raza, S. and Ding, C. (2021). News recommender system: a review of recent progress, challenges, and opportunities. *Artificial Intelligence Review*, 55(1):749–800.

Recasens, M., Danescu-Niculescu-Mizil, C., and Jurafsky, D. (2013). Linguistic models for analyzing and detecting biased language. In *Proceedings of the 51st Annual Meeting of the Association for Computational Linguistics (Volume 1: Long Papers)*, pages 1650–1659. Association for Computational Linguistics.

Riloff, E. and Wiebe, J. (2003). Learning extraction patterns for subjective expressions. In *Proceedings of the 2003 Conference on Empirical Methods in Natural Language Processing*, pages 105–112.

Stefanov, P., Darwish, K., Atanasov, A., and Nakov, P. (2020). Predicting the topical stance and political leaning of media using tweets. In *Proceedings of the 58th Annual Meeting of the Association for Computational Linguistics*, pages 527–537. Association for Computational Linguistics.

Sunstein, C. R. (2009). *Going to extremes: how like minds unite and divide*. Oxford University Press.

Tintarev, N., Sullivan, E., Guldin, D., Qiu, S., and Odjik, D. (2018). Same, same, but different: Algorithmic diversification of viewpoints in news. In *Adjunct Publication of the 26th Conference on User Modeling, Adaptation and Personalization*, pages 7–13. ACM.

Titov, I. and McDonald, R. (2008). Modeling online reviews with multi-grain topic models. In *Proceeding of the 17th international conference on World Wide Web - WWW '08*. ACM Press.

Vrijenhoek, S., Kaya Independent Researcher, M., Metoui Delft, N. T., Möller, J., Odijk, D., and Helberger, N. (2021). Recommenders with a Mission: Assessing Diver-sity in News Recommendations. 11.

Wang, H., Zhang, F., Xie, X., and Guo, M. (2018). DKN: Deep knowledge-aware network for news recommendation. In *Proceedings of the 2018 World Wide Web Conference on World Wide Web - WWW '18*, pages 1835–1844. ACM Press.

Wong, F. M. F., Tan, C. W., Sen, S., and Chiang, M. (2016). Quantifying political leaning from tweets, retweets, and retweeters. *IEEE Trans. Knowl. Data Eng.*, 28(8):2158–2172.

Wu, C., Wu, F., Qi, T., and Huang, Y. (2020). SentiRec: Sentiment diversity-aware neural news recommendation. In *Proceedings of the 1st Conference of the Asia-Pacific Chapter of the Association for Computational Linguistics and the 10th International Joint Conference on Natural Language Processing*, pages 44–53. Association for Computational Linguistics.

Zhang, X., Yang, Q., and Xu, D. (2021). Combining explicit entity graph with implicit text information for news recommendation. In *Companion Proceedings of the Web Conference 2021*, pages 412–416. ACM.

Zhou, T., Kuscsik, Z., Liu, J.-G., Medo, M., Wakeling, J. R., and Zhang, Y.-C. (2010). Solving the apparent diversity-accuracy dilemma of recommender systems. *Proceedings of the National Academy of Sciences*, 107(10):4511–4515.

Ziegler, C.-N., McNee, S. M., Konstan, J. A., and Lausen, G. (2005). Improving recommendation lists through topic diversification. In *Proceedings of the 14th international conference on World Wide Web - WWW '05*, page 22. ACM Press.

Zuiderveen Borgesius, F. J., Trilling, D., Möller, J., Bodó, B., de Vreese, C. H., and Helberger, N. (2016). Should we worry about filter bubbles? *Internet Policy Review*, 5(1).

7. Language Resource References

Card, D., Boydstun, A. E., Gross, J. H., Resnik, P., and Smith, N. A. (2015). The media frames corpus: Annotations of frames across issues. volume 2, pages 438–444.

Gaillat, T., Stearns, B., Sridhar, G., McDermott, R., Zarrouk, M., and Davis, B. (2018). Implicit and explicit aspect extraction in financial microblogs. In *Proceedings of the First Workshop on Economics and Natural Language Processing*, pages 55–61. Association for Computational Linguistics.

Hamborg, F. and Donnay, K.). NewsMTSC: A dataset for (multi-)target-dependent sentiment classification in political news articles. In *Proceedings of the 16th Conference of the European Chapter of the Association for Computational Linguistics: Main Volume*, pages 1663–1675. Association for Computational Linguistics.

Jangid, H., Singhal, S., Shah, R. R., and Zimmermann, R. (2018). Aspect-based financial sentiment analysis using deep learning. In *Companion of the The Web Conference 2018 on The Web Conference 2018 - WWW '18*, pages 1961–1966. ACM Press.

Miller, G. A. (1995). WordNet: a lexical database for english. volume 38, pages 39–41.

Pennington, J., Socher, R., and Manning, C. (2014). Glove: Global vectors for word representation. In *Proceedings of the 2014 Conference on Empirical Methods in Natural Language Processing (EMNLP)*, pages 1532–1543. Association for Computational Linguistics.

Pontiki, M., Galanis, D., Pavlopoulos, J., Papageorgiou, H., Androutsopoulos, I., and Manandhar, S. (2014). SemEval-2014 task 4: Aspect based sentiment analysis. In *Proceedings of the 8th International Workshop on Semantic Evaluation (SemEval 2014)*, pages 27–35. Association for Computational Linguistics.

Pontiki, M., Galanis, D., Papageorgiou, H., Manandhar, S., and Androutsopoulos, I. (2015). SemEval-2015 task 12: Aspect based sentiment analysis. In *Proceedings of the 9th International Workshop on Semantic Evaluation (SemEval 2015)*, pages 486–495. Association for Computational Linguistics.

Pontiki, M., Galanis, D., Papageorgiou, H., Androutsopoulos, I., Manandhar, S., AL-Smadi, M., Al-Ayyoub, M., Zhao, Y., Qin, B., De Clercq, O., Hoste, V., Apidianaki, M., Tannier, X., Loukachevitch, N., Kotelnikov, E., Bel, N., Jiménez-Zafra, S. M., and Eryiğit, G. (2016). SemEval-2016 task 5: Aspect based sentiment analysis. In *Proceedings of the 10th International Workshop on Semantic Evaluation (SemEval-2016)*, pages 19–30. Association for Computational Linguistics.

Steinberger, R., Hegele, S., Tanev, H., and Della Rocca, L. (2017). Large-scale news entity sentiment analysis. In *RANLP 2017 - Recent Advances in Natural Language Processing Meet Deep Learning*, pages 707–715. Incoma Ltd. Shoumen, Bulgaria.

Notes

[1]http://ec.europa.eu/digital-agenda/sites/digital-agenda/files/HLG%20Final

[2]https://www.newsguardtech.com/

[3]https://www.allsides.com/

[4]https://mediabiasfactcheck.com/

Proceedings of the First Workshop on Natural Language Processing for Political Sciences (PoliticalNLP), pages 86–90
Marseille, 24 June 2022

Creation of Polish Online News Corpus for Political Polarization Studies

[1]Joanna Szwoch, [2]Mateusz Staszkow, [3]Rafal Rzepka, [3]Kenji Araki

[1]Graduate School of Information Science and Technology, Hokkaido University,
[2]Mateusz Staszkow Software Development,
[3]Faculty of Information Science and Technology, Hokkaido University
[1,3]Sapporo - Japan, [2] Warsaw - Poland
joannaeleonora.szwoch.u0@elms.hokudai.ac.jp, mateuszstasz@gmail.com
{rzepka, araki}@ist.hokudai.ac.jp

Abstract

In this paper we describe a Polish news corpus as an attempt to create a filtered, organized and representative set of texts coming from contemporary online press articles from two major Polish TV news providers: commercial TVN24 and state-owned TVP Info. The process consists of web scraping, data cleaning and formatting. A random sample was selected from prepared data to perform a classification task. The random forest achieved the best prediction results out of all considered models. We believe that this dataset is a valuable contribution to existing Polish language corpora as online news are considered to be formal and relatively mistake-free, therefore, a reliable source of correct written language, unlike other online platforms such as blogs or social media. Furthermore, to our knowledge, such corpus from this period of time has not been created before. In the future we would like to expand this dataset with articles coming from other online news providers, repeat the classification task on a bigger scale, utilizing other algorithms. Our data analysis outcomes might be a relevant basis to improve research on a political polarization and propaganda techniques in media.

Keywords: Polish language, news corpus, classification, NLP, web scraping

1. Introduction

Nowadays, a piece of information is the most valuable asset. There is a growing problem of distinguishing valuable information from noise and fake news. In Poland it is significantly noticeable during the Russia-Ukraine conflict. One can see inaccuracies regarding the influx of Ukrainian refugees into the European Union, the course of the fighting or the actions of Western countries toward Russia.

In the 21st century we can observe a sociological phenomenon called the filter bubble (Cisek and Krakowska, 2018). Sometimes the same topic is presented in extremely different ways, depending on the news provider. Users tend to visit news sources matching their political attitudes and spend more time on biased content (Garimella et al., 2021). Manipulation is performed with a variety of language techniques and each language requires a tailored approach to detect them.

Polish language cannot be called a typical lesser-resourced language, but compared to others, such as English, German or Russian, it has a significantly smaller base of available corpora. Additionally, vast majority of text resources are paid and not disclosed to the public. The National Corpus of Polish[1] is one of few initiatives which provides a reference corpus containing roughly fifteen hundred million words for free. Sources include literature, newspapers, specialist magazines, transcripts of conversations and Internet texts. However, none of them are online news websites. Moreover, the project was finished in 2012 and has not been updated since. This means that all resources come from year 2011 or older, sometimes even reaching back to 1920s.

Modern languages are very flexible and their use changes constantly. That is why we think that the aforementioned corpora should be expanded by newer sources. Websites providing online news in Polish should therefore be perfect for that as they contain contemporary version of the language in everyday use. Another premise is that they are written in a correct manner, prepared by professional journalists, unlike other online sources such as blogs or social media.

Our dataset was created with the use of two online news websites, run by Polish major TV news providers, namely state-owned TVP Info[2] and commercial TVN24[3]. These are examples of the most watched TV news programs in Poland[4]. Aforementioned websites were scraped and news from years 2019-2021 from different categories were persisted into CSV files. This paper focuses on two tasks - data collection aspect and news outlet classification, which can be treated as a baseline for further experiments. It explains step by step how our corpus was created – we describe web scraping method which we find the most convenient,

[1]`http://nkjp.pl/index.php`

[2]`https://www.tvp.info/`

[3]`https://tvn24.pl/`

[4]`https://www.wirtualnemedia.pl/artykul/fakty-lider-ogladalnosci-luty-programy-informacyjne`

readable and therefore reproducible. Having created the dataset with scraped articles, we explain how to perform data cleaning to prepare the corpus for modeling. After lemmatization and tokenization, cleaned text is vectorized and classification task is performed with the use of several machine learning models. Unlike most of experiments concerning news articles processing, we trained models to predict which news provider wrote certain article, instead of predicting the article category. People often state that media which do not share their political views or opinions are biased and on the contrary, the ones that they follow are not. In the era of news flowing constantly from different sources it would be beneficial to be able to measure media bias objectively. It is claimed to be possible via data-driven analyses whose results should be free of subjectivity (D'Alonzo and Tegmark, 2021). This topic may be of particular interest in connection with the on-going war in Ukraine as reports about it are presented differently, sometimes to an extreme extend, depending on the source.
We think that this corpus is a good starting point for further analyses of contemporary Polish language. Although, the professional journalists should focus on conveying a clear message, holding subjective information only, we believe that news outlets could be examined whether they show any political bias and what kind of propaganda techniques are being used, if any. However, we want to direct our attention to that matter in our future works, with the use of this data set, possibly extended with more articles from other online news sources[5].
The rest of this paper is structured as follows. In Section 2 we focus on previous works which dealt with the problem of dataset creation, especially news corpora, as well as classification task in NLP. Section 3 describes our dataset, with details of each step of creation process that leads to its final form. In Section 4 we discuss methodology used for our models. Section 5 presents the results of our experiment, whose goal is to find the best way to predict which media outlet created certain piece of news. In Section 6 we summarize conclusions which can be drawn from this article and in the end, we mention our future work plans.

2. Related Works

In the past few years there was plenty of studies which tried to tackle the problem of collecting online text resources in an efficient manner. Researchers from MIT managed to collect over three million articles from 2019 and 2020 from about 100 online media outlets with the use of the open-source Newspaper3k[6] software (D'Alonzo and Tegmark, 2021). Another way to do it is web scraping. This process consists of a few steps: desired websites identification, URLs collection, HTML retrieval, text parsing and finally, persistence (Victoriano et al., 2022). One of the most popular and widely used Python libraries for imitating human alike behavior of entering the URL and retrieving necessary data is Beautiful Soup which automatically obtains data from HTML and XML files (Onyenwe et al., 2021).
Slovak Categorized News Corpus was created in a similar way. It contains words, automatic morphological as well as named entity annotations. It consists of almost five thousand articles, with over one hundred thousand sentences and million and a half of tokens (Hladek et al., 2014).
For text classification task itself, firstly, input data needs to be converted to a computer-readable form. BagofWords and TF-IDF word vectors are two possibilities to handle this task (Qader et al., 2019), (Vimal, 2020). Then, logistic regression can be trained on such data. Except for logit models, other methods include neural networks, support vector machines, random forests, or naive Bayes classifiers (Stein et al., 2020).

3. Corpus Creation

We decided to collect online articles from two Polish major TV news providers, TVP Info and TVN24. Firstly, we tried using Newspaper3k library for this task. Although library documentation states that it handles Polish language, it failed to parse chosen websites correctly and therefore we had to give up on this method. However, one feature that worked properly was listing the subcategories of the main website. In the end we decided to prepare a tailored solution for scraping these resources with Beautiful Soup library in Python, as it was suggested in other works (Onyenwe et al., 2021), (vanden Broucke and Baesens, 2018) (Al Qadi et al., 2019).

3.1. Data Collection

Aforementioned websites were scraped and news from different categories were collected between 1st January 2019 and 31st December 2021.
Data collection cleaning process consisted of the following steps:

- Identifying main pages of news providers
- Listing all contexts (website subpages)
- Web crawling to gather all URLs from designated time span
- Parsing websites to retrieve data from HTML files; first text cleaning with the use of regular expressions to filter markups from retrieved HTMLs
- Saving data to CSV file

The aforementioned process resulted in the collection of articles from two sources in the following amounts and categories presented in Table 1.

[5]Upon request, our dataset can be provided for research purposes.

[6]`https://newspaper.readthedocs.io/en/latest/`

Category	TVP Info	TVN24
POLAND	36,223	37,511
WORLD	19,982	28,318
SOCIETY	11,484	-
BUSINESS	4,488	12,629
WARSAW	-	12,532
SPORT	3,628	26,289
SCIENCE	2,297	108
CULTURE	1,698	-
MISCELLANEOUS	1,399	-
WEATHER	495	10,558
POLITICS	-	513
ENTERTAINMENT	-	69
TOTAL	81,694	128,527

Table 1: Number of articles within each category

Data is not evenly distributed and some categories existed only in one website, but not in the other one.
Datasets have the following structure as presented in Table 2.

Variable	TVP Info	TVN24
`url`	✓	✓
`magazine_title`	✓	✓
`website_category`	✓	✓
`title`	✓	✓
`description`	✓	✓
`authors`	✓	✓
`article`	✓	✓
`pub_time`	✓	✓
`mod_time`	✓	-
`hash_tags`	✓	-

Table 2: Extracted data

TVP Info dataset has two additional columns when compared to TVN24, namely modification time and hash tags. We decided to include them as they might be interesting to be examined in the future for other purposes. TVN24 dataset did not have any information regarding the modification time of the article and tags appeared only recently in their articles, therefore these columns were not added to this dataset.

3.2. Dataset Cleaning

Dataset cleaning process consisted of 5 steps in the following order:

- **Duplicates removal** - some articles were repeated during the web crawl.
- **Removing repetitions from retrieved text** - in some cases, description of the article appeared also in the article text which was not desired.
- **Filtering ad words** - most of the articles consisted of phrases which encouraged the reader to watch a related video or read an article whose topic is connected.
- **Deleting special characters such as punctuation, double spaces or tabulation as well as numbers** - regular expressions were used to eliminate all unnecessary elements from this group.
- **Stop words removal** - we used *stop-words* Python library[7] and a set listed by user *bieli* on GitHub[8] to create an extended collection of Polish stop words, as part of them were not included in *SpaCy* library.

As a result, we obtained fairly clean 197,606 articles from both TVP and TVN, consisting of 4,042,638 sentences and 44,528,641 tokens.

4. Methodology

In this Section all methods which were used to perform text classification task are briefly explained.

4.1. Dataset Preparation

Firstly, cleaned dataset has to undergo a few more processes before it is eventually used as an input to train classification models, namely:

- **Lemmatization** - *SpacyPL* handled this for Polish language, using a lemma dictionary imported from Morfeusz morphological analyzer[9].
- **Tokenization** - *nltk* Python library was used for this task.

As the website category groups were unevenly distributed, we decided to take 2,000 randomly selected articles both from TVN24 and TVP Info from the following four most numerous categories: WORLD, POLAND, BUSINESS and SPORTS. Eventually, we trained our models on a reduced subset of 16,000 online news. Dataset was then divided into two sets - training set which consists of 12,000 records and test set that has remaining 4,000 tuples.

4.2. Feature Extraction

Although classifying of text is not an easy task to be performed by computers, it can be done if input data is converted into a numerical representation.

- **Bag of Words (BoW)** - this method is considered to be simpler both computationally and conceptually than other methods. It is assumed that it could record higher performance scores on common used benchmarks of text (Qader et al., 2019).

[7] `https://github.com/Alir3z4/python-stop-words`
[8] `https://github.com/bieli/stopwords`
[9] `http://morfeusz.sgjp.pl/`

- **TF-IDF** - word vectors are also able to help with converting characters into a format that is processable by a computer (Vimal, 2020).

Both methods were implemented with the use of *Scikit-learn* library.

4.3. Algorithms

Based on the suggestions from previous works, we trained following four machine learning models:

- **Logistic regression** - commonly used for NLP classification tasks such as fake news detection (Yu et al., 2021)
- **Random forest** - recommended for news articles classification task, along with N-gram textual features (Liparas et al., 2014)
- **Support Vector Machine** - better results with high dimension data like large volumes of text, comparing with Neural Networks or Naive Bayes methods (Shahi and Pant, 2018)
- **Naive Bayes** - high accuracy in online news category classification task (Khine and Nwet, 2016)

Scikit-learn Python library allows us to use already built-in functions which perform all the calculations of the aforementioned supervised learning methods[10].

4.4. Model Quality Measurements

In order to check the performance of trained models, we calculated two of the standard metrics, namely **Accuracy** and **F1 Score** (Blagec et al., 2020). We also use *Scikit-learn* library for retrieval of these statistics.

5. Results

Having trained four different models with two possible types of feature extraction, we came with the following results as shown in Table 3.

	Feature Representation			
	BoW		TF-IDF	
Model	Accuracy	F-score	Accuracy	F-score
SVM	0.8668	0.8713	0.8598	0.8629
Random forest	0.8703	0.8798	**0.8745**	**0.8829**
Logistic Regression	0.8700	0.8729	0.7228	0.7790
Naive Bayes	0.8048	0.8013	0.7640	0.7627

Table 3: Performance measurements of models

The best results were achieved by random forest with TF-IDF vectorization method. Accuracy was 87.45% and F-score was equal to 88.29%. The worst results were obtained by logistic regression which also had features vectorized with TF-IDF method. Accuracy and F-score were equal 72.28% and 77.90% accordingly and these were the lowest scores among other models.

[10]`https://scikit-learn.org/stable/`

6. Discussion

TVN24 and TVP Info are two of the most watched news providers in Poland. Nonetheless, the way the information is conveyed by both is considered to be often much different from each other (Klepka, 2017), (Weglińska et al., 2021), (Batorowska et al., 2019). We believe it would be interesting to supplement social studies with machine learning techniques for measuring political bias. Another step to be considered is error analysis to check which words were most often confused when predicting the news outlet.
Our showcase study illustrated that there is still room for an improvement as others achieved over 90% accuracy scores in similar classification problems such as fake news detection (Alenezi and Alqenaei, 2021) or news categorization (Bracewell et al., 2009) as well as news topic analysis (Minaee et al., 2021).

7. Conclusions and Future Works

We introduced a collection of online news from two TV news broadcasters as the first step of building a full-fledged corpus containing modern, journalist-created and hopefully correct sample of Polish language. We showed that this corpus can be used for such a task like news outlet classification based on news article contents. Out of four trained models, random forest with TF-IDF vectorization achieved the highest accuracy and F-score metrics. Our next step is to compare these results with a few more prediction methods including Convolutional Neural Networks or Polbert language model (Kłeczek, 2020).
American news outlets have already been analyzed in terms of political polarization problem (D'Alonzo and Tegmark, 2021). Our dataset is unique and we hope our contribution will become a base for other tasks, such as news category prediction or also sentiment analysis in Polish language. With this corpus of distinctly different sources we also look forward to encouraging researchers to use it to study polarization of Polish society and to develop methods (e.g. for automatic summarization) freeing information of political biases and possible manipulation. In the future, we want to extend the dataset with articles coming from other online news outlets from the same period of time to study the full scale of political gradation of Polish media. It would allow us to focus on further research regarding political bias and detection of propaganda techniques.

8. Bibliographical References

Al Qadi, L., El Rifai, H., Obaid, S., and Elnagar, A. (2019). Arabic text classification of news articles using classical supervised classifiers. pages 1–6, 10.

Alenezi, M. and Alqenaei, Z. (2021). Machine learning in detecting covid-19 misinformation on twitter. *Future Internet*, 13:244, 09.

Batorowska, H., Wasiuta, O., and Klepka, R. (2019). *Media jako instrument wpływu informacyjnego i manipulacji społeczeństwem*. 02.

Blagec, K., Dorffner, G., Moradi, M., and Samwald, M. (2020). A critical analysis of metrics used for measuring progress in artificial intelligence. *CoRR*, abs/2008.02577.

Bracewell, D., Yan, J., Ren, F., and Kuroiwa, S. (2009). Category classification and topic discovery of japanese and english news articles. *Electr. Notes Theor. Comput. Sci.*, 225:51–65, 01.

Cisek, S. and Krakowska, M. (2018). The filter bubble: a perspective for information behaviour research, 10.

D'Alonzo, S. and Tegmark, M. (2021). Machine-learning media bias. *CoRR*, abs/2109.00024.

Garimella, K., Smith, T., Weiss, R., and West, R. (2021). Political polarization in online news consumption, 04.

Hladek, D., Stas, J., and Juhar, J. (2014). The Slovak categorized news corpus. In *Proceedings of the Ninth International Conference on Language Resources and Evaluation (LREC'14)*, pages 1705–1708, Reykjavik, Iceland, May. European Language Resources Association (ELRA).

Khine, A. H. and Nwet, K. T. (2016). Automatic myanmar news classification using naive bayes classifier.

Klepka, R., (2017). *Ewolucja Wiadomości TVP1: od medialnej stronniczości do propagandy politycznej?*, pages 244–253. 03.

Kłeczek, D. (2020). Polbert: Attacking Polish NLP tasks with transformers. In Maciej Ogrodniczuk et al., editors, *Proceedings of the PolEval 2020 Workshop*. Institute of Computer Science, Polish Academy of Sciences.

Liparas, D., HaCohen-Kerner, Y., Moumtzidou, A., Vrochidis, S., and Kompatsiaris, I. (2014). News articles classification using random forests and weighted multimodal features. volume 8849, 11.

Minaee, S., Kalchbrenner, N., Cambria, E., Nikzad, N., Chenaghlu, M., and Gao, J. (2021). Deep learning–based text classification: a comprehensive review. *ACM Computing Surveys (CSUR)*, 54(3):1–40.

Onyenwe, I. E., Onyedinma, E. G., Nwafor, C. A., and Agbata, O. (2021). Developing products update-alert system for e-commerce websites users using HTML data and web scraping technique. *CoRR*, abs/2109.00656.

Qader, W. A., Ameen, M. M., and Ahmed, B. I. (2019). An overview of bag of words; importance, implementation, applications, and challenges. In *2019 International Engineering Conference (IEC)*, pages 200–204.

Shahi, T. B. and Pant, A. K. (2018). Nepali news classification using naïve bayes, support vector machines and neural networks. In *2018 International Conference on Communication information and Computing Technology (ICCICT)*, pages 1–5.

Stein, A., Weerasinghe, J., Mancoridis, S., and Greenstadt, R. (2020). News article text classification and summary for authors and topics. pages 1–12, 11.

vanden Broucke, S. and Baesens, B., (2018). *Examples*, pages 197–298. Apress, Berkeley, CA.

Victoriano, J., Pulumbarit, J., and Lacatan, L. (2022). Data analysis of BulSU faculty research engagement based on Google Scholar data using web data scrapping technique. *International Journal of Computing Sciences Research*, 26:1–12, 01.

Vimal, B. (2020). Application of logistic regression in natural language processing. *International Journal of Engineering Research and*, V9, 06.

Weglińska, A., Szurmiński, , and Wasicka-Sroczyńska, M. (2021). Politicization as a factor of shaping news in the public service media : A case study on public television in poland polityzacja jako czynnik w kształtowaniu przekazu medialnego w tvp sa - studium przypadku. *Athenaeum Polskie Studia Politologiczne*, 72:29–51, 12.

Yu, P., Cui, V., and Guan, J. (2021). Text classification by using natural language processing. *Journal of Physics: Conference Series*, 1802:042010, 03.

Proceedings of the First Workshop on Natural Language Processing for Political Sciences (PoliticalNLP), pages 91–97
Marseille, 24 June 2022

Annotation of expressive dimensions on a multimodal French corpus of political interviews

Jules Cauzinille, Marc Evrard, Nikita Kiselov, Albert Rilliard
Université Paris-Saclay, CNRS, Laboratoire Interdisciplinaire des Sciences du Numérique (LISN)
Campus universitaire – bat. 507 Rue du Belvedère – F-91405 Orsay cedex
{jules.cauzinille, marc.evrard, nikita.kiselov, albert.rilliard}@lisn.upsaclay.fr

Abstract

We present a French corpus of political interviews labeled at the utterance level according to expressive dimensions such as Arousal. This corpus consists of 7.5 hours of high-quality audio-visual recordings with transcription. At the time of this publication, 1 hour of speech was segmented into short utterances, each manually annotated in Arousal. Our segmentation approach differs from similar corpora and allows us to perform an automatic Arousal prediction baseline by building a speech-based classification model. Although this paper focuses on the acoustic expression of Arousal, it paves the way for future work on conflictual and hostile expression recognition as well as multimodal architectures.

Keywords: expressive speech, affective computing, automatic prediction of Arousal, political speech processing

1. Introduction

This paper presents a new corpus of French political interviews annotated on expressive dimensions. We conducted a primary annotation on a subset of a corpus consisting of 7.5 hours of automatically transcribed audio-visual recordings of French broadcast programs. Arousal levels were manually annotated on speech segments. A baseline models for speech-based automatic Arousal prediction is also proposed.

In this paper, we mainly focus on defining annotation guidelines, studying our preliminary labeling, and setting the future work that will be carried out on the complete corpus. We first present the specific characteristics of this political corpus and make a literature review on similar projects. We then describe the methodology of our preliminary annotation and baseline model in Section 2 and showcase the first results in Section 3. In Section 4, we finally discuss these results and their implications for future work.

1.1. Political Scope and Context

The specific nature of political talks, interviews, and speeches makes them an appealing topic for researchers in affective computing and expressive speech processing. Such corpora provide the advantages of studio-quality audio while being expressively diverse and overcoming the limitations of read and acted speech. Professional speakers, such as politicians, produce a particular type of speech that could be described as semi-spontaneous, in the sense that displayed expressive behaviors are part of the politician's communication strategies without being completely scripted and enacted.

This political context also presents a limited variety of expressions. Some projects focus on conflictual and hostile discourse (Kouklia, 2019), arguing that it is the most frequent expressive style in political debates, thus offering a prolific ground for the study of affective expressivity linked to controlled aggression, cold anger, dispute, and hostility.

In this work, we focus on a dimensional model of expressivity, which is inspired by Russel's psychological *circumplex* model of affect (Posner et al., 2005) and Barrett's theory of *constructed emotion* (Barrett, 2016), by Gussenhoven's biological codes (Frequency and Effort codes) (Gussenhoven, 2004), and by the dimensional description of affective meaning proposed by Osgood (Osgood et al., 1975). Although the final goal of this project would be the study of conflicting expressive behaviors in spoken interactions, here we present a preliminary annotation of Arousal, seen as the amount of energy physically displayed in speech and movement. Valence labeling was left for future work as many difficulties arose during the annotation of this dimension in this political context.

1.2. Previous Work

Although our corpus was annotated with a focus on expressive labeling, it resembles datasets belonging to the affective computing domain in general. The majority of such resources are in English, with widely cited affective corpora such as IEMOCAP (Busso et al., 2008) and RAVDESS (Livingstone and Russo, 2018)—both multimodal, acted, and labeled with categorical emotions. Closer to our work would be the large MSP-Podcast dataset (Lotfian and Busso, 2019) based on semi-spontaneous speech from radio shows and podcasts. On top of categorical emotion labels, it presents annotations along the Arousal and Valence dimensions. For French, some of the most used and cited affective corpora are RECOLA (Ringeval et al., 2013) and AlloSat (Macary et al., 2020). RECOLA is a continuously annotated corpus of spontaneous speech with Valence and Arousal labeling for 46 speakers. It gives an insight into the difficulties and limitations of such affective annotations. A major difference between our corpus and RECOLA is its focus on an affective definition of Arousal and Valence compared to our expressive point of view. We rely on a definition of Arousal based on speech production and the concept of vocal effort that may be linked to Gussenhoven's *Effort Code* (Gussenhoven, 2004), or Liénard's definition of vocal effort (Liénard, 2019). Another difference is the context of the spoken interactions, as RECOLA consists of video conference recordings of individuals performing collaborative tasks, while we target broadcast political interviews. RECOLA also proposes a continuous annotation framework while we performed our annotations on discrete segments. We expect that considering entire speech segments allows for a more consistent labeling process, as such annotations are complex and may require several passes over a segment for the annotator to make a decision. More information about the segmentation process can be found in Section 2.

A notable work on French political expressive speech was carried out by Kouklia (Kouklia, 2019) on debates recorded in a French town hall in 2013. The author presented an extensive survey of affective expression in a political context with prosodic analyses carried out on a corpus of annotated speech. It showed the importance of studying affective expressions in political speech for many research areas beyond affective computing and speech processing, while stressing the number of perspectives opened up by the annotation of such data.

2. Methods

2.1. Annotation Framework

The complete corpus consists of 7.5 hours of political interviews from two French television channels: *BFM TV* and *France 2*. It includes 30 different speakers—and 4 interviewers—for an average of 20 minutes per interview for *BFM TV* and 8 minutes for *France 2*. These sequences contain video, studio-quality audio, an automatic transcription aligned at the word-level, and manually annotated speech turns and overlaps. We present an annotation on a subset of the whole corpus: 5 minutes extracts from 12 different interviews for a total of 1 hour. This work focuses on the Arousal dimension although an attempt was made at annotating Valence.

The annotation was carried out with the *PRAAT* and *ELAN* software programs. *PRAAT* allowed speeding up the segmentation task using only the audio and its transcription, while *ELAN* allowed for the use of visual information to perform a genuinely multimodal expressive annotation.

2.1.1. Segmentation

Most available datasets labeled on similar dimensions, such as RECOLA (Ringeval et al., 2013), were annotated in a time-continuous way, resulting in evolving Arousal and Valence trends spanning entire sound files. In other datasets, such as in Kouklia (2019), single labels will be assigned to speech utterances that can often be quite long, possibly yielding multiple emotional and expressive states within a single annotated segment.

In this regard, we first tried to settle on a syntactic segmentation. Because, contrary to written text, speech transcriptions cannot generally be segmented into sentence-like units with clear punctuation boundaries (Ostendorf et al., 2008), we identified short syntactic units consisting of several words that could be isolated as meaningful syntagms, usually separated by discourse markers or pauses.

Unfortunately, this approach tends to produce segments of various sizes, which is unpractical both for the annotation process and for the implementation of computational models.

With this in mind, we adapted our segmentation approach by following three criteria: a boundary is added either when the annotator perceives a significant expressive variation, when a semantically meaningful unit can be found, or when the segment exceeds a fixed threshold. We found that a duration of about 3 seconds was optimum for the annotation task (resulting in a median of 2.14 seconds per segment).

2.1.2. Expressive Dimensions

As previously said, we adopted Arousal and Valence dimensions as the main variables of vocal expression. Our definition is inspired by studies emphasizing the role of Arousal in the vocal expression of emotions (Goudbeek and Scherer, 2010), and the importance of vocal effort as a characteristic of the voice (Liénard, 2019; Titze and Sundberg, 1992). We adapted this, as well as previously cited psychological models, to serve the concept of Arousal as a vocal feature. In this respect, it should be seen as the degree of vocal effort and energy displayed by a speaker along a given utterance. It is cued at different levels within speech: on syllable-sized segments, short utterances (which correspond to our approach), or longer units of discourse. We broadened Rilliard et al. (2018)'s description of Arousal on syllable-sized units to our longer segments. In this perspective, low Arousal is characterized by a slow speech rate, low intensity, and steady fundamental frequency due to slower vibration of the vocal folds. Low Arousal may also lead to specific voice qualities such as creaky and breathy voices. The high energy Arousal, on the contrary, is cued by greater variability in speech rate and f_0, large f_0 span, high intensity levels, and an increased overall vocal effort. Of course, most of these vocal events may not be directly linked to an Arousal level, which is instead signaled by a combination of several features. For instance, although they can be seen as typical cues of Arousal, speech rate and pause frequency or duration may fail to show a strict correlation with it, especially in the context of political speech (Madureira and de Camargo, 2019; Kouklia, 2019).

After experimenting with different options for the description of levels of Arousal, we settled on a 7-level Likert scale (Joshi et al., 2015) from -3 to 3, although both minimal values (-3 and -2) were never encountered in our annotation process. With neutrally aroused speech—0 in such a scale—usually being the minimally aroused expressive style in a political context, levels corresponding to truly sleepy, extremely depressed, and underactivated speech are, as expected, barely used in our annotation. Political expression is indeed typically characterized by positive Arousal, as shown by Vázquez et al. (2019). We still kept a 7-level scale, including negative Arousal, for better generalization of our annotation method.

A remaining question regarding this scale is to decide on the neutral Arousal level for each speaker, as some of them tend to be more or less active when they speak with seemingly neutral expressivity. We answered this problem by asking annotators to base their labels on a common neutral Arousal value of 0 (which would correspond to a "typical" speaker) and annotate speakers showing higher than normal neutral speech styles with corresponding higher levels. This common scale applies to every speaker and allows building computational models without the additional difficulty of predicting speaker-dependent labels.

As we previously mentioned, we attempted to annotate vocal Valence. Unfortunately, compared to the expression of Arousal, Valence is defined by a very complex set of acoustic features and is considered, as shown by Belyk and Brown (2014), to be highly dependent on emotional contexts, which are not the main focus of our annotation. It is also a more variable dimension, as for its acoustic characteristics (Goudbeek and Scherer, 2010), typically dependent on Arousal. In addition to that, the political context of our corpus makes Valence labeling particularly difficult to grasp (Vázquez et al., 2019). We still conducted a preliminary Valence annotation to get an idea of the statistical distribution of values over part of the corpus.

2.2. Baseline Models

Based on our annotations, we built two baseline models for automatic vocal Arousal classification. The first consists in using the self-supervised learning framework wav2vec 2.0 (Baevski et al., 2020) for feature extraction (encoding each segment of speech into a fixed size matrix embedding). A subsequent Gated Recurrent Unit (GRU) architecture was then trained on top of these representations to predict the arousal values.

The second consists in a Convolutional Neural Network (CNN) trained on top of Mel-Frequency Cepstral Coefficients (MFCC) representations of each segment. This model serves as a comparison with the pre-trained approach and allows us to test if the corpus contains enough information to train a simple neural network on spectral features.

2.2.1. Wav2vec-Based Models

The model is based on pre-trained wav2vec 2.0 feature extraction from the multilingual *facebook/wav2vec2-large-xlsr-53* (Conneau et al., 2020). We also tested a french version, *LeBenchmark/wav2vec2-FR-1K-large* (Evain et al., 2021), which showed significantly lower performances. The wav2vec 2.0 representations were extracted with the *Huggingface* module and all models are built with *Pytorch*. All feature matrices were trimmed and zero-padded to obtain a segment size of 3 seconds, corresponding to embeddings of size (150×1024), with 50 wav2vec features of size 1024 for each second. The best performing model was a GRU trained on these sets of features. It is built with one layer, a hidden size of 128, sigmoid activation, and 10% dropout.

2.2.2. MFCC-Based Model

A set of 13 MFCCs was extracted for each segment with the *Librosa* package. The segments were padded or trimmed to be 120 frames long (40 per second for 3 seconds segments). They were subsequently processed by a CNN with three 2D convolutional layers and three linear layers.

The best-performing CNN's architecture and hyperparameters were inspired by models found in the literature, such as Zhao et al. (2019), and through empirical testing.

Each layer consists in a convolution kernel of size (3×3) with a ReLU activation function and, respectively, 64 and 128 filters. Two (2×2) max-pooling layers are added after each convolution. Three fully connected linear layers are then applied with 30% dropout.

3. Results

3.1. Inter-Annotator Agreement

Inter-annotator agreement may be assessed in different ways for expressive dimensions labeling. Considering a strict correspondence of each segment with a defined *class* is not coherent with the *degrees* of an Arousal scale, and the distance between these degrees should be taken into account when measuring the annotator's agreement.

Although more than two annotators would be required to build a robust annotation, our preliminary labeling shows promising results when agreement is tested through the quadratic-weighted Kappa (Artstein and Poesio, 2008) metrics: $\kappa_w = 0.546$. This value was obtained by concatenating the annotations of all interviews. The resulting Kappa score may be considered as a *moderate* agreement.

3.2. Annotation and Segmentation Distribution

A first step in investigating our preliminary corpus is to study the distribution of annotated values in order to describe Arousal dynamics. The reported values are the average of those given by both annotators. Over the whole dataset, Arousal tends to be positive, with an average of 0.7 (on the $-3/+3$ scale) for the 12 interviews. As expected in the context of political speech (Vázquez et al., 2019; Kouklia, 2019), Arousal distribution is dominated by positive values: 51.2% of segments showed an Arousal between 0 and 1, 41.4% between 1 and 2, and only 5.3% from 2 onward. Negative values are relatively rare as only 2.1% of the data was labeled below 0, and no segments were given a value below −1. The global distribution of the Arousal levels can be seen in Table 1 and Fig. 1. Violin plots for each interview are shown in Fig. 2.

Arousal interval	Count	Percentage
$[-1.25, -0.75)$	3	0.18%
$[-0.75, -0.25)$	33	1.94%
$[-0.25, 0.25)$	465	27.37%
$[0.25, 0.75)$	408	24.01%
$[0.75, 1.25)$	503	29.61%
$[1.25, 1.75)$	202	11.89%
$[1.75, 2.25)$	70	4.12%
$[2.25, 2.75]$	15	0.88%

Table 1: Distribution of Arousal levels for all segments in the dataset. Arousal values are the average of those given by both annotators.

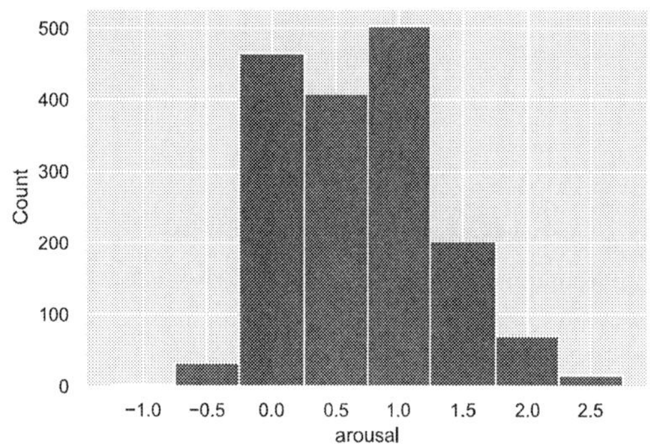

Figure 1: Distribution of Arousal levels for all segments in the dataset. Arousal values are the average of those given by both annotators.

Regarding the segmentation process, the median segment length is 1.81 seconds (see Fig. 3), and 97% of them are under the 3 seconds threshold that we defined as the upper bound.

3.3. Baseline Results

The performance scores obtained by our two models can be seen in Table 2. They were computed on the entire annotated dataset through a 12-folds cross-validation procedure (each fold containing 11 interviews for the training set and 1 for the test set). This allowed us to obtain a representative performance and to limit the bias implied by the small size of the corpus, as testing the models on different interviews may yield different results.

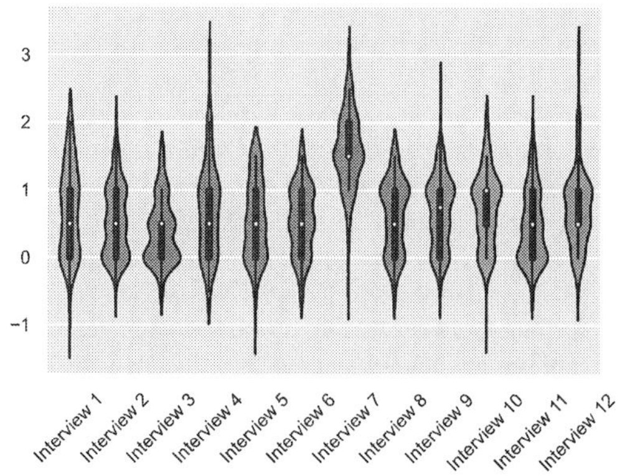

Figure 2: Violin plots of Arousal levels for segments in the 12 interviews. Arousal values are the average of those given by both annotators.

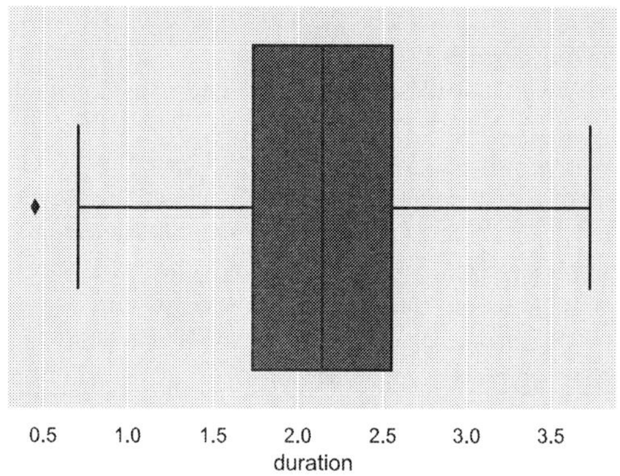

Figure 3: Distribution of segments lengths in seconds.

In addition to the mean squared error (MSE) that was used as a loss function for the training process, which yielded better results than L1 loss, we computed traditional regression metrics such as root mean square error (RMSE) and mean absolute error (MAE).

Model	RMSE	MSE	MAE
MFCCs+CNN	0.555	0.322	0.464
	(0.064)	(0.081)	(0.053)
Wav2vec+GRU	0.577	0.336	0.461
	(0.062)	(0.073)	(0.051)

Table 2: Mean results for automatic Arousal prediction on the 12-folds cross-validation, with the standard deviation in brackets.

4. Discussion

The general trend of the annotation is quite similar between both annotators, with the majority of differences rarely exceeding one degree on the scale, as shown by shaded area heights in Fig. 6 and 7. The obvious solution to merge both annotations was to compute their average. In fact, if a segment is labeled higher by one annotator and lower by another, then the corresponding level of Arousal is most certainly ambiguous and should be averaged to an intermediary level. This observation also raises the important question of soft-labeling that may be applied to this type of annotation. The idea would be to take into account a certainty degree on each annotation value in order to address the problem of variability in subjective annotations. We leave these considerations for future work.

With regard to the distribution of Arousal and Valence labels, we observed good correspondence with our first intuition, as well as previous work carried out by (Vázquez et al., 2019; Kouklia, 2019). Expressive political speech shows a tendency to express conflict and hostility, denoted by these generally positive values of Arousal and negative values of Valence. In addition to these metrics, it is also interesting to compare speakers' behaviors, keeping in mind that a 5 minutes annotation is not perfectly representative of a one's expressive style. As shown in Fig. 4 and 5., interviews considered to be more conflictual by the annotators exhibit significantly different distributions when compared to the more neutral ones.

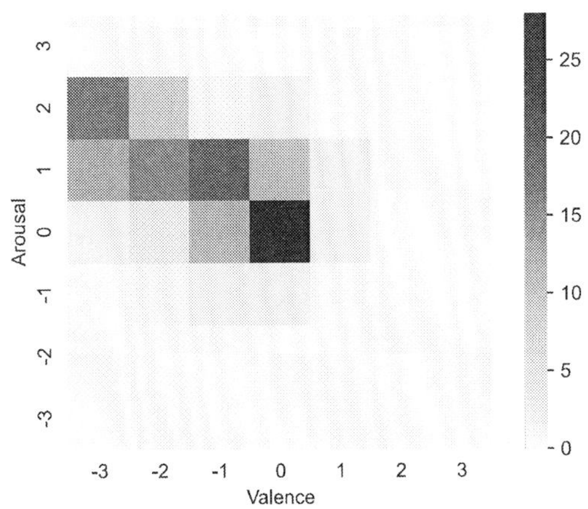

Figure 4: Heatmap of the Arousal-Valence distribution for a "conflictual" interview (Interview 7).

Finally, one can observe the variation of Arousal levels throughout a given extract, as in Fig. 6 and 7.

Regarding the automatic prediction of Arousal levels from speech, the obtained results showed that convergence is possible but that more work needs to be carried out on a variety of architectures to handle the task thoroughly. Both the Wav2vec transfer learning approach

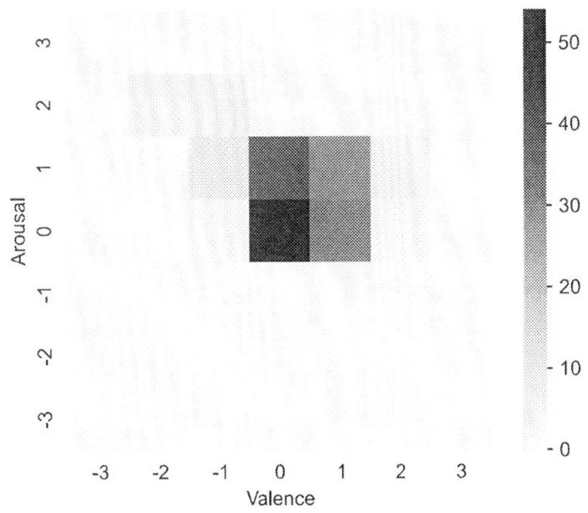

Figure 5: Heatmap of the Arousal-Valence distribution for a "neutral" interview (Interview 4).

and the MFCC-based CNN showed promising performances given the scarcity of data on which they were trained. Fig. 8 shows the similar tendencies of predictions and labels in one of the interviews.

Although very different in their architecture and feature extraction process, both models exhibit very similar performances (see Table 2), with differences within the margin of error. This tends to confirm that we may have reached an upper limit on the dataset in its current state.

5. Conclusion

In this work, we discussed the challenge of creating a stable and coherent annotation framework for political interviews. We have seen that dimensional labels, such as the amount of expressed Arousal, are well suited for labeling political speech expressivity and can lead to future annotation and implementation of more specific speech-based conflict recognition models. We also argued that a discrete approach with segmented extracts of speech, each labeled on Arousal, is an effective way to ease the annotation process and allow for efficient training of computational models.

We presented a preliminary corpus annotated on the Arousal dimension for 12 speakers and conducted several statistical experiments to describe the annotation distribution. Finally, we proposed two regression models, exploiting wav2vec 2.0 feature extraction and MFCC-based architectures as a first baseline for automatic Arousal prediction.

After validating our annotation process, we plan on performing it on the entirety of the 7.5-hour corpus with a higher number of participants. The complete annotation would also benefit from an extended study of the Valence dimension and a more precise definition of its annotation. It will also include a new label, dependent on the ones we already discussed, exploring conflict

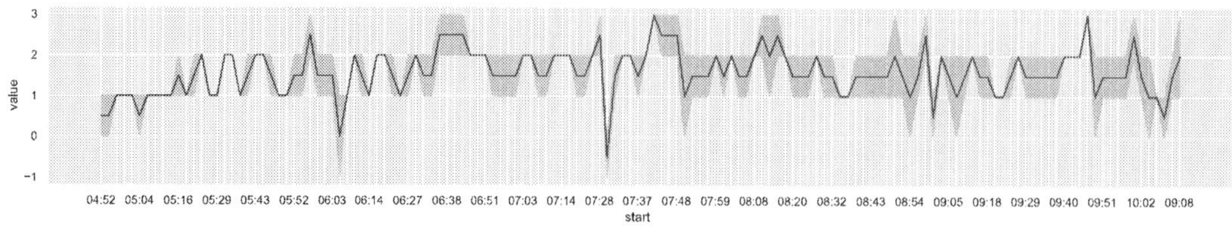

Figure 6: Averaged Arousal from both annotators for a typical "conflictual" interview (Interview 7). The shaded area shows the differences between values chosen by the annotators.

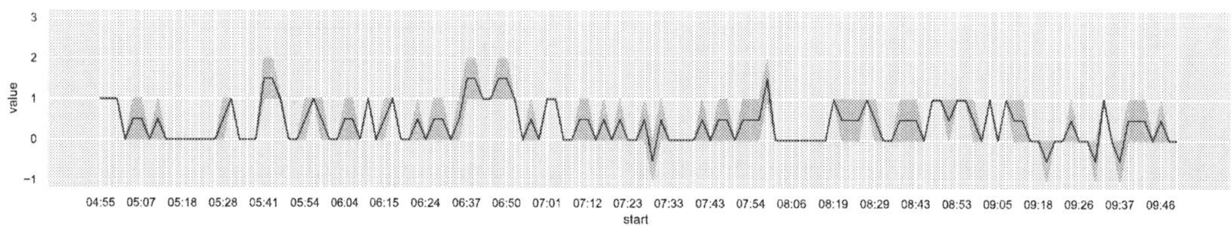

Figure 7: Averaged Arousal from both annotators for a typical "neutral" interview (Interview 3). The shaded area shows the differences between values chosen by the annotators.

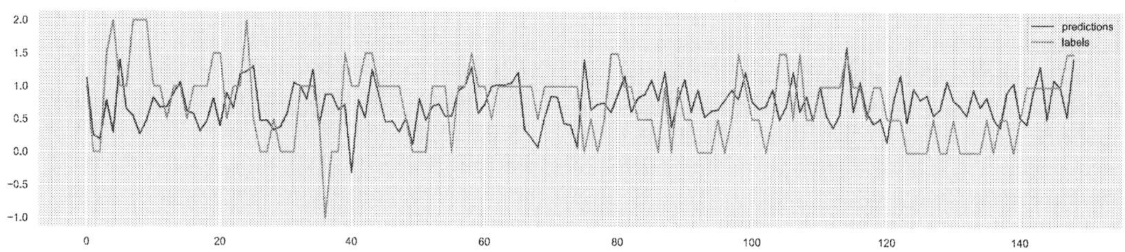

Figure 8: Visual representation of predictions and labels for the MFCC-based CNN (Interview 10).

versus complicity expression or the degree of approval and hostility between speakers.

6. Acknowledgments

This research was supported by the DATAIA/MSH Paris-Saclay "Excellence" grant "OTELO", and was part of a cooperation of the CESSP (Paris Panthéon-Sorbonne University, CNRS), the Institut national de l'audiovisuel (INA), and the LISN (Université Paris-Saclay, CNRS) through the OOPAIP project under the DIM STCN (Ile de France). The corpus was initially built with the OKAPI platform developed by INA, thanks to the work of Steffen Lalande and Abdelkrim Beloued.

7. Bibliographical References

Artstein, R. and Poesio, M. (2008). Inter-coder agreement for computational linguistics. *Computational linguistics*, 34(4):555–596.

Baevski, A., Zhou, Y., Mohamed, A., and Auli, M. (2020). wav2vec 2.0: A framework for self-supervised learning of speech representations. *Advances in Neural Information Processing Systems*, 33:12449–12460.

Barrett, L. F. (2016). The theory of constructed emotion: an active inference account of interoception and categorization. *Social Cognitive and Affective Neuroscience*, 12(1):1–23, 10.

Belyk, M. and Brown, S. (2014). The acoustic correlates of valence depend on emotion family. *Journal of Voice*, 28(4):523.e9–523.e18.

Busso, C., Bulut, M., Lee, C.-C., Kazemzadeh, A., Mower Provost, E., Kim, S., Chang, J., Lee, S., and Narayanan, S. (2008). Iemocap: Interactive emotional dyadic motion capture database. *Language Resources and Evaluation*, 42:335–359, 12.

Conneau, A., Baevski, A., Collobert, R., Mohamed, A., and Auli, M. (2020). Unsupervised cross-lingual representation learning for speech recognition. *CoRR*, abs/2006.13979.

Evain, S., Nguyen, H., Le, H., Boito, M. Z., Mdhaffar, S., Alisamir, S., Tong, Z., Tomashenko, N., Dinarelli, M., Parcollet, T., et al. (2021). Lebenchmark: A reproducible framework for assessing self-supervised representation learning from speech. In *INTERSPEECH*.

Goudbeek, M. and Scherer, K. (2010). Beyond arousal: Valence and potency/control cues in the vocal expression of emotion. *The Journal of the Acoustical Society of America*, 128:1322–36, 09.

Gussenhoven, C. (2004). *The Phonology of Tone and Intonation*. Cambridge University Press, 07.

Joshi, A., Kale, S., Chandel, S., and Pal, D. K. (2015). Likert scale: Explored and explained. *British journal of applied science & technology*, 7(4):396.

Kouklia, C. (2019). *Dominance, hostilité et expressivié vocale dans le débat politique: étude perceptive et acoustique du conseil municipal de Montreuil (93100)*. Ph.D. thesis, Université Sorbonne Paris Cité.

Liénard, J.-S. (2019). Quantifying vocal effort from the shape of the one-third octave long-term-average spectrum of speech. *The Journal of the Acoustical Society of America*, 146(4):EL369–EL375, October.

Livingstone, S. and Russo, F. (2018). The ryerson audio-visual database of emotional speech and song (ravdess): A dynamic, multimodal set of facial and vocal expressions in north american english. *PLOS ONE*, 13:e0196391, 05.

Lotfian, R. and Busso, C. (2019). Building naturalistic emotionally balanced speech corpus by retrieving emotional speech from existing podcast recordings. *IEEE Transactions on Affective Computing*, 10(4):471–483, October-December.

Macary, M., Tahon, M., Estève, Y., and Rousseau, A. (2020). AlloSat: A New Call Center French Corpus for Satisfaction and Frustration Analysis. In *Language Resources and Evaluation Conference, LREC 2020*, Marseille, France, May.

Madureira, S. and de Camargo, Z. A. (2019). Exploring sound symbolism in the investigation of speech expressivity. *International Speech Communication Association*, page 105.

Osgood, C. E., May, W. S., and Miron, M. S. (1975). *Cross-Cultural Universals of Affective Meaning*. University of Illinois Press, Baltimore, MD, June.

Ostendorf, M., Favre, B., Grishman, R., Hakkani-Tur, D., Harper, M., Hillard, D., Hirschberg, J., Ji, H., Kahn, J., Liu, Y., Maskey, S., Matusov, E., Ney, H., Rosenberg, A., Shriberg, E., Wang, W., and Woofers, C. (2008). Speech segmentation and spoken document processing. *Signal Processing Magazine, IEEE*, 25:59 – 69, 06.

Posner, J., Russell, J., and Peterson, B. (2005). The circumplex model of affect: An integrative approach to affective neuroscience, cognitive development, and psychopathology. *Development and psychopathology*, 17:715–34, 02.

Rilliard, A., d'Alessandro, C., and Evrard, M. (2018). Paradigmatic variation of vowels in expressive speech: Acoustic description and dimensional analysis. *The Journal of the Acoustical Society of America*, 143(1):109–122.

Ringeval, F., Sonderegger, A., Sauer, J., and Lalanne, D. (2013). Introducing the recola multimodal corpus of remote collaborative and affective interactions. In *2013 10th IEEE International Conference and Workshops on Automatic Face and Gesture Recognition, FG 2013*, pages 1–8, 04.

Titze, I. R. and Sundberg, J. (1992). Vocal intensity in speakers and singers. *The Journal of the Acoustical Society of America*, 91(5):2936–2946, May.

Vázquez, M. d., Justo, R., Zorrilla, A. L., and Torres, M. I. (2019). Can spontaneous emotions be detected from speech on tv political debates? In *10th IEEE International Conference on Cognitive Infocommunications*, page 289.

Zhao, J., Mao, X., and Chen, L. (2019). Speech emotion recognition using deep 1d & 2d cnn lstm networks. *Biomedical signal processing and control*, 47:312–323.

Proceedings of the First Workshop on Natural Language Processing for Political Sciences (PoliticalNLP), pages 98–103
Marseille, 24 June 2022

TransCasm: A Bilingual Corpus of Sarcastic Tweets

Desline Simon[2], Sheila Castilho[2], Pintu Lohar[2] and Haithem Afli[1]
ADAPT Centre
[1]Department of Computer Sciences, Munster Technological University, Cork, Ireland
[2]School of Computing, Dublin City University, Dublin, Ireland
{firstname.lastname}@adaptcentre.ie

Abstract

Sarcasm is extensively used in User Generated Content (UGC) in order to express one's discontent, especially through blogs, forums, or social media such as Twitter. Several works have attempted to detect and analyse sarcasm in UGC. However, the lack of freely available corpora in this field makes the task even more difficult. In this work, we present "TransCasm" corpus, a parallel corpus of sarcastic tweets translated from English into French along with their non-sarcastic representations. To build the bilingual corpus of sarcasm, we select the "SIGN" corpus, a monolingual data set of sarcastic tweets and their non-sarcastic interpretations, created by (Peled and Reichart, 2017). We propose to define linguistic guidelines for developing "TransCasm" which is the first ever bilingual corpus of sarcastic tweets. In addition, we utilise "TransCasm" for building a binary *sarcasm* classifier in order to identify whether a tweet is sarcastic or not. Our experiment reveals that the *sarcasm* classifier achieves 61% accuracy on detecting *sarcasm* in tweets. "TransCasm" is now freely available online and is ready to be explored for further research.

Keywords: Sarcasm, parallel corpus, translation

1. Introduction

Sarcasm is an extremely ambiguous form of wit, extremely hard to analyse for a machine but as well as for the average human reader. Sarcasm is even harder to be analysed in written form, as the tone of voice (pitch, heavy stress), gestures or facial clues (hand movements, rolling the eyes, etc.) which are important to detect sarcasm in spoken form, cannot be considered in textual communication. Sarcasm is an indirect way to communicate negation using a contradiction between a sentiment and a situation. It is usually used to express the opposite of one truly wants to say. In fact, its structure very often consists of a contrast between positive or intensified sentiment words to convey a negative feeling - a very strong one most of the time - such as insult, irritation, hostility, disagreement, mockery, etc. Sarcasm is a particular form of irony, but with the intention and consciousness not to be explicit to express a negative feeling or aggressive attitude (acrimony, bitterness). In the example "I love being ignored", a very positive word *love* is used in a negative context *being ignored.* The particular structure of a positive word followed by a negative situation is often a strong indicator of sarcasm.

Currently, sarcasm is extensively used in UGC in order to express one's discontent, especially through blogs, forums, or social media such as Twitter. The importance and need to detect sarcasm is real. It is attracting interest in many application domains. In fact, BBC reported[1] on January 5th, 2014 that the US Secret Service is seeking a Twitter sarcasm detector. The motivation of our present work comes from the challenges in processing sarcastic tweets. We develop a first ever corpus of bilingual sarcastic tweets for the English–French pair. On top of it, we also build a binary sarcasm classifier using the corpus in order to mitigate the difficulties in detecting sarcastic tweets.

[1]https://www.bbc.com/news/technology-27711109

2. Related work

Twitter sentiment analysis has attracted many researchers during the last few years (Agarwal et al., 2011; Zimbra et al., 2018; Branz and Brockmann, 2018). Parallel twitter corpus has also been developed for Twitter sentiment translation (Afli et al., 2017; Lohar et al., 2017). The sarcasm phenomena has been well-studied in linguistics, psychology and cognitive science (González-Ibáñez et al., 2011; Gibbs, 1986). But in the natural language processing (NLP) literature, automatic detection of sarcasm is considered a difficult problem (Pang and Lee, 2008) and has been addressed in several works. Bouazizi and Ohtsuki (2015); Reyes and Rosso (2012) use sarcasm detection to enhance the efficiency of after-sales services and consumer assistance through understanding the intentions and real opinions of customers when browsing their feedback or complaints.

Inspired by the advances on sentiment analysis (SA) (O'Connor et al., 2010) and figurative language processing research (Reyes et al., 2012), the field of sarcasm detection has started to benefit from using SA (Ghosh et al., 2015). To the best of our knowledge, no parallel corpus of sarcastic tweets is available till date. In this work, we propose to define linguistic guidelines for building a first ever bilingual corpus of sarcastic tweets, based on the extension of the unique corpora created by Peled and Reichart (2017). In addition, we train a sarcasm classifier using this corpus in order to detect whether a tweet is sarcastic or not. We conduct initial experiment on sarcasm detection and measure its performance.

3. Method

3.1. SIGN Corpus

To build the bilingual corpus of sarcasm, we have selected the SIGN corpus, a monolingual data set of sarcastic tweets and their non-sarcastic interpretations. The SIGN corpus was created by Peled and Reichart (2017) and consists of $3,000$ sarcastic tweets containing text only, where the average sarcastic tweet length is 13.87 utterances and the vocabulary size is $8,788$ unique words. The authors used Twitter API[2], and collected tweets with the hashtag *#sarcasm* from January 2016 to June 2016. Following the collection, the authors asked five human judges to write honest, non-sarcastic interpretations of those tweets to capture the original meaning behind them. Therefore, a monolingual parallel corpus was created in which sarcastic English tweets were translated into non-sarcastic English. For example, a sentence "How I love Mondays. #sarcasm" would generate interpretations such as "how I hate Mondays' or "I really hate Mondays". Table 1 shows examples of sarcastic tweets and their interpretations.

Quite often, the human judges would interpret the sarcastic tweets in the same manner, getting the same meaning behind the sarcasm, but at times, the interpretation would greatly differ from each other, which is a strong indicator that sarcasm is extremely complex to analyse and interpret, even for humans. As the non-sarcastic interpretations composed for each tweet might help the task of sentiment analysis - since those honest interpretations capture the meaning behind the original sarcastic utterances - we also decided to translate a few of those interpretations. However, due to time constraints, no more than three interpretation per tweets were translated. The decision on what interpretation to translate depended on the vocabulary encountered, and the overall relevance of those interpretations.

3.2. Creating the TransCasm Parallel Corpus

The corpus is being translated from English into French with the help of MateCat[3] , a web-based open source tool. Figure 1 shows the translation set-up. In the corpus, the same tweet is presented each time their interpretations are presented. Both the original and the interpretations are separated by a comma. As the SIGN corpus is normalised, that is, the hashtag (#sarcasm), capital letters and all punctuations of any kind are cleaned, the interpretation of the tweets was challenging, and in consequence, their translation. The topics in the SIGN corpus are greatly eclectic considering that the method to extract them was only based on the query #sarcasm. The topics we were able to identify while translating include:

- weather

  e.g.1 ' really looking forward to more rain today', " i'm hoping that there won t be more rain today"

  e.g.2 ' 96 degrees one of the great benefits of living in california', ' 96 degrees california is too hot for me'

- traffic and transport

  e.g.1 ' delays on the piccadilly line yayyyyyyy', ' oh no there are delays on the piccadilly line'

  e.g.2 ' ah yes i love replacing a tire at 9 in the morning', ' i hate replacing tires especially early in the day'

- work

  e.g.1 ' almost lunchtime i get a half hour away from this paradise', ' almost lunchtime i get a half hour close far this terrible workplace'

  e.g.2 " don't you just love when people takes the credit for something you did ? yeah ? me too", ' i hate people taking credit for something i did'

- school

  e.g.1 ' finals are so nice like omg best thing ever to happen to my life like love studying', ' i hate studying for the final exams'

  e.g.2 " making flash cards for my exams tomorrow i'm having fun", ' i am not enjoying making these flash cards for my exams tomorrow'

  e.g.3 " it's teacher appreciation week and the lovefest is in full swing at my school", " it's teacher appreciation week but they are not getting any love at my school"

- health

  e.g.1 ' dentists make money off of people with bad teeth so should we really trust the toothpaste they recommend ?', " we shouldn't trust dentist"

  e.g.2 ' a nice long wait in the doctors office should calm my nerves', ' waiting at the doctor office will stress me out'

- sports (especially American football, baseball, ice hockey and football (soccer))

  e.g.1 ' did bartolo colon hit a hr tonight ? i didnt see it mentioned anywhere on twitter ?', ' did bartolo colon hit a hr tonight ? it was mentioned everywhere on twitter'

  e.g.2 ' terry got sent off ? maybe hiddink needs to have more control over his players', ' hiddink already has a lot of control over his players'

  e.g.3 " cavs aren't getting any calls this is new", " cavs aren't getting any calls as usual"

[2]https://dev.twitter.com

[3]https://www.matecat.com

Sarcastic Tweets	Honest Interpretations
What a great way to end my night #sarcasm	1. Such a bad ending to my night 2. Oh what a great way to ruin my night 3. What a horrible way to end a night 4. Not a good way to end a night 5. Well that wasn't the night I was hoping for
Staying up till 2 : 30 was a brilliant idea, very productive #sarcasm	1. Bad idea staying up late, not very productive 2. It was not smart or productive for me to stay up so late 3. Staying up till 2 : 30 was not a brilliant idea 4. I need to go to bed on time 5. Staying up till 2 : 30 was completely useless

Table 1: Example of two sarcastic tweets augmented by five non-sarcastic interpretations

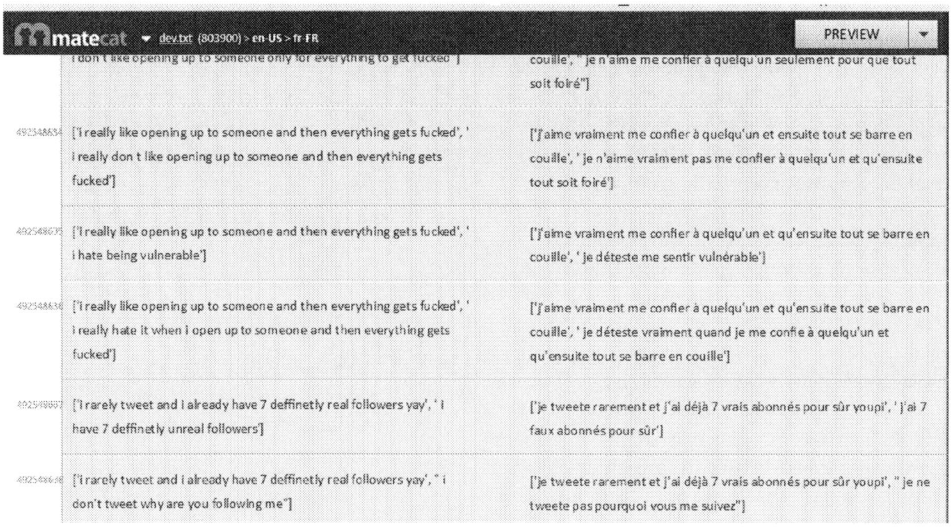

Figure 1: Translation process using the Matecat tool

- politics (especially the American Republican Party and the then candidate Donald Trump)

  e.g.1 ' now trump is bringing up bill clinton 90 s affairs because we all know there are no current day pressing matters to focus on', ' there are important matters to focus on instead of bringing up affairs of bill clinton from the 1990 s'

  e.g.2 " so trump won the republican nominee so that's that good job america", " so trump won the republican nominee so that's that shameful job america"

  e.g.3 ' obviously a well prepared speech by trump', ' obviously a poorly prepared speech by trump'

- social relationships (love, friends, family and co-workers)

  e.g.1 ' being left out is such an amazing feeling', ' being left out is such a painful feeling'

  e.g.2 " really don't know what i'd do without you", ' i am doing great without you'

  e.g.3 ' some people are just really brilliant', ' some people are just really dumb'

  e.g.4 " many people don't know this but you can actually read a book or go to the gym without announcing it on facebook", ' people need to understand that nobody cares of what you do stop trying hard on facebook'

As sarcasm is very often, if not all the time, used to express frustration about being in unpleasant situations, undesirable states, and unenjoyable activities, it is not surprising that the corpus contained the topics listed above.

3.2.1. Complexity of the Translation Task

Each social media platform has its own idiosyncrasies, and occasionally even new dialects. Twitter is no exception to that rule, as writing a tweet is limited to 280 characters. The length constraint has created a new way of communicating, especially considering the massive use of acronyms, abbreviations, slang, phonetisation, onomatopoeia and interjections, words contractions, etc. Moreover, the informal nature of tweets which of-

ten lack grammatical structure (spelling errors, syntax problems) frequently leads to misunderstanding issues, which in turn, leads to translation issues.
The lack of context, and the lack of knowledge about the real intentions when writing the tweet, is another issue faced. The collected tweets are not linked to each other and the order they are presented are random. This issue was also shared with Peled and Reichart (2017), as at times, the human judges could not understand the meaning of sarcasm and, therefore, unable to write an interpretation. In this case, they were told to skip the tweet. These issues described above had an impact on the translation as each time an unknown acronym, or the use of technical vocabulary used by people to comment were found, added to the lack of context, it meant that the translator needed to research those specific terminology, which in turn, affected the translator's efficiency.

3.2.2. Guidelines

Considering the issues we found during translation, a set of rules was agreed upon in order to keep the translation to the same standard:

1. Length: even if the translation exceed the 280 characters, find the best equivalent in French.

2. Structure: keep the original structure of the original corpus. The original tweet is displayed first between quotations followed by its interpretation, separated by a comma [' ', ' '].

3. Capitalization: keep the original capitalization found int he corpus.

4. Accents: write the translations using the French diacritics/accents, even if the tweets appear unstructured or ungrammatical, implying that the language register used by the author is casual or informal.

5. Slangs or Onomatopoeia: find the best French equivalent.

   'ass hat' = 'tête de nœud'
   'that sucks' = 'ça craint' or 'c'est nul'
   'wow' = 'ouah'
   'yuck' = 'beurk' or 'pouah'
   'boo' = 'bouh'

6. Acronyms and abbreviations: find the best French equivalent, but if not possible, leave the original acronym untranslated.

   'bc' for 'because' = 'pcq' for 'parce que'
   'omg' for 'oh my god' = 'omd' for 'oh mon dieu'
   'lol' for 'lot of laugh' = 'mrd' for 'mort de rire'
   'thk' for 'thanks' = 'mrc' for 'merci'
   'btcr' or 'btr' for 'bcttcr'= 'mx' for 'mieux'

7. Metaphors and idioms: translate metaphors and idioms focusing on the adequacy/equivalence of the translation, by finding the best French equivalent.

   doublespeak' = 'langue de bois'
   'wipe the floor' = 'mordre la poussière'
   'like taking candy from a baby' = 'c'est enfantin' or 'c'est un jeu d'enfant'
   'bet the farm' = 'tout miser'

8. graphemic stretching: keep the same number of repeated letters in the best French equivalent translation.

   'greeeat' = 'génialllll'
   'realllly' = 'vraimentttt'

These rules were applied for the set of the corpus that has been translated so far. We believe that further rules will be added as the translation advances.

4. Initial experiments with TransCasm

In addition to developing the "TransCasm" corpus, we also utilise it in sarcasm detection. As mentioned earlier, each sarcastic tweet in English is transformed into at most 5 non-sarcastic interpretations. Some of the tweets contain less than 5 interpretations. Sometimes it is very difficult to transform a sarcastic tweet into many different interpretations, a single non-sarcastic representation is enough in these cases. TransCasm consists of $1,831$ different non-sarcastic interpretations of 860 unique sarcastic tweets in English. These unique 860 sarcastic tweets and their $1,831$ non-sarcastic interpretations are translated into French. The corpus statistics is shown in Table 2.

Language	#Sarcastic Tweets	#non-sarcastic interpretations
English	860	1,831
French	860	1,831

Table 2: corpus statistics

In our experiment of binary sarcasm classification, we use 610 out of 860 unique sarcastic tweets as the training data set and held out the remaining 250 as the test data set. These 610 sarcastic tweets are then mixed with randomly selected 610 non sarcastic representations so that our training data becomes an equal distribution of sarcastic and non-sarcastic tweets. Similarly, the test data set is created by mixing the 250 non-sarcastic tweets with 250 sarcastic tweets. We use multinomial naive bayes (MNB) classification approach to train our sarcasm detection model. The model is automatically tuned by randomly selecting the 20% of the training data itself during the training process. The data distribution of the whole experiment is shown in Table 3.

5. Results

Although the main objective of this work is to develop the first ever bilingual corpus of English–French sar-

Distribution	#sarcastic	#non-sarcastic
train	610	610
test	250	250

Table 3: Data distribution

castic tweets, we conduct an initial experiment on sarcasm detection using this data set and obtain interesting results. We apply our binary sarcasm detection model to the test data set of 500 mixed tweets (both sarcastic and non-sarcastic) to see how the system performs in identifying sarcastic tweets. Our system achieves an accuracy of 61% in identifying whether a tweet is sarcastic or not. Table 4 shows the detailed results with accuracy for each category. We can observe that the

Tweet type	#of tweets	#Correctly classified	Accuracy
sarcastic	250	169	67.6%
non-sarcastic	250	136	54.4%
all	500	305	61%

Table 4: Experimental results

sarcasm classifier obtains an accuracy of 67.6% for sarcastic and 54.4% for non-sarcastic tweets, respectively. However, we note that this is a preliminary phase of our experiments and further research directions with this data set is planned.

6. Conclusion and Future Work

The main contribution of this work is to present an ongoing translation project that aims at building the first ever parallel sarcasm corpus - "TransCasm" corpus - by fully translating the SIGN corpus, a freely available corpus of sarcastic tweets and their non-sarcastic interpretations, from English into French.

We translated 860 unique sarcastic tweets in English into French. Each of the tweets, having at least 1 and at most 5 interpretations was translated, which amounted to $1,831$ translations of the interpretations. Due to the informal nature of the tweets and the issues found during translation, we developed guidelines in order to aid the translation process. In addition to developing TransCasm, we utilised this corpus for sarcasm detection in Tweets.

We built a binary classifier using the MNB classification algorithm. In the initial experiments, our classifier achieved an accuracy of 61% for the test data of 500 tweets, which can be considered a good mark given that this is the beginning of our work on "TransCasm". There is no such corpus available according to the best of our knowledge, therefore, "TransCasm" may become very useful resource in the NLP community, especially those working with the twitter data.

For future work, we intend to extend the corpus, as well as the translation of the interpretations. Upon extension we will also build the first sarcasm translation system (TransCasm MT). In addition, we will aim to build more robust sarcasm classifier with the extended data set and compare with the state-of-the-art sarcasm detectors. We will also apply deep learning techniques to further refine our sarcasm detection model. Moreover, we believe that annotating the text features in which sarcasm can be identified, would be beneficial and make the corpus useful for multilingual sarcasm detection as well sentiment translation research. We have released the "TransCasm" corpus online[4] to facilitate further research on this data set.

7. Acknowledgements

This research was conducted with the financial support of the Horizon 2020 project ITFLOWS under Grant Agreement No. 882986 and the ADAPT SFI Research Centre at Munster Technological University. The ADAPT SFI Centre for Digital Media Technology is funded by Science Foundation Ireland through the SFI Research Centres Programme and is co-funded under the European Regional Development Fund (ERDF) through Grant 13/RC/2106. The project was partially supported by the Horizon 2020 projects STOP Obesity Platform under Grant Agreement No. 823978.

8. Bibliographical References

Afli, H., McGuire, S., and Way, A. (2017). Sentiment translation for low resourced languages: Experiments on irish general election tweets. In *Proceedings of the 18th International Conference on Computational Linguistics and Intelligent Text Processing*, Budapest, Hungary.

Agarwal, A., Xie, B., Vovsha, I., Rambow, O., and Passonneau, R. (2011). Sentiment analysis of twitter data. In *Proceedings of the Workshop on Languages in Social Media*, LSM '11, pages 30–38, Portland, Oregon, USA.

Bouazizi, M. and Ohtsuki, T. (2015). Sarcasm detection in twitter: "all your products are incredibly amazing!!!" - are they really? In *GLOBECOM*, pages 1–6. IEEE.

Branz, L. and Brockmann, P. (2018). Sentiment analysis of twitter data: Towards filtering, analyzing and interpreting social network data. In *Proceedings of the 12th ACM International Conference on Distributed and Event-based Systems*, DEBS '18, pages 238–241, Hamilton, New Zealand.

Ghosh, A., Li, G., Veale, T., Rosso, P., Shutova, E., Barnden, J. A., and Reyes, A. (2015). Semeval-2015 task 11: Sentiment analysis of figurative language in twitter. In *SemEval@NAACL-HLT*, pages 470–478, Denver, Colorado, USA.

Gibbs, R. W. (1986). On the psycholinguistics of sarcasm. *Journal of Experimental Psychology: General*, 115(1):3 – 15.

[4] `https://github.com/HAfli/TransCasm_Corpus`

González-Ibáñez, R. I., Muresan, S., and Wacholder, N. (2011). Identifying sarcasm in twitter: A closer look. In *The 49th Annual Meeting of the Association for Computational Linguistics: Human Language Technologies, Proceedings of the Conference, 19-24 June, 2011, Portland, Oregon, USA - Short Papers*, pages 581–586, Portland, Oregon, USA.

Lohar, P., Afli, H., and Way, A. (2017). Maintaining sentiment polarity in translation of user-generated content. *The Prague Bulletin of Mathematical Linguistics*, 108(1).

O'Connor, B., Balasubramanyan, R., Routledge, B. R., and Smith, N. A. (2010). From tweets to polls: Linking text sentiment to public opinion time series. In *Proceedings of the Fourth International AAAI Conference on Weblogs and Social Media*, pages 122–129, Washington D.C., USA.

Pang, B. and Lee, L. (2008). Opinion mining and sentiment analysis. *Found. Trends Inf. Retr.*, 2(1-2):1–135, January.

Peled, L. and Reichart, R. (2017). Sarcasm sign: Interpreting sarcasm with sentiment based monolingual machine translation. In *Proceedings of the 55th Annual Meeting of the Association for Computational Linguistics (Volume 1: Long Papers)*, pages 1690–1700, Vancouver, Canada.

Reyes, A. and Rosso, P. (2012). Making objective decisions from subjective data: Detecting irony in customer reviews. *Decision Support Systems*, 53(4):754 – 760.

Reyes, A., Rosso, P., and Buscaldi, D. (2012). From humor recognition to irony detection: The figurative language of social media. *Data Knowl. Eng.*, 74:1–12, April.

Zimbra, D., Abbasi, A., Zeng, D., and Chen, H. (2018). The state-of-the-art in twitter sentiment analysis: A review and benchmark evaluation. *ACM Trans. Manage. Inf. Syst.*, 9(2):5:1–5:29, August.

Author Index

Association for Computational Linguistics
209 N. Eighth Street
Stroudsburg, Pennsylvania 18360

CURRAN ASSOCIATES INC.
proceedings.com

ISBN 978-1-7138-6133-1
9 781713 861331

6th Workshop on Indian Language Data: Resources and Evaluation (WILDRE-6)

Held at LREC 2022

Marseille, France
20 – 25 June 2022